T0386770

DARK SIDE
OF THE CUT

DARK SIDE

OF THE CUT

A HISTORY OF CRIME ON BRITAIN'S CANALS

SUSAN C. LAW

For the thousands of forgotten navvies who dug out the cut, and generations of decent, hard-working canal-boat families who endured a tough existence with dignity and humour, to survive the hardships of that lost way of life.

First published 2023

The History Press
97 St George's Place, Cheltenham,
Gloucestershire, GL50 3QB
www.thehistorypress.co.uk

British Library Cataloguing in Publication Data.
A catalogue record for this book is available from the British Library.

ISBN 978 1 8039 9330 0

Typesetting and origination by The History Press
Printed and bound in Great Britain by TJ Books Limited, Padstow, Cornwall.

Trees for LYfe

CONTENTS

INTRODUCTION

As you sit peacefully at a canal-side pub, sipping a cool drink in the sunshine while dappled shadows play gently across the grass, it's hard to imagine the darker side of the water. But crime, poverty, drunkenness and violence were facts of everyday life in past centuries.

Today, canals are tranquil places to escape on a narrowboat or take a relaxing stroll along the towpath, enjoying countryside, trees and wild-life. For us they mean freedom, leisure and a chance to get away from the stresses of work. Step back in time to the early years of the water-ways in nineteenth-century Britain and it was a very different story.

The canal network was the lifeblood of the Industrial Revolution and a vital trade route for goods in the new consumer society. But this expanding prosperity had its price. The dark side was crime and many sinister figures lurked in the shadows. Inside rough beer shops scattered along canal banks, the poor and desperate huddled in front of crackling log fires, drowning their sorrows in pint pots of tepid ale. Almost half of violent crime today is caused by alcohol, but in Victorian Britain, when heavy drinking was common, nine out of every ten offences were said to be committed under the influence of intoxicating liquor.

There is something strangely compelling about the waterways. Isolated places set apart on the edge of society, they have always had their own distinctive way of life and a certain shady reputation. Ever since the earliest days, canals seemed to attract crime. And often there were no witnesses. Whenever a dead body was found floating in the water, it might have been the victim of an accident, murder or suicide – there was always room for doubt.

So, facts became tangled with rumours, to create myths and intriguing murder mysteries. Colourful myths were handed down through generations about 'the Cut', as the canal was known, and working boatmen – roving water gypsies, who were too often condemned for their hard drinking, fighting and dishonesty – lived tough lives by their own rules. Decent, hard-working boat families found their reputation was tarnished by the crimes of a notorious rogue minority.

Canals were the silent witnesses to shocking stories of passion, tragedy, greed and revenge – smooth, untroubled waters, stretching out through bustling cities, placid villages and lonely green fields, just watching and waiting as so many different people passed by. Now you can follow the echoing footsteps of forgotten characters along the towpath and discover what life was really like back then.

1

ROUGH JUSTICE

Right from the start, canals were dark and dangerous places to be. Shovelling tons of mud and stones to dig out 'the cut' was tough work. And for hundreds of navvies, it meant long days of gruelling labour in all weathers, with the constant risk of accidents, serious injury or death.

They were rough men, with a fearsome reputation as hard workers and heavy drinkers, who terrorised the countryside with their fighting, cursing and stealing. When they went looking for trouble things could really get out of hand, and that was exactly what happened one spring afternoon in March 1795, when a riot broke out in the Leicestershire village of Kibworth.

A gang of labourers working on the Leicester & Northampton Union Canal decided to have some fun by attacking a detachment of guards from the Leicester Fencibles, trying to liberate two army deserters who were in their charge. Rioting and chaos quickly spread through the streets as the frightened villagers panicked. Around 3 p.m., the mayor summoned Captain Heyrick to bring in the troops and disperse the crowd. A horn sounded with the call to arms, and within ten minutes the Leicester troop of volunteer cavalry had assembled in the marketplace as the volunteer infantry marched into Kibworth with fixed bayonets.

Meanwhile, a few miles away on the Oadby turnpike road, soldiers were informed that a breakaway group had run off, taking the two deserters with them, and were now holed up in the Recruiting Sergeant public house at Newton Harcourt. The cavalry charged into the village to be met at the pub door by rioters, defending the premises with long pikes and refusing to surrender.

Mr Justice Burnaby, one of the local magistrates, read aloud the official words of the Riot Act and with that, cavalry officers dismounted, rushed inside the pub and frantically searched every room. But the deserters could not be found anywhere. Four navvies were arrested and sent off to Leicester under armed guard, while the cavalry galloped out of Newton Harcourt to scour the surrounding country-side, making their way up the line of the canal through Fleckney and Smeeton. By the time they arrived back in Kibworth at 7 p.m., all the rioters had disappeared.

Early next morning, the cavalry set out again to hunt down the ringleaders. They rode along the path of the canal under construction, scrutinising the working labourers to try and identify the culprits. Nine navvies were eventually dragged away under arrest, including Red Jack and Northamptonshire Tom, 'two fellows notorious for being a terror to every country they have resided in', according to the *Northampton Mercury*. The newspaper reported that on 2 April the offenders all appeared before the magistrate, who committed four men for trial but freed the others.

Navvies were a tough breed of men, surviving in the harshest of conditions. They could be reckless and violent but had their own code of conduct and refused to be pushed around, enforcing their own kind of rough justice when they felt they had been badly treated. Living on the edge of villages, in scattered makeshift camps of wooden shacks near the canal, they existed alongside respectable country folk in an uneasy truce.

Many villagers resented this alarming intrusion into their lives, but well-paid navvies brought much-needed cash into the parish, which shopkeepers and innkeepers were eager to get their hands on. The migrant workforce wore distinctive clothing of moleskin breeches, neck-erchiefs and brightly coloured garments in yellow, red or blue. Unusual nicknames and their own private language, similar to cockney rhyming slang, set them apart from mainstream society with a formidable gang identity. This made them easy scapegoats when trouble erupted.

A few months later, in August 1795, canal boats carrying grain down from Liverpool were hijacked by townsfolk in Stafford, while at Barrow-upon-Soar in Leicestershire, the locals stopped a wagon loaded with corn. These were just some of the many riots sweeping Britain during the turbulent years around the turn of the century, when a series of bad harvests left thousands hungry. It was a time of unrest and desperate poverty, when angry protests about food shortages and high prices often ran out of control, ending in pitched battles. The authorities in Leicestershire and Derbyshire even cancelled annual races and parish feasts to prevent excessive drinking, which could set off riots.

There was no sympathy for rioters, and the *Derby Mercury* noted grimly, 'Led on by the vicious and abandoned, the people have committed acts of outrage and violence which can only tend to increase the distresses of which they complain, and heap calamity on their heads.'

In the Barrow-upon-Soar protest, villagers drove the corn wagon away to the church and refused to surrender their load to magistrates. The Riot Act was read, and the Leicester troop of cavalry arrived, but the mob assailed them with brickbats and began firing shots from adjacent houses. The soldiers fired back, leaving three dead and eight dangerously wounded.

The village was right alongside the canal and navvies were blamed for the whole incident, as an indignant contributor to the *Gentleman's Magazine* wrote:

> The disturbance at Barrow on Soar ... has indeed been productive of the most fatal consequences; but this, it should be recollected, was among that newly-created, and so wantonly multiplied set of men, the *diggers* and *conductors* of *navigations*, or as they are called in the language of the country, *navigators*.

They were weather-beaten and muscular, big, powerful, boisterous men who needed an outlet for enormous energies in their rare hours of freedom. Their amazing capacity for hard drinking soon created a notoriety that the newspapers enjoyed sharing with readers. The rowdy Kibworth navvies made news again when the *Chester Courant* reported:

> ... a singular instance of depravity, which may perhaps operate as a useful example to others. Several men employed upon the Union Canal, usually called *Navigators*, had stolen from a public-house in Kibworth, a keg of gin, about four gallons, and not having prudence

to make a temperate use of their booty, they proceeded to drench themselves till the whole was emptied, and one of them died upon the spot … they have all been compelled to flee the country, to avoid a prosecution.

Other law-breakers did not escape punishment so easily, however, such as Joseph Hunt, a canal labourer known as Wild Nathan, who was found guilty at the court sessions in Boston, Lincolnshire, of stealing a silver pint mug from the landlord of The Plough public house and sentenced to seven years' transportation overseas.

Alcohol was usually the cause of any trouble, as canal companies knew only too well. In Scotland, the Caledonian Canal Committee did their best to address the problem by keeping a herd of cows and setting up a brewery at Corpach near Fort William, when work began on site, to try and persuade their navvies to drink fresh milk or beer instead of whisky.

Another foolhardy case of binge-drinking reached the newspapers in April 1793, when the *Leeds Intelligencer* noted, 'a dreadful instance of the effects of excessive drinking', discovered one Sunday morning at a public house in Tipton near Birmingham. Two canal labourers had gone to the pub on Saturday night, got drunk and asked the landlord if they could stay the night. But instead of going to sleep, they sneaked down to the cellar when the house was quiet, drank a great quantity of spirits and took more supplies upstairs to the kitchen. Next morning, the pair were found 'in a state of the strongest stupefaction' and a surgeon was sent for, but despite trying bleeding and other means of recovery, 'both of them soon after expired'.

Despite all the problems caused by a volatile workforce, nothing could stop the progress of a massive national construction plan to create a waterway network to carry raw materials and goods for the new industrial centres, linking them to major ports via the River Thames, River Severn, the Trent and the River Mersey. In a letter to the *Gentleman's Magazine* of September 1795, signed 'A Friend to the Improvement of his Country', the proprietor of a new canal being cut from Walsall said that during the past thirty years in Staffordshire, 200 miles of canal had been completed. It was now a busy route for boats transporting coal and limestone, adding £100,000 per annum to the county's income.

It was the same all over Britain. Canals were spreading inexorably across the countryside, with mile after mile of land being dug out by the navvies. As one commentator explained, 'Inland navigation, to a manufacturing country, is the very heart's blood and soul of commerce.' Shorter routes cut the price of goods, but they had to be completed as quickly and cheaply as possible. What really mattered was money.

†††

A dispute over pay brought mayhem to a Devon village, some years later, when navvies went on the rampage at Sampford Peverell, near Tiverton, where some very strange and spooky things had been happening for months in the house of shopkeeper John Chave. The haunted house had previously been used by smugglers. At night, there were loud thumps and crashes, footsteps pacing the floor and bed-hangings agitated so violently that the brass curtain-rings rattled.

The 18-year-old domestic servant, Sally Case, was slapped round the face by an invisible hand as she slept, and swore she glimpsed a large disembodied, white arm suspended over her bed. In another bed chamber, a large iron candlestick crossed the wooden floorboards with an eerie grinding noise, threw itself at the bedstead and fell onto the pillow. It was all very peculiar.

Thanks to a series of letters printed in the *Taunton Courier* from a Tiverton clergyman, describing what he had witnessed in Mr Chave's house, the Sampford Ghost soon became a national celebrity and featured in more than 100 press reports. Some people believed it was merely a clever trick to scare off an unwanted tenant, while others said it was a deliberate hoax to con gullible visitors into paying a fee to look round the house. Newspapers vied with each other to solve the mystery for their readers and even offered a substantial cash reward to anyone who could reveal the ghost's true identity. The *Taunton Courier* ridiculed 'the pretended visitations of the monster', and the *Evening Mail* in London condemned Chave as a huckster acting out a 'vile farce'.

Meanwhile, hundreds of navvies were hard at work digging out the new Grand Western Canal, which was being cut right through the centre of Sampford Peverell. It was common practice for employers to pay them in tokens, which shopkeepers would exchange for goods or cash, although some tradesmen did not trust canal companies to redeem the tokens and would not accept them.

One Saturday, a large group assembled in Wellington, but after being refused change for their wage tokens, they started boozing and getting rowdy. On the following Monday, they went to the cattle fair at Sampford Peverell for an all-day session of heavy drinking, and by early evening 300 drunken navvies were still loitering in the village. The mood hardened suddenly when some of them recognised Mr Chave being driven home in a cart. Jeering and shouting abuse, they followed him along the road.

We don't know exactly why the mob turned on Mr Chave. Shopkeepers were never popular with navvies anyway. Perhaps they had been overcharged for goods in his shop or been tricked into paying for one of his so-called ghost tours after dark. Perhaps they were hoping to uncover the truth about the hoax, to claim the huge reward being offered. But Mr Chave was by now a known huckster and infamous character, suspected of perpetuating a dreadful fraud. Travelling alone on the road accompanied only by his carter, he must have seemed like a natural target to a gang of aggrieved navvies in a fuddled, alcoholic haze.

Chave jumped down from the cart, dashed into his house and managed to slam the door just in time. He was followed by a hail of stones from the encroaching mob, who surrounded the carter and badly beat him. Windows were smashed and the furious navvies threatened to pull down the whole building, brick by brick. Terrified of what they might do next, Chave fired a pistol into the crowd and shot dead a navvy named George Helps. Another shot severely wounded a second man.

Eventually the mob dispersed of its own accord and returned to camp. But the *Taunton Courier* expressed the anger of locals, who felt they had been abandoned and left defenceless by the authorities, reporting:

It is impossible not to feel the deepest abhorrence for the proceedings of a savage ungovernable banditti, whose ferocious behaviour we hope will be visited by the heaviest punishments of the law. Let Mr Chave's conduct have been ever so criminal, it will form not a shadow of excuse for the daring outrage of which these men have been guilty. The fate of their companions is of their own seeking, and to their conduct is it alone to be attributed. Chave has acted as most men would have done in defence of their home; nor will, or ought, the law to injure a hair of his head for the vigorous resistance he made to this attack. It is a most extraordinary circumstance that the whole neighbourhood should have been kept in a state of the greatest terror and commotion for more than twenty-four hours, and no efforts of the Police or Military made to quell the tumult. In the name of Justice, where are the Magistrates!

Predictably, Chave was not held liable for murder. At an inquest into the death of George Helps, before Devon coroner, Charles Daly Pugh, several witnesses were called to recount events leading up to the fatal shooting, but the jury returned a verdict of justifiable homicide.

The mystery of the Sampford Ghost was never solved, but it lived on to haunt the imagination in a popular ballad performed in the London theatres. The unlucky navvy was buried in the village churchyard of St John's, close to the canal he was employed on – just one forgotten casualty of a small battle, in a much larger campaign to build Britain's waterways.

†††

In fact, he was only one of hundreds of navvies killed during the many decades of canal construction. Although the men could earn wages of 2 shillings a day in the 1790s, which was far more than farm labourers received, the work was well paid because it was physically much harder and highly dangerous.

Incredibly fit and strong, navvies worked on site for long days in appalling conditions, many clad in leaky boots and sodden clothing drenched by driving rain. Hot weather or freezing winters made things even worse. To fuel all this hard labour, they existed on huge quantities of oatmeal, bread and potatoes, washed down with 8 pints of ale every day. Using only basic picks, shovels and wheelbarrows, it was estimated that each man could move 12 cubic yards of earth and stone a day, which weighed a hefty 18 tonnes. For the impatient contractors, however, the work was never fast enough.

A total of 165 Canal Acts were approved by Parliament between 1758 and 1802, a third of which were agreed from 1792 to 1795 during a short-lived enthusiasm known as 'canal mania'. Investors were constantly pressing canal companies to complete the work as rapidly as possible, and the safety of the workforce was not a priority. Pushed to work faster in harsh conditions, it is not surprising that serious injuries and deaths were commonplace. They were accepted merely as an inevitable part of construction and few, if any, records of accidents were kept because they were simply too numerous to count.

Some sections of canal were particularly difficult to build, and men faced the greatest danger of all in the tunnels. Probably the most ambitious and expensive project was the Blisworth Tunnel on the Grand Junction Canal, near Stoke Bruerne. Work to cut through nearly 2 miles of stone beneath the Northamptonshire hillside started in 1793, but there were a series of technical problems which engineers struggled to solve, floodwater was seeping in and the line of the tunnel veered off course due to contractors' errors.

Then, in 1796, real disaster struck. A gang of navvies hacking away the rocky outcrop in a shadowy underground cavern, lit only by candlelight, suddenly struck quicksand with their pickaxes and the whole roof collapsed, piling tons of clay and boulders down onto them. Fourteen men were buried alive beneath the rubble. There was nothing more to be done. The ill-fated tunnel was hurriedly bricked up with the bodies inside and work stopped for the next six years.

No one can be sure what actually happened down there in the darkness, 140ft deep underground. Labourers were usually blamed for causing accidents through their own carelessness, though in many cases the contractors had clearly failed to anticipate obvious dangers or take adequate precautions to safeguard their workers. There was no chance of dubious incidents like the one at Blisworth being properly investigated, or criminal charges being brought against employers held liable for gross negligence.

In all, more than sixty men are believed to have been killed during the construction of the tunnel, which was the last section of the canal to be completed. It was eventually opened with joyful public celebrations attracting large crowds on a warm spring day in March 1805.

The *Sun* newspaper in London reported that the Northamptonshire Militia band struck up as canal proprietors and local dignitaries, on a procession of boats, made their way through the tunnel lit by flaming torches where 'the company seemed lost in contemplating the stupendous efforts by which this amazing arch of brick-work ... had been completed'. More than 5,000 happy, cheering people gathered to watch them emerge at Stoke Bruerne and go down the locks. Later on, more than 100 special guests sat down to an excellent dinner at the Bull Inn, Stoney Stratford, and raised their wine glasses to drink a series of toasts. 'The utmost harmony and conviviality prevailed ... till near twelve o'clock, when they broke up. All the other inns in Stoney Stratford were filled with company, and many of the parties did not separate till a late hour.' The navvies would have loved it.

Since then, many boaters passing through the dank and eerie tunnel, its brickwork dripping with icy water, have told of ghostly happenings. Rough shouts have been heard echoing along the walls, and the glow of flickering candles has been seen lighting up a fork in the canal where the old, abandoned tunnel entrance was sealed off.

The long-gone navvies have at least won their place in canal mythology, as one Victorian traveller later wrote:

We entered Blisworth tunnel, about which all sorts of ghost stories, frightful apparitions, dreadful murders, and a thousand other things, enough to make your hair stand on end, have been said, and by the superstitious seen. Some boatmen of the present day still believe in them.

2

WATER GYPSIES

Secretly emptying a few pints from barrels of liquor was easy enough after plenty of practice. One of the hoops was deftly prised off and two small boreholes pierced in the wood to siphon out the pure spirits. Then water was poured in to refill the cask, the holes pegged up with greased cork and the hoop replaced to hide the damage. As simple as that.

Boxes and packages were just as easily plundered for sugar, china or cutlery, with stones or bricks added to make up the weight, before they were carefully retied with matching twine. Even large bales of valuable silk or wool could be tackled with a length of thick cord and a hook which pulled out pieces from the middle, while leaving the bale apparently intact.

The same furtive thieving was happening on boats all over the waterways. Sometimes in the dead of night, but usually in broad daylight, crates were being broken open and sacks of wheat, yards of cloth or parcels of just about anything were disappearing from canal boats loaded with cargoes too tempting to ignore. In fact, nothing stowed away in the hold was entirely safe from the skilful smuggling methods of old hands, who could disguise any theft, so it was not discovered until long after the goods were delivered.

Many such small, audacious acts of robbery taking place throughout the country added up to enormous losses from stolen property that could be sold on for ready cash. And the main culprits were the boatmen themselves, who soon came to be known as a rootless, lawless group of men capable of the worst sort of behaviour. Usually, they got away with it as most crimes went undetected, with only perhaps one offence in every 100 being prosecuted or even known about. Loads were passed between so many different workers that goods could go missing anywhere along the way and few thefts could ever be traced back to the true culprits.

Nineteen-year-old Benjamin Thompson and Richard Gibbert, aged 20, were among those hapless boatmen who were caught and punished, after stealing 140 yards of cloth valued at £17 10s from their boat on 29 September 1802. The package containing five pieces of printed calico was being returned by Samuel Croughton, a London dealer in bedding, to Lancashire clothmakers Jacksons in Preston, on one of the many boats run by leading canal carriers Pickfords. The material was packed up at Croughton's by John Oliver and handed in to Pickfords' porter John Meakin, who signed the receipt and sent it on by wagon to the warehouse clerk at Paddington, who, three days later, helped load it on board a boat at the wharf.

Boatman James Wright led the horse along the towpath pulling the boat, and about 8 miles along the canal he noticed Gibbert taking calico out of the parcel then refilling the hole with a piece of sheeting pulled off another package. At ten o'clock in the morning, they moored up at Berkhamstead to take a sick horse to the farrier, then went on to the Cow Roast public house. On the road, the boatmen met saddler William Bailey, who offered to take the animal for a good price if it did not live. Thompson asked if he might be interested in buying handkerchiefs or cloth, and that afternoon called in at his shop and offered a sample of calico for sale. The saddler became suspicious when Thompson promised to return at midnight with more cloth and he decided to tip off the local constable.

The men didn't turn up that night, however, but appeared at the shop door before six o'clock next morning, when William Bailey quietly gave his assistant the nod to run and fetch the constable. Gibbert waited outside, while Wright and Thompson were taken into a small back room, where they initially agreed to sell all the calico 'by the lump' for £4, plus a pot of beer apiece. Gibbert then insisted it had to be 4 guineas. Pretending to go along with the deal, William Bailey said he would meet them at a public house with the cash, and the boatmen set off to feed their horses.

Shortly afterwards, Bailey and the constable apprehended the felons on their way back from the pub. At a brief hearing in the Old Bailey criminal court on 12 January 1803, Croughton's clerk, George Bateman, was able to identify the calico because the official crown mark required by the custom house had been omitted by mistake on those pieces. Gibbert denied everything and merely said in his defence, 'I know nothing about it, but am innocent. Thompson asked me to go and drink with him, I went, and we were coming down the town, when they took me along with him.'

Both men were found guilty of grand larceny and sentenced to seven years' transportation overseas. It was a common sentence for thefts even that small and was supposed to deter other would-be offenders. Wright was not charged with any crime, probably because he gave evidence against the others. Although he did admit to carrying one of the bundles of stolen calico, he swore rather unconvincingly in the witness box that he never had any intention of sharing in the money.

Plenty of other thefts did not turn out quite as planned. A barge master and his four crew, working the Paddington Canal, were all charged with the theft of valuable fine china from their boat on its way to London from the Spode manufactory at Stoke-on-Trent. When the crates were unloaded, they had obviously been tampered with, and the stolen china was found hidden in the cabin.

By the early 1800s, canal boatmen had become notorious for dishonesty, flagrant acts of theft and rough behaviour. Like the navvies, they too had to be tough characters to survive on the waterways where relentless hard work and punishingly long hours were the norm. There were also constant time pressures to contend with, as men were only paid on delivery of the cargo, so violent punch-ups would often erupt whenever boats were held up at tunnels and locks, and after fighting it out, the toughest crews went through first.

Derbyshire clergyman, Reverend Stebbing Shaw, writing about a memorable journey by candlelight through the tunnel beneath Harecastle Hill on the Trent & Mersey, vividly described the oaths and curses of boatmen carrying coal that he encountered:

The voices of the workmen from the mines were rude and awful, and to be present at their quarrels, which sometimes happen when they meet, and battle for a passage, must resemble greatly the ideas we may form of the regions of Pluto.

In Greek myth, Pluto was the god of the underworld, which was said to be separated from the kingdom of the living by a river, and Reverend Shaw's words conjure up a powerful image of the canal as a forbidding otherworldly realm inhabited by ruffians.

On wharfs there could also be tussles over who unloaded first, and angry disputes with toll collectors or lock-keepers often led to assaults. One canal company agent who had to deal with boatmen on a daily basis, at the busy Braunston Wharf on the Grand Junction in Northamptonshire, summed them up as a 'vile set of rogues'.

There was widespread criticism of the boatmen's unruly behaviour, and they were condemned not only as habitual thieves, but for their general lifestyle, drinking, brutality and 'decided wickedness'. This bad reputation gradually worsened over the years, until eventually a crime would take place that was so shocking it seemed to confirm all the worst fears about the waterways.

†††

From the earliest times, boatmen working on the rivers traditionally had a bad name, and this ill repute seems to have been passed down to canal men. A popular ballad entitled *Will the Waterman* recounted a sorry tale of lowlife robbery to impress a cunning harlot, in which young Will confessed:

> I went a thieving night and day, to maintain her fine and brave,
> All I could get I valu'd not, to her I freely gave.
> At last to Newgate I was sent, fast bound in fetters strong,
> About my heels they do remain, she laughs to see me wrong.

The ballad ended with Will repenting of his wrongdoing:

> I shall be reckon'd a Newgate bird among the boatmen all,
> And to jeer me will be the word, among both great and small.

I must needs own the fact is true, dear brothers all, I pray,
Pity the folly of my youth, that first led me astray.

The first boatmen came onto the waterways from many different backgrounds. Some were farmers, labourers, carters or navvies who stayed to work on the cut, and some had previously been river boatmen. But as more boats needed more crew, hirers could not afford to be choosy, employing unsavoury characters wanting casual labour and men escaping justice by working on the hoof. Of course, there were still many decent, hard-working boatmen, but unfairly, they all came to be seen as a disreputable and separate underclass living outside society – outlaws.

This was particularly true when the original slow boats carrying iron and coal were joined in the 1790s by flyboats, the fast non-stop delivery service of goods between ports, towns and cities. One of the largest flyboat companies was run by the Pickford family, who had built up a successful road transport business as waggoners, before moving onto the waterways with their distinctive boats marked with a diamond painted on the sides. Starting with ten vessels in 1795, Pickfords rapidly expanded the fleet to nearly 100 boats and established a London base at Paddington with extensive wharfs and warehouses.

Flyboats were manned by crews of four who did shifts around the clock, taking turns to snatch a few hours' sleep in the cabin. They travelled long distances using relays of horses to pull the boat, working seven days a week and fifteen or more hours a day.

Boatmen had their own jargon of slang words which were heavily laced with expletives, using terms such as 'down a thick and through the 'ole', which meant to travel down a flight of locks then under a bridge, and to 'bell oil', something which meant the boat had hit it hard.

According to popular mythology, boatmen were of Romany Gypsy blood and had left their colourful painted caravans for life on the cut. They soon became known as water gypsies, but although little evidence supported such romantic ideas about their origins, the folklore persisted. Perhaps it was because of a certain intriguing mystique attached to boatmen with their distinctive clothes, wooden horse-drawn boats and roaming lifestyle. They were a secretive and rootless set of men travelling freely about the country at a time when most people rarely ventured further than the nearest market town. Inevitably, they were regarded with suspicion, as outsiders who could not be trusted.

Casual poaching and petty thefts from farmland alongside canals were regular occurrences. They took poultry, turnips, grass or clover for horse fodder, clothes left outside to dry, and there were even reports of boatmen milking farmers' cows in fields at night. Only a small minority of unlucky culprits were apprehended, like the barge-man Edward Crawford, who was committed to Oxford Gaol in January 1803, charged with stealing six geese from Binley in the city suburbs, the property of Samuel Seckham. We don't know his fate, but those convicted of theft could expect extremely harsh sentences.

Petty larceny cases involving goods worth less than a shilling were usually tried at local quarter sessions courts and could be punished with a maximum sentence of transportation. Where goods valued at more than 1 shilling were stolen, the offence was deemed to be grand larceny, which could bring the death penalty, although courts had substantial discretion in sentencing.

Boatman John Peggs and 10-year-old Thomas Key were convicted of stealing hay worth 3 shillings from a field in Chelsey, 2 miles from Paddington. Farmer Joseph Smith had employed a watchman after repeatedly having his crops stolen, and one June night the boatmen were seen taking a large haycock and loading it into their barge, which was moored on the canal. The pair were found guilty and, as the age of criminal responsibility was then 7 years old, there was no special leniency for the boy. Both were sentenced to be confined in the House of Correction for one year and publicly whipped. Whipping was a typical punishment for minor crimes like this, with felons being stripped down to the waist and flogged at a public whipping post.

In another case, bargemaster John Morgan, aged 20, and his three boat hands, Richard Chapman, Joseph Cook and Joseph Daniels, were all charged with feloniously stealing six live geese, valued at £1 5s, and two goslings, valued at 6 shillings, on 2 August 1808. The geese were kept by farmer William Mason, who lived a mile from the canal at Hillingdon in Middlesex, with his sister, Elizabeth Cox, and her husband. Mrs Cox was woken between two and three o'clock in the morning by the noise of geese in the barnyard, and jumped out of bed, calling to her brother that they were being stolen. William Mason ran outside to find the gates were open, six geese missing and a trail of foot-prints leading down to a barge on the water.

At six o'clock the Hillingdon constable, William Read, tracked four sets of prints, some of bare feet, down to the canal and noticed traces of geese dung and feathers on the boat. Some fowls and ducks were lying on deck. The men were at breakfast and Morgan, the bargemaster, said he was welcome to search the fore cabin as he was sure there was nothing there.

The constable later described the violent tussle that ensued when he had handcuffed Morgan and boat hand Joseph Cook:

> … made use of desperate words [and] said he did not mind two or three men; I took hold of his collar; he kicked me on my legs and kicked me on my private parts; I told him I would chop his head off if he resisted any more; after I secured him I broke open the cabin and there I found eight live geese, one hen and three or four ducks.

The boatmen were examined by the magistrate then locked up in the cells at Uxbridge, where they tried to bribe the constable by offering cash if he would get them off. At nine o'clock that night, another constable took the prisoners some beer, bread and cheese for supper, locked the cell door and stood outside to listen, where he overheard one of the boatmen say to another, 'If it had not been for your bare feet, they would not have found us in the morning.'

At their trial on 14 September, none of the accused men called char-acter witnesses in their defence. Daniels was found not guilty, but the other three were sentenced to be transported overseas for seven years.

Pilfering cargoes could be safely done, with little risk of being spot-ted, anywhere on a quiet stretch of canal with no passers-by or nearby houses. Boatmen regularly bartered buckets of coal and other goods with friendly lock-keepers in exchange for a few loaves of bread, a bag of plums or perhaps a pot of home-made jam. Theft of coal was par-ticularly common as it could readily be sold to cottagers, public houses or other acquaintances they met along the route.

Canal companies were aware of the many different fiddles being car-ried out and tried various measures to clamp down on the practices, usually without much success. Some lock-keepers on the Thames &

Severn Canal were known to be an easy touch, with boatmen buying their silence in return for gifts of alcoholic drink or meat, while at Birmingham an official notice was sent out warning that 'lock-keepers be not permitted upon any occasion to take coals for their own use off any of the Boats upon pain of being prosecuted'.

Small cottages were scattered along canals at flights of locks, built by each canal company to house its lock-keepers and their families. They had their own cottage gardens where they grew vegetables and fruit trees, kept a few poultry or pigs. Lock-keepers had to ensure waterway traffic stayed on the move, and to do so, they were on call to open lock gates at any time of day or night. After dark, they could keep a lookout for boats through a narrow, slit window set in the bedroom wall.

They were responsible for water control, maintaining canal property and preventing damage to the heavy wooden lock gates by impatient boatmen who crashed their boats into them or smashed gates against stone lock walls. This was a criminal offence, which could be prosecuted, and the Birmingham Canal Company sternly reminded its staff:

> You are expected to see the Passage of every Boat through the Locks under your care and in case of any damage ... occasioned by the negligence of any of the Boatmen ... that you do (on pain of dismissal) ... report the same that the offenders may be dealt with according to Law.

†††

There was bound to be constant friction between salaried canal company officials trying to enforce the rules and tired, angry boatmen in a hurry to reach their destination where they were paid. Many of the problems, the brawls and illegal activities, were undoubtedly caused by heavy drinking. Drunkenness was an inevitable part of working-class culture, as London magistrate Patrick Colquhoun noted in 1803:

> As the too prevalent habit of drunkenness among the lower classes of the people produces much misery and distress, both to themselves and families, ... while this vice tends not only to the corruption of morals, but to the commission of many criminal offences, it is the

bounden duty of all constables to admonish those persons who are particularly addicted to this evil habit.

Originally a merchant in the Glasgow linen trade, Patrick Colquhoun later moved to London and became a magistrate for Middlesex. He was an energetic campaigner for legal reform, producing a series of influential pamphlets on social problems, which included economic and crime statistics to support his arguments. Drawing on his experience in the courtroom, he was certain that alcohol consumption corrupted morals, health and family life, and frequently led to criminal offences.

Colquhoun proposed radical new guidelines for publicans to help curb unruly behaviour in public houses and disorderly alehouses. To discourage apprentices, journeymen and labourers from loitering away their time, he wanted a ban on unlawful taproom games such as cards, dice, shuffleboard, draughts, four corners, bumble puppy and ringing at the bull.

Colquhoun suggested that constables should regularly visit licensed houses 'to see that good rule and order are kept ... that the labouring people are not suffered to lounge and tipple until they are intoxicated'. All publicans were advised that premises should not stay open later than 11 p.m., and they should not harbour reputed thieves, rogues, vagabonds, common prostitutes or loose, idle and abandoned characters.

Alcohol was well known to cause social problems, but concerns about drunkenness were nothing new and had been around at least two centuries earlier. In the early seventeenth century, six different Acts of Parliament were passed to regulate alehouses and tackle excessive drinking by strengthening the licensing laws which were enforced by magistrates. A pamphlet published back in 1628 voiced fears that a huge increase in the number of alehouses was creating mass drunkenness and disorder in society. Titled *A Monster Late Found Out and Discovered*, it estimated that London had 122 churches but more than 3,000 alehouses, 'wherein the devil is daily served and honoured'.

As the population grew rapidly, so too did the number of outlets for alcohol. Licensed premises included large inns and posting houses used by travellers from coaches and wagons, taverns or houses of entertainment, hotels for lodging strangers, coffee houses, tea gardens licensed to sell ale, common alehouses and liquor shops selling only spirits.

By 1806, there were an estimated 50,000 licensed alehouses 'constantly holding out seductive lures to the labouring classes, in every part of the country'. London had one pub to every thirty-seven families living in the neighbourhood. Because there was so much competition for trade, some publicans resorted to any means necessary to attract customers:

> Thieves, burglars, highwaymen, pick-pockets and common prostitutes are harboured and encouraged; low games are introduced, and every device resorted to, which can excite a disposition to expend money, producing intoxication, quarrels, lewdness and every species of profligacy.

Ironically, a mini crimewave swept through alehouses in London and the surrounding villages, with customers habitually stealing the pewter pots they were drinking from. Vast numbers of these small thefts added up to £100,000 annually in stolen tankards, and landlords lobbied Parliament for tax relief to offset their losses. Colquhoun said these astonishing figures were 'shocking proof of the vast extent of petty offences and the depraved state of morals in vulgar life'. He criticised the 'habit among the labouring people, in every district in England and Wales, of spending the chief part of their leisure time in alehouses'.

All these drinkers consumed a staggering quantity of alcohol. In London alone, tipplers paying 5*d* a pot consumed roughly 1.2 million barrels of porter and ale in 1806, totalling £3.5 million. (It is difficult to calculate comparative values, but that is loosely equivalent to more than £210 million today.) In addition to the pints of ale, glasses of home-made spirits totalling £5 million were knocked back and a further £12 million worth of beer was purchased from public houses.

Boatmen were no different to other working men, and regularly stopped for a few pints by the fireside at one of the many canal-side inns with stabling for their horses. They enjoyed a drink, but it's fair to say that, like many others, they probably felt they needed the solace of alcohol to cope with the daily grind. Up at dawn, outside in all seasons, often working in pouring rain, dank fog or bitterly cold conditions, it could be a wretched and miserable existence with few comforts to look forward to, especially during the bleak winter months.

They trudged miles along muddy towpaths every day, leading the plodding horses on monotonous journeys they had made many times before. Only the dull thud of hooves and creaking leather harness broke the silence. At lock flights they uncoiled freezing ropes with numb, calloused fingers and wearily pushed solid oak beams to open immense, darkly dripping lock gates.

In tunnels, the boat had to be 'legged' through by two men lying flat on their backs with their boots on the side wall or roof, stepping slowly along in the gloom, sometimes for an hour or more. Equally tiring was 'shafting' the boat through a tunnel, using a long pole to press against the brick wall. On arrival at the wharf, boatmen were expected to unload their own heavy cargoes and on flyboats they immediately loaded up the hold with more goods and set off once again.

Although flyboat captains and master boatmen were well paid, for ordinary boat hands it was relentless hard, physical work on low wages, like most labouring jobs. But the constant travelling also meant that crews were only rarely able to visit their homes and families on land. Habitual drinking became a way of life to help men get through long working hours in harsh conditions. While boatmen put up with a grim existence, flyboats delivered welcome new prosperity to many other, more fortunate people.

3

MURDER MYSTERIES

It was warm and smoky in the Spotted Dog at Westbourne Green, a cosy refuge from the winter chill, and the public house was crowded one morning a few weeks before Christmas in 1802. The low hum of voices, with occasional bursts of laughter, rose above the noisy clatter of dishes and pewter pots.

A log fire was crackling in the broad stone hearth, blackened with soot, as George Foster sat at a table with his wife Jane and their baby daughter, tucking into plates of tasty beefsteak and sipping mugs of beer. A tall, well-built man of 32 years old, George was well paid as a skilled coachmaker in a respectable job and could afford to treat them both to a good dinner. Landlady Eleanor Winter noticed Jane, wearing an old, black bonnet and black gown, who seemed to be in very low spirits. She had been crying and was overheard saying to her husband, 'I have been here three times after a man who owes you money, and I am disappointed; I am determined I will never come again.'

The couple stayed there for over two hours and drank a large glass of rum each to keep out the cold. At around 1 p.m. they left the pub, setting off along the Paddington Canal, through the countryside and out of London. By now, it was little more than 4 degrees above freezing. After a 2-mile walk, they were shivering and weary when they reached the Mitre Tavern, built in a peaceful rural setting by the canal, opposite the solitary green expanse of Wormwood Scrubs Common.

The family arrived at 2 p.m. and spent several hours in the tavern, where they were served with a quartern of rum, and two more pints of porter beer with some bread and cheese. It was almost dark at 4.30 p.m. as they were leaving on that bleak afternoon, and the temperature was plummeting. Jane carefully wrapped up 9-month-old Louisa, who was dressed in a little straw bonnet and white bedgown. As they were going out, she threw her thin shawl over the baby for added warmth and said, 'This is the last time I shall ever come here.'

A minute or two later, George returned to the pub to look for a shoe which he said had dropped from his baby's foot, but it could not be found anywhere, and he followed Jane out into the darkness along the muddy canal bank. It was bitterly cold by the murky water. And very quiet.

†††

The next morning, around eight o'clock, bargeman John Atkins was travelling on the canal when he made the terrible discovery of a baby's small, frozen body beneath the bow of his boat, about a mile from the Mitre. He quickly raised the alarm and Sir Richard Ford, the magistrate, ordered him to drag the canal. It took three days of searching before a woman's body was found wedged in beneath the window of the Mitre Tavern, entangled in the branches of a loose bush.

The two bodies were identified and eventually the authorities tracked down George to tell him that his wife and child were dead. He explained that he last saw Jane walking away along the canal on Sunday, 5 December, and when they said goodbye, 'she was a little in liquor'. They parted ways, as she was going to her mother's lodgings, and he intended to start out on the long journey to Barnet. Despite his indignant protests of innocence, he was arrested and taken into custody at the Brown Bear public house in Bow Street. Here, the cellars were used to hold prisoners awaiting trial, as it was conveniently sited opposite the office of the city's magistrates and courthouse, just north of the River Thames.

What really happened out there on the deserted and muddy canal bank that winter afternoon? Could Jane simply have had an accident, slipping on the wet ground after the showery rain of the day before? Perhaps she stumbled in the dark, trying to clutch the baby tightly to her chest, and feeling more than a little tipsy after several hours drinking a potent alcoholic mix of rum and the popular dark, strong beer known as porter. Was it a case of murder, maybe even suicide, or just a tragic accident? Was her husband, in fact, completely innocent?

When George's employer, the coachmaker James Bushnell, heard the shocking news of the arrest, he went straight over to Bow Street to see if there was anything he could do to help. George said, if it was not too much trouble, he would thank him to find a witness who could provide an alibi for the Sunday afternoon and establish his innocence.

On Tuesday, 28 December, the *Morning Chronicle* reported that George Foster appeared before magistrates at the Public Office in Bow Street, along with several witnesses who had seen the couple together on the day of the tragedy, noting, 'He has a most excellent character with respect to his sobriety, humanity, good nature, and in every other respect, was considered as a very harmless man.' There were clearly many questions that needed to be answered, and after the hearing he was committed for further examination.

Early in the new year of 1803, a brief paragraph appeared in the *Sun*: 'George Foster, in custody on charge of suspicion of murdering his wife and child, was brought to the Office, underwent a final examination, and was committed for trial at the ensuing Sessions.'

†††

Ten days later, on Friday, 14 January, George was on trial at the Old Bailey criminal court, charged with the wilful murder of his wife and infant child by throwing them into the Paddington Canal, where they drowned. He stood silently in the dock of the packed courtroom as prosecution counsel Mr Knowles addressed the jury with his opening remarks, saying the charge was one of the most awful that could be brought against any human being. He told jurors that 'no distinct fact would be proved against him' and there was no direct evidence of the crime, but he stressed that circumstantial evidence was often the most convincing sort to prove guilt.

The first witness to be called was the victim's mother, Mrs Hobart, who said her daughter had been living with her at lodgings in Old Boswell Court since November. Before that, Jane had been forced to go into the workhouse, where her baby was born, because she was separated from her husband. The couple had four children – one who was dead, two now in the workhouse at Barnet and baby Louisa, who drowned. Jane usually went to stay with him every Saturday night. She left for his lodgings just before four o'clock that Saturday and never returned.

The rocky marriage was confirmed by Joseph Bradfield, at whose house George lodged in North Row, near the wealthy area of Grosvenor Square. He said that from the manner in which the couple spoke to one another, they appeared not to be on good terms, because Jane wanted to live with her husband again. The deceased used to call round once or twice in the week, besides every Saturday evening, he supposed for the purpose of getting some of the week's wages. He remembered she arrived with her child and slept there on 4 December. Next morning, they breakfasted and went out together about ten o'clock and George returned alone between eight and nine o'clock that night.

The waiter at the Mitre, John Goff, recalled how he had stood at the kitchen window and watched the Fosters walk from the tavern towards London on that side of the canal where there was no footpath, which was rather an unusual way. They had no clock in the house, but he had no doubt of the time because it began to grow dark. The Mitre's landlady, Hannah Patience, recollected serving drinks to the couple and said they left about half-past four, as far as she could judge.

A little girl of 9 years old, Sarah Daniel, was called into the witness box and recounted how she went to the Mitre to buy a candle for her master on that Sunday. She met the prisoner with a woman carrying a child in her arms, walking along the banks of the canal. Could it have been three o'clock? No, she was certain it could not be so early, as it was nearly dark and so late in the evening that the people were at tea.

Charles Weild, who worked in the coachmaker's shop with George, said they met on the Sunday evening in question, at about half-past six o'clock in Oxford Street, and went to the Horse Grenadier public house for a drink. While they were chatting, he asked, 'Why can't you live happy with your wife, as I do with mine?' and George replied that he should never live with her again. He made no mention of having been with his wife that day and did not seem to be flurried.

The magistrate, Sir Richard Ford, was called next to produce the prisoner's signed statement. Foster's story was that he went with his wife to the canal at Paddington on some business and had something to drink at the Mitre. They asked the landlady about a bed for the night but were told they must pay 2*s* 6*d*, which they thought too much, and his wife said she would go home to her mother. Foster said he left his wife immediately after coming out of the Mitre at about three o'clock and set off for Barnet to see two of his children in the workhouse there. But after walking an hour and a half through the bylanes, it was so dark when he reached the village of Whetstone that he decided to turn back. He arrived in London between seven and eight o'clock, stopping only at the Green Dragon in Highgate for another glass of rum. He had not seen his wife since.

Coachmaker James Bushnell said George was a sober, honest man, and one of the most diligent men he had employed, earning a guinea or 24 shillings a week as a journeyman. At the prisoner's request, he visited the Green Dragon to try to find a witness for Sunday, 5 December, and spoke to the landlady, Elizabeth Southall. She confirmed the prisoner had been there with a woman and child on a Sunday evening about dusk but could not tell him what Sunday it was.

That closed the prosecution case and George was asked if he wanted to speak in his own defence, but he simply said he would leave it to his counsel. The Middlesex coroner, George Hodgson, said a verdict of accidental death was recorded at the inquest into the deaths of Jane and Louisa Foster. There were no marks of violence found on their bodies and the child's arm was not broken, as had been wrongly reported.

Three other witnesses were called by defence counsel Mr Alley, all testifying to Foster's excellent character and declaring him to be a humane man, 'a good husband and a tender father'. One of them cast doubt over Jane's character, saying that when the Fosters lodged in his house she had stolen and pawned some trifling articles, but George behaved kindly, forgave her and paid for the missing items.

In his summing up, the presiding judge said the whole case depended on circumstantial evidence, which was often as strong and satisfactory as direct proof. He told jurors they must particularly consider the hour when the prisoner was proved to have left the Mitre, and whether it was possible in the two hours before he met his acquaintance in Oxford Street that a man could have walked over 19 miles. As to his having called at Highgate, it must have been some other Sunday when his wife was with him.

So, was this just a straightforward case of murder by a callous husband? Was he infuriated to such a degree by his wife's constant appeals for cash that he deliberately plied her with alcohol in a remote canalside pub and made sure they stayed there until dark when he had the best chance of knocking her into the water unseen?

Or was George really the kindly, reliable man his friends and workmates believed him to be? Perhaps he was not lying after all, and in the shock of the tragedy had just muddled the times and events of that Sunday when Jane slipped and accidentally plunged into the icy canal. Certainly, accidental death had been the verdict at the coroner's inquest. He might have seen the incident take place, panicked and made up the clumsy lies to avoid being blamed.

There was always the other possibility that Jane had taken her own life. Abandoned by George while she was pregnant and only recently out of the workhouse, she was destitute without her husband's grudging charity, and with a baby to care for was unable to find work. She was in very low spirits at the Spotted Dog, and what had she meant by her words, 'This is the last time I shall ever come here'? Jane was undoubtedly struggling in a miserable existence, but to most people listening to all the evidence at the Old Bailey that day, suicide now seemed to be unlikely. What, then, was the truth?

†††

It took the jury only fifteen minutes to return a verdict of guilty. The writer for *The Times*, who was in court reporting the trial, noted how Foster stood calmly in the dock, awaiting the verdict with apparent composure. But when the jury foreman uttered the fatal word, the prisoner 'turned excessively pale and seemed dreadfully agitated'. When the court clerk asked if he had anything to say as to why he should not have judgement to die, Foster replied, 'Nothing. I certainly should.' The judge pronounced the death sentence and ordered that the prisoner 'be hanged by the neck until he is dead'.

The press was naturally eager to publish all the lurid details of crime stories that readers enjoyed so much and which were always guaranteed to boost sales. Murders were especially popular. The *Morning Post* report of the Paddington Canal case covered more than two broadsheet columns, while accounts of the trial appeared in many other national newspapers and in regional papers as far afield as the *Staffordshire Advertiser*, the *Newcastle Courant* and the *Stamford Mercury*.

Four days later, on the morning of Tuesday, 18 January, Foster was brought up from the narrow, dimly lit condemned cell in Newgate Prison, wearing a brown greatcoat buttoned over a red waistcoat. He was led outside to the gallows looking 'dejected in the extreme', where a crowd had gathered beneath the platform to watch the execution. There was just time to say a short prayer with Dr Ford, the prison chaplain, before the thick rope was put round his neck by the hangman and a cap pulled over his eyes. The stage beneath him fell away sharply and as his body dropped, several friends watching by the scaffold grabbed and violently pulled down on his legs to end the suffering as quickly as possible.

The *Sun* printed one final grim paragraph:

Yesterday morning at ten minutes past eight o'clock was executed before the Debtors' door, Newgate, George Foster, for murder of his wife and child by throwing them into the Paddington Canal. On Saturday he confessed he was guilty of the crime.

But hanging was not the end of the matter, because Foster had been sentenced to what most people thought was an even more horrible fate. Since the Murder Act of 1752, judges could order a murderer's body to be taken to surgeons for medical research. In most cases, this meant the corpses were used for dissection, often in public anatomy lessons given to fascinated spectators. Foster, however, was destined to take part in a ground-breaking new experiment.

According to an account in the *Newgate Calendar*, Foster's body was cut down from the gallows and taken to a nearby house, where the renowned Dr Aldini wanted to follow up his recent successful trial on a dead dog, by demonstrating on a human being. He had presented a paper to the Royal Society about the effects of electric currents on muscles and there was much optimism that this scientific discovery could eventually be used to revive people after drowning or suffocation. As a group of medical men watched intently, Dr Aldini attached wires to the body and applied a galvanic current so that:

... the jaws of the deceased criminal began to quiver, and the adjoining muscles were horribly distorted, and one eye was actually opened ... the right hand was raised and clenched, and the legs and thighs were set in motion.

The gruesome experiment to further medical knowledge may indeed have 'offered most encouraging prospects for the benefit of mankind', but it must have been equally successful as a powerful deterrent to crime. Surely anyone reading about George Foster's dreadful fate would think twice about committing murder.

The case was one of hundreds featured in *The New Newgate Calendar*, a best-selling book of the most brutal and shocking crimes, compiled from newspapers and trial transcripts and published in five volumes. They included illustrations of courtroom and execution scenes and were usually spiced up to enthral readers with dramatic but often fictitious accounts of the convicted criminal's last hours, pitiful remorse and confession. The report of Foster's melancholy end was almost certainly fictitious:

He fully confessed the horrible crime for which he suffered: confessed he had unhappily conceived a most inveterate hatred for his wife, that nothing could conquer, and determined to rid himself and the world of a being he loathed. ... even at the awful moment of his approaching dissolution, he seemed to regret more the loss of his infant, than the destruction of the woman he had sworn to cherish and protect. He was questioned if jealousy had worked him up to the horrid act, but made no reply except saying that he ought to die.

True-crime stories like this gave everyone the satisfaction of moral judgement on a terrible deed and the comforting reassurance that justice had been done.

††

Harsh punishments for crime were deliberately planned to create maximum public horror and have enough impact to deter other would-be villains. In some cases, the bodies of executed murderers were hung up in chains and left out on display in the parish where the murder was committed.

Public executions took place once or twice annually in the counties and eight times each year in London, when huge, noisy crowds from all classes of society jostled excitedly in the packed streets around Newgate Prison to watch proceedings. The gallows in London were originally at Tyburn (where Marble Arch now stands), but in 1783 were relocated to Newgate Street, where the Old Bailey Central Criminal Court is today. A total of 35,000 criminals in England and Wales are estimated to have been sentenced to death from 1770 to 1830. Although the majority were reprieved and either transported to Australia or imprisoned, about 7,000 people were executed.

Not everyone in Georgian England accepted the death penalty merely as an inevitable but routine practice. Many people were giving the matter serious thought and questioning punishments that seemed to some like a barbaric inheritance from the medieval era. An anonymous letter writer to *The Times* in February 1804 protested at the unnecessary cruelty inflicted:

> I became last week an accidental spectator of the execution at Newgate and cannot well express my indignation and surprise, at the barbarous expedient of hanging the malefactor from a cart. The objections to this new mode appear to me so numerous and weighty, that I am actually astonished at its adoption.

The writer had heard that traditional hanging from a scaffold on a high platform was discontinued simply because it was too much trouble for idle officers to set up. Explaining the old method's advantages, he said:

> By the suddenness and violence of its fall, the sufferings of the victims were terminated at once; by its elevation, an extensive moral impression [was made] on the multitude, the great object of all public executions, [and] wretched sufferers were enabled to receive religious consolation almost to the last moment.

However, the new method of a shorter drop from gallows on a low cart not only increased suffering, but 'the effect produced on the populace from a gibbet scarcely elevated above the heads of the immediate by-standers must be extremely limited'.

The year after this letter appeared in *The Times*, national crime figures for 1805 showed that 350 people were condemned to death, but only 68 of them were executed. One of the undeniable problems with capital punishment was its finality. There was no second chance if mistakes were made and the accused was not guilty at all.

Thomas Done, captain of a barge carrying goods on the Cheshire canals, spent one August Sunday evening in a Manchester public house with his workmate Robert Holroyd, drinking with two local girls, Betty Eckersley and her friend from the village of Lymm. As they left, Done asked Betty to go onto his boat, and when she refused, he carried her forcibly aboard.

The next day, she was seen lying on the bed in the captain's cabin looking very pale, and may have been asleep, as the barge travelled slowly down the Bridgewater Canal, reaching Lymm about ten at night. Robert Holroyd put their horse into the stables at the public house, stayed for a swift pint of ale and left soon afterwards. Around midnight, the landlord heard the shrieks of a female in distress coming from further along the canal, and an exclamation of 'O Lord Jesus!' A woman living nearby also heard the dreadful screams and cries but could not distinguish the words. Neither of them ventured outside in the darkness to investigate further.

When the innkeeper got up at seven o'clock in the morning, Done's horse and boat had gone. It was another week before Betty's body was found wrapped in a sack, sunk in the canal, with her hands tied across her chest, her neck dislocated and marks of violence on her arms and breast. A large stone weighing more than 50lb was roped round her middle.

At the trial a few months later, 28-year-old Yorkshireman Robert Holroyd was acquitted of any involvement in Betty's murder. Done made no defence and only his father appeared in court to testify to his character. When the death sentence was passed, he said to the judge, 'I am as innocent of the murder as your lordship', and to the jury, 'I forgive you all', then turning round to his acquaintances in court he called out, 'Farewell to you, lads.' He was imprisoned in Chester Castle and, two days later, taken on a cart to the scaffold behind the city's gaol. After the hanging, his body was delivered to surgeons for dissection and then put on public view.

The *Chester Chronicle* reported that on the morning of his execution, Done was visited in the cell by his mother and sister, receiving the sacrament with the utmost devotion. Although he admitted being guilty of tying the girl in the sack and of almost every other crime, he strenuously denied the killing and 'persisted to the last in declaring his innocence of the murder'. The newspaper insisted that, contrary to unfounded rumours circulating in the town, 'a person more penitent or resigned to his unhappy fate never left this world'. We can only guess what Betty endured throughout the twenty-four hours she spent in the barge cabin. The most likely chain of events on the Bridgewater Canal at Lymm can be pieced together, but with Betty and Thomas Done both dead, no one was ever going to know the whole truth about that night.

†††

Canals were by now beginning to earn an unsavoury reputation as perfect places to commit crime. Anyone plotting to get rid of an unwanted body could usually count on being alone if they loitered on the long, isolated stretches of towpath or beneath a shadowy bridge. There was always an opportunity for sudden violence, with little chance of being caught in the act.

In most cases, however, a body found in the water was more often the victim of an accident, such as the unfortunate Thomas Walton from Stansfield near Halifax, who was last seen at a public house in Todmorden on a Saturday night 'much disguised in liquor', and was eventually found dead in the Rochdale Canal, or the mother carrying her child, who fell into the water and drowned at Bramley near Leeds as she crossed a wooden board from a canal boat onto the bank.

So many unlucky men, women and children seemed to be ending up in the water that the Royal Humane Society stepped in to offer help. Established 'for the recovery of persons apparently drowned or dead', the society announced in April 1802 that it had chosen the King's Arms near the city's Grand Junction Canal as one of its official receiving houses, and deposited there with the landlord, 'the drags and modes of treatment for restoration of life'.

The Times reported the good news that two apparently dead children had recently been pulled out of the canal and both were 'providentially restored to life and to their fond parents. The parties recommended by Mr Ward, Medical Assistant, have been rewarded by the managers of this excellent institution.'

Bodies in canals always made news, and readers particularly loved a mystery. An intriguing case headlined 'Suspicion of Murder' occurred one autumn when Londoners were puzzled by evidence of a crime with no victim and no suspects. Around seven o'clock one morning, passers-by noticed a park bench covered in blood and a little white dog sitting by the water, as if forlornly waiting for his lost master. Ominous splashes of blood were also found on the iron spikes of railings along the canal bank.

As a crowd of curious onlookers gathered to stare, a surgeon called to the scene examined the gory mess and pronounced it was definitely human blood. 'All eyes were then directed to the canal, into which it was not doubted that the murdered body had been thrown.' Alarm quickly spread through the neighbourhood at the prospect of a desperate killer at large, and although permission was given to drag the canal, no body could be found.

Several watchmen who had been on duty during the night were arrested and questioned but were unable to cast any light on the matter. Finally, a young shopman who came to find out what was going on told everyone that the previous evening he saw a butcher's man put his basket of sheep heads down on the bench, where it toppled over, and blood poured out. Despite this apparently plausible explanation, suspicions of murder lingered on.

Some murders, of course, were far more obvious and much easier to solve. One such case was reported in the *Staffordshire Advertiser* in April 1805, when a body was found in the canal near Swindon with the skull perforated by a hole the size of a pistol ball, and a heavy stone tied to the neck which 'too plainly indicated he had been foully murdered'. The victim was Mr Bailey, who had gone missing from his home in Holt six weeks previously, and the crime was discovered after:

> … some extraordinary particularities in the behaviour of a man who had worked on the navigation, excited a suspicion that he knew the deceased had been murdered and thrown into that part of the canal, which occasioned it to be dragged.

The guilty navvy was taken into custody and committed to prison.

Thankfully, not all attempted crimes succeeded. The poignant story of a child abandoned near Water Street in Birmingham appeared in *The Times*, which reported that at ten o'clock one Saturday night he was found by the canal, dressed in cheap clothing to disguise his wealthy background. The engaging little boy with a Scottish accent said he was nearly 4 years old:

> He states in the most simple manner, that a lady left him near the place where he was found, that she took off his frock and the gold band from his hat, and desired him to stop till her return. He says his name is George Barrasankey and that his father wears a red coat and sword – that John cleaned his father's horse and waited at table, that he went to school and that Mrs Ross cut his hair. He is a fine boy, possesses much animation and [has] been used to genteel life. From the situation in which he was found, many persons suspect he was conveyed there for the purpose of being lost or destroyed. ... every friend of humanity will sincerely hope the parties may be discovered and brought to punishment.

It was only by sheer luck that a passing boatman noticed him standing alone in the darkness, just a few yards from the edge of the canal. George was safe, but the whole story only emerged five months later in January, when his mother Charlotte Turner appeared at Warwick quarter sessions, charged with abandoning her bastard child.

The court heard that she came to Birmingham with her son by the Nottingham coach and went to the Rose Inn around seven o'clock in the evening. At nine o'clock, she left with the boy, who was wearing a white muslin frock and expensive beaver hat with a gold band, tied by green ribbons. An hour later, when the boatman found him beside the canal at Snow Hill, the boy was dressed in a cheap, coarse, hurden pinafore, 'which appeared to have been made for the occasion'. His frock had been taken off, and the gold band removed from his hat.

Meanwhile, Charlotte Turner had gone to the Bird in Hand Inn at Dale End, where she supped and slept the night, before leaving early next morning on the Lichfield mail coach. In court, Charlotte said she had lost her son in a crowded street and, being in a strange place, did not know where to look for him. She admitted, however, that she made no enquiries about the missing boy and did not mention him to the land-lady at supper.

It was a meticulously planned crime, with the change of clothing to disguise the victim's identity, and two different inns and coaches so that any witnesses would not think it strange she returned without the child. It was clear that Charlotte travelled far from home deliberately to go to the canal, where she had the best chance of getting rid of her son.

Why did she do it? Had she perhaps been abandoned by the boy's father herself? He was, according to George, a soldier and may have gone off with his regiment. But Charlotte offered no explanation at all in court, nor any clues about her situation.

Newspaper reports of the trial expressed disgust that any mother could abandon her own offspring and hoped that 'this melan-choly instance of human depravity, will be a warning to the young and thoughtless, to avoid the first steps into the paths of vice'. The *Staffordshire Advertiser* noted, 'It is solely to be ascribed to Divine Providence, that the crime of Murder was not the consequence of this inhuman and barbarous act.'

The court sentenced Charlotte to twelve months' imprisonment in the common gaol confined to a solitary cell, where she too would be abandoned and alone like the son she had deserted. It was a sort of natural justice that echoed her crime.

There was a happier ending for lively little George, who could so easily have drowned or been left in the workhouse. The *Advertiser* confirmed, 'It is with true pleasure we learn, that the child is likely to be taken under the protection of a lady of distinction in the neighbourhood.'

4

PERKS OF THE JOB

Canals ran right through the very heart of Britain, underpinning every activity of daily life by carrying the goods needed to meet the insatiable demands of the Industrial Revolution. In the early days, virtually everyone had been enthusiastic about the new and growing canal network.

One letter from 'A Friend to Commerce', in the *Gloucester Journal* on 23 June 1794, applauded the 'astonishingly great' quantity of goods already being conveyed from northern manufacturers and predicted that boat traffic would rapidly increase when the Worcester & Birmingham Canal opened. Cost-cutting was the big advantage of canal transport. Goods could be carried for 18s a ton, instead of over 33s a ton by wagons and river freight – almost half the price. 'Trade will benefit by so cheap and regular a conveyance, by one carrier all the way, which will cut up the nefarious practices of pilfering now carried on to a considerable amount.'

Although, as it turned out, crime actually increased on canals, many other writers extolled all the positive benefits of a waterway network. And there was a great sense of pride in heroic national achievements, echoing the classical engineering feats of the Romans who built the first canals in Britain, including the Foss Dyke in Lincolnshire linking up the River Trent with several towns.

There were always a few carping critics on the side-lines wanting to have their say, like the writer signing himself 'An Enemy to Useless Canals' in a long, rambling letter to the *Gentleman's Magazine* of November 1795. While in favour of canals in general, he was annoyed by the disruption caused in cutting the Staffordshire Canal, which had left some local roads at Pipe Hill impassable, and by the blatant profiteering going on. 'I am sorry to say, too many canal schemes originate not merely from a wish to serve the country, but to serve the purposes of interested individuals.'

On the whole, however, canals were seen as a welcome feature of progress. The naturalist and traveller, Thomas Pennant, detailed the social impact he observed on his annual trip from Chester to London. He said that despite initial protests from people living beside the planned canal route, 'now content reigns on its banks and plenty attends its progress'. He paid tribute to 'that rare genius', the engineer James Brindley, known as the father of canals, who in 1759 had masterminded the first project to construct the Bridgewater Canal, carrying coal from mines on the Duke of Bridgewater's estate at Worsley into Manchester.

Pennant kept a diary of his trip and vividly described how cottage roofs previously 'half-covered with miserable thatch' were now secured with tiles or slates brought from the distant hills of Wales or Cumberland, barren fields were fertilised with cheaper manure, and places which had only scanty supplies of coal or corn were now plentifully supplied, all thanks to canals. 'These and many other advantages are derived to individuals and the public from this internal navigation. The profit arising from tonnage is already very considerable; and there is no doubt but they will increase annually.'

Another keen advocate for canals was the Derbyshire clergyman, Reverend Stebbing Shaw, who declared, 'The general utility of all inland navigations, the prosperity of agriculture, trade and manufactures arising from them, are too well known to admit any further doubt.' He described how, along the Staffordshire canal, 'new buildings and new streets spring up in many parts ... where it passes, the poor no longer starving ... and the rich grow greatly richer'.

Such major changes had been taking place all over the country. But there were winners and losers in a fiercely competitive marketplace as everyone fought for their own share of the profits. Proprietors of the Trent & Mersey Navigation were sued for negligence by cotton merchants Messrs Hyde and Fletcher, after parcels of cloth valued at £522 were destroyed by fire one night in a Manchester Canal warehouse. At a court hearing before Lord Kenyon and a special jury at

London's Guildhall in July 1793, there were complex legal arguments about the liability of carriers for goods they conveyed by land and water, but damages for compensation were finally awarded against the defendant. Canals serviced England's lucrative cotton industry, which was growing rapidly in the boom decades from 1780 to 1815, but it was a high-risk business and 80 per cent of Manchester manufacturers went bust.

There was no masterplan for a nationwide waterway network and canals grew piecemeal, with new stretches planned and funded by local businessmen and landowners who saw an opportunity. Canals were built to carry tons of extra coal from the new coalmines in Lancashire, south Wales and the Midlands, which were needed to stoke the furnaces of industry and warm the domestic hearths of an expanding population.

A section of canal was cut linking the Staffordshire & Worcestershire to the town of Stourbridge, to carry raw materials and finished products for the area's thriving glassmaking industry. At its peak, there were more than twenty glassworks producing fine cut crystal and cameo glass for international export. Stourbridge Canal, from Stourton Junction, was later linked to Dudley and then on to Birmingham. Eventually, separate canals were connected to form a complete circuit of 74 miles round the Black Country, Worcestershire and the Midlands, known as the Stourport Ring. This was typical of the organic, sometimes haphazard growth of the canal network to support industry.

One celebration took place after another, as more sections of canal were opened in different parts of the country. A crowd of 2,000 cheering spectators gathered at a grand ceremony in April 1798, when the Herefordshire & Gloucestershire Canal was completed as far as Ledbury. The *Gloucester Journal* described the procession of boats and the usual boozy dinner for local dignitaries at the George Inn, Ledbury, 'where the utmost conviviality prevailed and many appropriate toasts were drank'. The report concluded, 'In short, every real lover of his country will congratulate the Proprietors upon the completion of so material a part of a scheme, promising great and extensive benefits to the community.'

The most important trade route was that connecting Birmingham with London. A day of festivities was held in July 1801 for the opening of Paddington Basin, which marked the arrival of the long-awaited Grand Junction Canal in the capital. Newspapers everywhere carried reports of the procession of barges carrying officials and a whole band of musicians, several vessels with large parties of ladies, followed by pleasure boats with flags and streamers flying. A salute of cannon fire on Westbourne Green Bridge greeted the cavalcade's arrival at the Great Dock where, 'after three huzzas, the company landed, and walked in procession, preceded by the Buckinghamshire band playing God Save the King'. An excellent dinner and plenty of drinks rounded off the merrymaking.

In the early days, canals seemed to usher in an exciting new era of wealth and opportunity for all, which was celebrated at each triumphant opening ceremony. In many ways, it was true, although it was not the whole story. The popular image of canals as places of benevolent prosperity was an appealing fiction that people wanted to believe in. But gradually, disturbing facts emerged to shatter the myth and reveal the hidden, darker aspects of poverty, alcohol addiction, hardship and crime.

†††

As the waterway network spread, snaking out to link up yet more towns, rivers and docks, the sheer scale of the enterprise, with more boats carrying more cargoes, inevitably created more problems with crime. Pilfering was regarded by many workers simply as a legitimate perk of the job.

Pickfords' boatman Edward Hutchinson was lucky to be acquitted in court of stealing a sack worth 2 shillings and four bushels of wheat valued at 25 shillings, from a wharf owned by Thomas and George Osborne on the Grand Junction near Uxbridge. He was charged on the dubious evidence of William Radley, a 14-year-old on the boat who was initially arrested for the theft. Although the boy claimed he saw Hutchinson take the sack on board about 10.30 p.m., the master boatman and crew swore he did not do so.

A similar case had a different outcome. Boatman Philip Goodenough was sentenced to seven years' transportation at his trial in January 1801 for stealing four bushels of wheat, valued at 30 shillings, from a cargo he was carrying to a mill, after letting a man come aboard the boat at Southall to collect the sack.

Theft was already so well established in 1802 that a group of fifteen leading canal carrying companies, including Pickfords, banded together to form the Inland Navigation Association for Apprehending and Prosecuting Felons. It was, in effect, an attempt to set up a spy network of informers, who were promised a reward of 5 guineas for information about offences that led to a conviction. Accomplices in crime were offered the same payment, together with a free pardon. Whether it helped to reduce the number of offences is not clear, but two years later, the association decided to cast the net wider, this time advertising an even larger, more tempting reward of 20 guineas for information on receivers of stolen goods.

Receivers were an essential link in the chain of crime, and they could be found everywhere. They ranged from professional receivers in known shops (often kept by grocers and chandlers) to casual buyers who did smaller deals in pubs, country lanes and secluded alleyways.

Convicted receivers could expect longer sentences than their criminal suppliers. Waggoner Edward Caseltine was given seven years' transportation for stealing coal worth 5 shillings from a London wharf, while Sarah Michael, who kept a greengrocer's shop in Whitechapel was sentenced to fourteen years' transportation for receiving, after the coal sacks were emptied in through her cellar window one night.

Were boatmen any more criminally inclined than other members of the poor labouring classes? Certainly, they had more opportunities for crime, working alone and unsupervised with valuable cargoes of goods in a roving life where boats were literally here today and gone tomorrow. Flyboat crews working all night had more chance of committing offences that would go undetected. However, as social outsiders, boatmen were also easy scapegoats to blame, even when they were completely innocent of any wrongdoing.

In the hard times of the early nineteenth century, it was difficult to make ends meet for people in work but struggling to exist on meagre wages. Survival of the fittest entailed doing anything to buy food or coal, and that included petty theft, dealing or other criminal activities, when necessary, even among basically honest folk who wanted to make a few shillings on the side.

A visit to the pub was a good place to start for anyone seeking an opportunity. All along canals like the Grand Junction were dozens of public houses where men could meet over a beer, some bread and cheese or a slice of pie, to catch up on the latest gossip. Boatmen gathered in popular hostelries at busy wharfs, lock flights and canal intersections, such as the quaintly named Stewponey Inn alongside Stourton locks, where Stourbridge Canal joins the Staffordshire & Worcestershire. Talk was about the activities of carrying companies, who was hiring, stoppages and cargoes on the cut, where you could ask a favour, find work, plan a dodgy deal, or pick up a cheap bag of nails with no questions asked.

A few pints with an old mate brought trouble for bargeman Ellis Harvey in January 1800. He usually ferried chalk loads out to Egham and beyond, but freezing weather had stopped canal traffic and he went instead to London where, at the Bowl and Pin in Thames Street, he met up with Henry Miles, a warehouseman who worked at Hambro's Wharf in the city. They went round to Miles' lodgings at the Cart and Horse, where they sat drinking together until half-past ten before going upstairs to bed. Ellis Harvey stayed overnight and when he awoke early next morning, Miles handed over a large, brown-paper parcel of cloth, asking him to take it away to dispose of and send 15 shillings as soon as possible.

Ellis Harvey later recalled in court:

He asked me if I had any money in my pocket; I said I had but ten-pence; he persuaded me to carry some of it to Marlow; I asked him how he came by it; he said he came by it very honest, he found it; he told me there was no danger to carry it, for he had cut the names off so that nobody could swear to it, for my safety, if anybody took me; my wife disposed of it, and I disposed of a little of it.

A week later, Miles turned up with a sack on his shoulders at Ellis Harvey's home in Great Marlow, Buckinghamshire, and asked the bargeman's little daughter to go and pawn a bit of cotton. The girl took 3 yards of printed calico to Mr Puddeford's pawnbroker's shop and returned with 6 shillings, 3 halfpence for Miles, who thanked Ellis Harvey with some ale at the White Hart.

Not long afterwards, John Winterpigeon, employed by Messrs Sills at their warehouse on Hambro's Wharf, discovered a bale of cotton had been cut open and a large quantity removed. Suspicion fell on Miles, who went absent from work without leave, and after asking around for information the stolen material was traced.

At the Old Bailey court hearing, Mr Winterpigeon described how he went to Ellis Harvey's house with a search warrant but found nothing, until he noticed the bargeman's daughter wearing a frock of the same pattern as the stolen cloth. Further pieces were retrieved from respectable townsfolk, including butcher's wife Mrs East, who had 2 yards of printed cotton, shopkeeper Mrs Plumridge, who paid for 9 yards of blue Irish linen, and several others who had bought cloth from Mrs Harvey. They all played a part, however unwittingly, in the casual black market subsistence economy that was simply an accepted part of working-class life.

Giving evidence at the trial, Ellis Harvey said:

> I know the prisoner at the bar very well ... he told me if I would bring a punt to the Hambro Wharf he knew how to get some more out. ... he put it in his smock-frock, and brought it home to his lodgings in the dusk of the evening.

Miles tried to lay all the blame on the bargeman, accusing him of proposing to rob the wharf and other offences, including the theft of some fowls, but said, 'I am as innocent of the charge as an unborn baby.'

Miles was found guilty of grand larceny and was sentenced to seven years' transportation. Ellis Harvey managed to avoid being charged with any offence by making it clear he had not benefited from the proceeds of theft:

> I know my wife disposed of what I brought from London; my wife put the money into a little wooden dish, and I gave it into his hand, it was silver and halfpence and a seven shilling piece; it was kept apart from my own.

†††

Canal trade created all kinds of opportunities for theft, not just by boatmen but by any of the vast army of workers employed on canal wharfs and in warehouses. John Howarth, a casual worker at a London warehouse storing thousands of hogsheads of raw sugar, tried to steal some of the sugar he was weighing, stuffing a bundle under his apron. But he was caught after a scuffle with the wharfinger's man and sentenced to be whipped.

John Pyman, a labourer at Brook's Wharf, was found guilty of theft after delivering a basket of nails worth 25 shillings to Briley's old iron shop in Cow-cross, London, for watchman James Webb on Wednesday, 25 July 1804. He blamed Webb for regularly stealing bags of nails over twelve months and selling them on to Briley and to a bargeman called Jack Duck.

Construction sites also offered easy pickings. The *Oxford Journal* reported that one of the navigators, George Harpur, was apprehended at Hoddesdon in Hertfordshire, charged with stealing a great quantity of wheelbarrows from the canal at Paddington, the property of the Grand Junction Company, 'whose loss from that neighbourhood of such articles within the last year, is supposed to be £200'.

Regular thefts continued from London canals, and a year later, labourer John Fenton stole a pickaxe valued at 2s 6d on the day he was discharged from work, claiming he had not been paid full wages. The contractors who employed him confirmed they kept large quantities of tools, shovels and other equipment totalling £2,000 on site and had lost upwards of £200 through theft. The pickaxe, marked with a 'C', was found in Fenton's rooms. Although twelve witnesses in court gave him a good character, he was sentenced to six months' confinement in the House of Correction, with a 1 shilling fine. In Scotland, the *Aberdeen Press and Journal* noted that Donald Peterson was found guilty of stealing planks from the Crinan Canal, sentenced to pay a fine and imprisoned until payment.

Pilfering was widespread in most workplaces, among all types of employees, from tradesmen and clerks to agricultural labourers and domestic servants, but few were ever caught. It is difficult to ascertain the number of cases that came to court because no official annual crime figures were published until 1810. The magistrate Patrick Colquhoun estimated that 3,555 people in England and Wales were charged with larceny offences in 1805. But the full extent of criminal activity was unknown because most crimes were never prosecuted, and many victims chose instead to seek redress through the payment of compensation or by taking revenge on the offender, perhaps by giving them a beating.

Newspapers wanted to print crime stories involving distinctive characters or unusual places that would interest readers, therefore, canal incidents were more likely to be covered. In January 1807, the *Derby Mercury* reported that boatman Thomas Glover appeared at the quarter sessions charged with robbing a canal boat, but he was permitted to enter the army without trial. Courts sometimes chose to send convicts into military service during times of war to provide much-needed cannon fodder, while at the same time conveniently exiling unwanted felons. Glover would have enlisted for the Napoleonic Wars, which had, by then, been going on for fourteen years.

Several publications carried news of an unpleasant case in December 1809, where an unnamed Pickfords' boatman was taken before the magistrate at Stockport in Cheshire, charged with 'inhumanly and unmercifully beating, wounding and bruising' a horse towing the boat. He was committed to hard labour for one calendar month in the House of Correction at Middlewich. The *Manchester Mercury* was appalled by the cruelty, commenting:

> We have greatly to lament the prevailing brutality of a *certain class* of persons, who necessarily, but unfortunately, must be entrusted with the care of animals much more valuable than themselves. Not influenced by any of those beneficent principles of Religion and Humanity, (to which Cowards and Tyrants are always strangers) they mistake their trust for absolute power and dominion, which they exert without mercy towards the poor brute, whom they know cannot complain or resist.

Sometimes boatmen were themselves the victims of crime. In May 1805, the *Oxford Journal* told the sorry tale of an anonymous bargeman who went to Smithfield Market, where he purchased a mare for £10. On his way home, he stopped at a public house in the Barbican and handed the horse over to the care of a stranger, who rode off with it. 'To add to his misfortune, he picked up a lady of easy virtue, who stripped him of his cash amounting to £12.' Whether this was true, or merely an anecdote concocted by someone with a low opinion of boatmen, is debatable.

A bundle of clothing, including a coat, two petticoats, a gown, four waistcoats, a shirt, three handkerchiefs and a pair of stockings, was stolen from the cabin of a boat left moored up at Paddington in November 1811. Boatman John Reeves and his wife Elizabeth were alerted to the robbery by the publican of the Green Man, who noticed a man leave a bundle in the gateway of the yard. When they returned to the boat, they found the cabin broken open and their property gone. The culprit was John Heath, an unemployed man who had asked if he could help unload the boat that morning but was turned away. He was sentenced to seven years' transportation.

The Green Man was once again the scene of crime three years later, when the landlord Mr Strange was offered a couple of large Cheshire cheeses weighing 60lb by two men who came into the pub kitchen with a bag. Samuel Conliffe and John Cooper initially said they would sell for 50 or 60 shillings, but then halved the price and eventually agreed to take 6 shillings and return next day for the rest of the money. The landlord heard the cheese had been stolen from Edward Powell's barge near Paddington Wharf and had the thieves taken into custody. They were later found guilty of grand larceny and transported for seven years.

Committing crime after dark, when most people had gone to their beds, was the best way to get away with it. One boatman had a lucky escape from an arson attack as he slept on his vessel laden with cotton next to a warehouse in Castle Field, on the Duke of Bridgewater's Canal near Manchester. The *Derby Mercury* reported:

> Some wicked incendiary one night last week put lighted tar ropes into a boat … Providentially the boatman was sleeping in the cabin, and the smell of burning cotton waking him, he instantly removed the boat from under the warehouse, and extinguished the fire, otherwise the consequences might have been dreadful.

Perhaps the attempted murder was revenge by someone with a grudge against the boatman. A convicted incendiary would face the death penalty, but in this case, nobody was caught.

Far more dramatic was another inflammable incident, where two boatmen made a fatal error and became the victims of their own crime. A Pickfords' boat, fully loaded with barrels of brandy, rum and ten casks of gunpowder, was travelling along the Paddington Canal on its way to the country one Friday night in April 1809, manned by a crew of four. About 5 miles out of London, near Twyford, two of the boatmen fancied a nightcap at ten o'clock and decided to help themselves to some liquor.

Working on deck by the flickering candlelight of a lantern, they bored a hole with a gimlet in one of the gunpowder barrels by mistake. It immediately caught fire:

> The boat blew up with a most dreadful explosion. The two men were killed on the instant. One of them was blown to a distance of more than 60 yards, his entrails torn out … The shock was dreadful in the vicinity, and the houses were agitated as though by an earthquake.

The blaze spread into a nearby field of haystacks, burning three ricks to the ground. Incredibly, one boatman who was asleep in the cabin at the stern escaped completely unharmed.

5

DESPERATE REMEDIES

The raw, jagged sounds of splintering wood and locks being smashed to pieces echoed across the yard as the warehouse gates were forced open by a gang of hired hands. They broke into the premises of trader Augustus Cove at No. 2 Wharf, Paddington, during a traumatic week at the end of June 1808. Shouting abuse, they tore down fences, entered buildings, seized furniture, roughly bundled up piles of paper and carried off boxes.

Then, on Saturday evening, the men fastened a chain and padlock on the gates, locking up Cove inside the building. At noon on Monday, two of the ruffians, George Sharrat and John Weston, alias 'the Butcher', returned to collar him as a thief and launched a violent assault. In fear for his life, Cove repeatedly shouted, 'Murder!', eventually managing to throw open the chamber window and leap out to escape. Covered in blood and dirt, he staggered to safety and tried to clean himself up, dipping his handkerchief into the canal and wringing out the water to dab ineptly at his clothes while a surgeon was sent for to dress his wounds.

The terrifying attack was not, however, the work of criminals. It was a deliberately planned tactic to forcibly evict Cove from the warehouse in what he believed to be a conspiracy hatched between the Grand Junction Canal Company, who owned the wharf, and Pickfords, who wanted to take over the lease. As Cove stood, angry and shaken, on the wharf, he saw Pickfords' Chief Clerk John Wright and complained that the intrusion was 'as illegal as it was barbarous'. Wright and his workmen simply made off, taking the keys with them and leaving Cove imprisoned on the wharf amid the wreckage of his prosperous business.

But the whole shocking incident was far from over, and soon after eight o'clock two men arrived to arrest him on the orders of the Grand Junction Company, who issued a warrant for an outstanding debt of over £85. Astounded, Cove asked, 'Where are you going to take me?'

The officer said simply, 'To Newgate.'

A crowd of onlookers had gathered, but none of the neighbouring wharfingers could be persuaded to stand bail for him as they were reluctant to take his side against the company. Helpless to resist or defend himself against the charge, Cove was led off to prison. On the way, he was allowed two minutes to call in at his home in Chapel Street to inform his wife, then he was taken to Newgate, going in through the felons' door like a common criminal after 10 p.m., when it was too late to get either supper or a bed.

He was released on bail a few days later, only to find that his cart horse and wharf dog had been turned out on the public road and had both disappeared. For many people, that would have been the end of the matter. But for Cove, the events of that week marked the start of a long David-and-Goliath-type battle for justice against Pickfords and the Grand Junction Canal Company, which went on for years. It seems to have become an all-consuming obsession for Cove, who refused to let himself, as a small trader, become the victim of his large and powerful opponents.

Cove proved to be a fierce and persistent fighter, determined to seek compensation from his oppressors, although as a practising Quaker he was supposed to live by the pacifist principles of the Nonconformist group known as the Society of Friends. A family man in his early forties, he was assisted by his son Thomas in the profitable business he had built up on the strength of the Staffordshire coal trade. He had owned the Paddington Wharf lease since purchasing it for 1,000 guineas in 1804, with a verbal promise of renewal. Instead, the lease was granted to Pickfords, who, Cove alleged, took the law into their own hands to secure vacant possession, although we only have his side of the story to go on. The verbal agreement was not legally binding. But he could not accept that, while the eviction was unfair and heavy-handed, it was lawful.

Firstly, Cove had Sharrat and Weston, the two heavies who attacked him, charged with assault and convicted at Clerkenwell court, but their fines were paid by the company. Next, he sued the eight men who broke into his premises, only to be awarded the nominal sum of 1 farthing. Then he kept turning up uninvited at the six-monthly meetings of those 'gigantic tyrants' the Grand Junction proprietors, demanding recompense, but he was ignored.

Eventually, after four years of unsuccessful legal tussles, he took an action for damages of £8,000 against Pickfords' clerk John Wright to the Court of Common Pleas but lost the case. The trial was reported by several newspapers including the *London Statesman*, in an account almost certainly written by Cove or a friend and sent to the press, noting:

> Mr Augustus Cove pleaded his own cause, which occupied more than one hour and a half in the delivery ... He displayed a considerable portion of eloquence, not unfrequently mixed with a clear and acute reasoning.

According to Cove, the judge actually nodded off and was fast asleep during this long speech.

The following year, he published an indignant seventy-page pamphlet, *The Tocsin Sounded, or A Libel Extraordinary*. The front page was crammed full of accusations in furious capital letters against 'A GRAND-JUNCTION OF VICES, An Horde of desperate Villains and Scoundrels', whose crimes against 'AN OUTLAW WITHOUT A CRIME!' included swindling, forgery, fraud, bloodshed, housebreaking, false imprisonment and robbery.

A tocsin is a bell rung as an alarm signal and Cove wrote:

> I find public Companies (some of them) tolerate, and even promote, doing those Things in their collective Capacity, when cloathed in a Coat of *Darkness,* and *Invisibility* ... which individually they would be afraid to practise or abhor.

He also cited another similar case where a poor, lame former wharfinger in his eighties was 'cruelly robbed and plundered of all his property' by the Grand Junction Company. This publication was followed by *The Tocsin Sounded a Second Time!* which included a verse:

When *Rogues* unite, and form a *Junction Grand*;
Truth falls a *Victim*, Reason cannot stand.
Even *Courts of Law*, (or Justice) can become,
AS LOTTERY PROJECTS, and as *Snares to some*.

It was Cove's final riposte and his warning to others, born of painful personal experience, that too often it was the rich and powerful who won.

Bitter disputes over conflicting interests on the canal were commonplace and usually involved lengthy legal wrangling about compensation for losses. These lawsuits could involve canal companies and carriers like Pickfords, warehouse owners, merchants, manufacturers and industries producing materials like stone, lime or coal.

London had hundreds of canal wharfs and they were noisy, bustling places filled with activity from dawn until late at night. Shouted orders rang out, heavy wooden boxes thumped down, horses' hooves clattered and cartwheels rumbled across cobbled yards cluttered with stacks of barrels, coils of rope and piles of packages in all shapes and sizes. Queues of waggons were needed for the relentless flow of boats, and scores of sweat-stained labourers in worn leather boots loaded and unloaded the cargo, often working by lamplight into the early hours.

Paddington had originally been 'simply a mere high road thoroughfare into Buckinghamshire, and the western parts of Hertfordshire, and was rather celebrated for the nursery and market gardener's grounds in its vicinity', according to travel writer John Hassell. The painter and self-confessed drunkard George Morland once lived there, sketching the rustic scenes he was well known for from the windows of his house opposite the White Lion Inn, which depicted the carters and labourers who gathered there drinking.

Now the Grand Junction Canal brought a steady stream of laden fly-boats, heavy barges and coal craft into Paddington Basin, described by Hassell as:

A large square sheet of water occupying many acres, with warehouses on either of its sides, and so commodiously sheltered, that goods of every kind, can be shipped or unloaded without the danger of being wetted. Since the canal has come to Paddington, this place has become an extensive and well frequented market for cattle, sheep, butter, poultry &c.

Canals meant cash and there were plenty of different ways for everyone to make money, both lawful and unlawful. Theft continued to be the scourge of waterways trade, despite all the best efforts to prevent it. Staff on the wharfs were always on the lookout for suspicious activities, but sometimes it was safer to keep silent and avoid trouble.

A vigilant porter employed at Pickfords' wharf was followed by three bargemen as he walked home with his wife along the Edgware Road in London, one Wednesday night in August. After arriving at their house, the men 'attacked both of them, cutting and beating them dreadfully; and in order to get at them again after retreat, two doors were broken open'. Yelling 'Murder!', the porter grabbed hold of one man named Cotton until the cries brought help.

Cotton appeared before the magistrate at Marlborough Street charged with felonious assault with intent to murder, where he was committed for trial and taken off to gaol in irons. Apparently, Cotton had vowed revenge because the porter 'excited his enmity as well as that of several of his comrades, in consequence of detecting and putting an end to several of the evil practices of the bargemen'.

†††

Thomas Homer was a fortunate man. He had the enviable knack of seeing an opportunity and making ideas into lucrative projects. Everything he touched turned to gold. And when, in 1811, he approached the architect John Nash with a bold scheme for a new London canal, success was assured. It would be an expensive and risky venture but promised high returns for investors.

There was no doubt about Homer's all-round experience of the waterways. A solicitor and canal speculator, he had established himself as a canny businessman. He also possessed that vital winning combination of intelligence, credibility, personal charm and the luck of being in the right place at the right time.

Born on 27 March 1761 at Birdingbury in Warwickshire, he was one of seventeen children of the village rector and prominent classical scholar Henry Sacheverell Homer. At 16, he began legal training as an articled clerk to a local solicitor but, prompted by his father's enthusiasm for canal investment, soon recognised the exciting opportunities opening up on the new canal network. He took a job as joint clerk on the Coventry Canal, before being appointed by the Grand Junction Canal Company to oversee accounts and general management. He was a stickler for detail, and his investigations into vast overspends on the ill-fated Blisworth Tunnel led to the abrupt dismissal of the works contractor and several relatives.

Homer was on a generous salary, which he needed to provide for his wife Mary and their children, but he began to cultivate a variety of interests, practising as a solicitor in London while also investing in barges and wharfs to trade as a coal merchant at Paddington. By the age of 43, he was a prosperous, well-respected public figure and had taken over the lease to run a popular daily passenger service of three pleasure boats on the Grand Junction from Paddington to Uxbridge, known as the Paddington Packet.

The *Morning Chronicle* noted his charitable donation to the Royal Humane Society:

> It is strongly reported that Mr Homer, of the Grand Junction Canal will bring out a handsome new Passage Vessel; and ... the benevolent owner has determined to present its benefits to that excellent institution the Humane Society. Since the opening of the Canal, many children have been rescued from the watery grave, and the Rewards of the Society paid to the providential preservers of their lives.

Despite this amiable public image, Homer was a stubborn opponent, when necessary, in the inevitable disputes that arose in canal trade, asserting his legal rights for the slightest offence. On one occasion, he pressed charges against William Messenger, a father of five small children, for stealing coal worth just 3 shillings from one of his boats moored at Linslade. The man was sentenced at Buckinghamshire quarter sessions in Aylesbury to seven years' transportation. However, after he had served two years' hard labour in prison, petitions for his release were signed by more than thirty people, who confirmed his previous good character and asked for clemency on the grounds that he was now contrite and very ill, and his aged father of 70 was in great distress. The judge granted Messenger a free pardon.

Another, even smaller theft, of coal valued at 2s 6d, by 20-year-old boatman William Painter, was also prosecuted. Two nightwatchmen noticed him taking coal from a heap on Homer's wharf at Paddington and accosted him after he put it into his own barge loaded with dung. Painter retorted, 'Well, I will take it back again, it was only one piece of coal.' But although he did carry the coal back to the wharf, he was still charged and later sentenced to be publicly whipped.

Homer also won other lawsuits, such as the two actions against him by ship owner William Booth, claiming compensation for extra wages paid to coal heavers when his vessel *Nancy* was delayed in Paddington Basin.

Thomas Homer did not usually accept defeat. Always quick to grasp an opportunity, he originally came up with the idea for a new London canal in 1802, but it was rejected as too costly. When he revived the ambitious project, this time along a different route through fields north of the city, he soon found some enthusiastic supporters. He was now nearing 50, at the peak of his career and full of confidence.

In early 1811, he went to the architect John Nash, asking him to incorporate proposals for a canal in the exclusive Marylebone Park estate, which he was developing. It was to be called Regent's Park, in honour of the Prince Regent (later King George IV), who was an acquaintance of Nash but a widely unpopular figure, cuttingly described by *The Times* as a 'hard-drinking, swearing man who at all times would prefer a girl and a bottle to politics and a sermon'.

The new Regent's Canal would be just over 8.5 miles long and run from an area now known as Little Venice, just north of Paddington Basin, to connect the Grand Junction with the River Thames at Limehouse in east London. The estimated cost of land acquisition and building would be far higher than any other canal construction project so far, but Homer anticipated an impressive return for investors of more than 15 per cent.

John Nash immediately recognised the scheme's potential and took charge, drawing up a detailed report with plans to raise capital through subscriptions and forming a committee with Thomas Homer as secretary. Everything was falling into place. But Homer had a secret. A secret so dangerous, it threatened to destroy everything he had. It was imperative that no one should find out.

Initially, plans for the canal were delayed by opposition in Parliament, when some Members objected that development of Marylebone Park would exclude the labouring classes, who gathered for recreation to enjoy their free time in the public houses and meadows. One MP protested that the canal 'would break in upon a large and salubrious space of ground, of the utmost consequence to the health and comforts of the inhabitants of the Metropolis'. However, the Act of Parliament approving the canal was passed in July 1812 and construction started in October.

Work was progressing steadily until, in the spring of 1815, a series of completely unexpected events put the whole scheme in jeopardy. Trouble first erupted when a gang of twenty navvies began digging out the cut at Camden through land owned by a barrister named William Agar, who had repeatedly tried to prevent the work going ahead and was demanding huge sums in compensation. At ten o'clock on a Monday morning in late March, Agar's team of gardeners confronted the navigators; fences were torn down and fighting broke out. Three of the navvies were taken to Bow Street, charged with riot and violent assault, but magistrates dismissed the case. Agar responded by serving a writ against the Regent's Canal Company directors.

Then, less than a week later, came revelations about an entirely different matter. An anonymous note was delivered on Tuesday evening to Charles Monro, the company's chairman, which made some damning allegations about Homer. Alarmed, but reluctant to believe the incredible accusations, the following morning Monro spoke to the project's engineer, James Morgan, and sent word to Homer that he would be expected to show evidence of his accounting at a meeting the next day.

On Thursday, Homer turned up with some of the payment vouchers and explained he had mislaid other documents, which he would bring in at the end of the week. Their suspicions growing, Monro, director Joseph Delafield and company solicitor John Edwards arrived at the offices on Saturday for the critical meeting and waited for Homer. He did not come. Instead, he had a letter delivered with the excuse that he could not bring in the missing vouchers because he had left them in the country, but would do so on Monday. That lie bought him some extra time, although not enough. The game was up.

The secret that Homer had tried so desperately to hide for the past three years was out in the open. He was bankrupt. And worse still, he had been using the company's money in a desperate effort to pay off his debts. He explained that he had been declared a bankrupt before he applied for the job as Secretary to the Regent's Canal but did not mention it to the directors for fear it might prejudice his appointment. Since then, he had been continually harassed by creditors to repay his debts.

In a long, rambling letter full of remorse, dated 3 April and addressed to Monro, he confessed everything. And by the time Monro unfolded the scrawled pages of this hurried letter, Homer was long gone. He fled to Europe but was turned back when attempting to land at Ostend. This was probably due to the chaos of war, as troops and supplies were arriving at the Belgian port where a large British garrison was preparing for the Battle of Waterloo, which would be fought that June. Instead, he returned to London briefly, before setting off again for Scotland.

Meanwhile, the directors had issued a reward of 100 guineas for the fugitive's capture, and with news of his arrival north of the border, they immediately sent an officer in pursuit by mail coach. Details of the arrest appeared in the press, including the *Caledonian Mercury* of 6 May, which reported:

> Mr Homer, Secretary to the Regent Canal Company, a defaulter, as it is represented, to the amount of £4,000 was apprehended by Thomas Foy, whilst taking a comfortable dinner at Edinburgh, on Tuesday last. … He left his home about a month since, and so much confidence was placed in him that his absence excited no suspicion, until his defalcation appeared. He is turned 60 years of age, and is now in confinement in London.

Although he was only 54 when locked up in Bridewell as a debtor, the defeated and penitent Homer undoubtedly felt years older after the strain of the past months. He pleaded guilty to embezzlement at his trial at the Old Bailey on 15 May and was sentenced to seven years' transportation. Newspapers reporting his disgrace included the *Oxford Journal*:

> In the list of prisoners sentenced to be transported for seven years, it grieves us to report Mr Homer, formerly in the service of the

Grand Junction, and recently of the Regent's Canal Company, for embezzling and running away with considerable sums of money, the property of the latter.

It was the end of everything Homer had worked so hard to achieve. He was taken to Newgate as a prisoner, where he was held for several months and then moved on to one of the forbidding prison ships known as 'the hulks', which held offenders awaiting passage overseas.

In a final effort to salvage something from the wreckage of his life by having his sentence reduced, he wrote three letters to the Regent's Canal Company directors asking them to intervene, but they were unmoved. By then, they had discovered the full extent of his fraud, which was much more serious than they had realised. Homer had to pay for his crimes like any common thief and transportation to Australia had been the usual punishment since 1787.

An identical sentence of seven years' transportation was imposed on two pickpockets, John Keith, aged 20, and James Eves, 18, for stealing a dozen handkerchiefs worth 1 shilling each, from people in the London canal-side crowds at the August Fair and others watching fireworks in the park. They were followed into a public house by police officer Benjamin Johnson and had just ordered a pot of beer when he came over to search them and found the pocket handkerchiefs hidden under their clothes.

In another case, where canal boatmen John Turner and Thomas Fuller smashed a board in the corner of a coal merchant's warehouse on the Grand Junction to steal two bushels of coal, they were also transported for seven years.

The majority of convicted thieves belonged to the poor, labouring classes. Although Thomas Homer's sentence was the same as these petty offenders from the lowest levels of society, as a wealthy white-collar fraudster, he was viewed not as part of the despised criminal class but as a corrupt exception from the ranks of respectable middle-class morality. Social distinctions meant nothing, however, on board the rotting old hulks that had been used for decades as a convenient solution to prison overcrowding.

Even before felons set out on the long voyage to Australia, they had to endure life in the grim conditions on these dank, disease-ridden former war ships, such as the *Justicia*, moored on the Thames at Woolwich. In the daytime, men did hard labour onshore, digging or dredging silt from the riverbed, and at night they lay in cramped rows of hammocks inside the chilly, rat-infested decks.

In fact, less than a third of convicts sentenced to be transported were actually sent abroad, and it appears that Homer stayed in England after all. From the few known facts, it seems likely that he instead served at least part of his sentence on a prison hulk and may later have been transferred to debtors' prison. Certainly, two years later, on 22 April 1817, *The Times* reported a trial at the Court of King's Bench when Homer was said to be 'now on board the hulks, under sentence of transportation' and therefore unable to be called by the court to explain the exact methods of his embezzlement.

The case was one of several unsuccessful lawsuits taken by the Regent's Canal Company against its shareholders to try to recover some of the money milked off by Homer. At this trial, the company alleged Lord Dundas, one of the canal investors, was liable to pay £800 in overdue share instalments. Thomas, 1st Baron Dundas, was a Scottish politician who inherited his father's interest in canals, becoming governor of the Forth & Clyde Canal Company and commissioning the first steamboat. Lord Dundas denied any liability, saying he had paid the money in to Homer.

The Times reported that Mr Warren, counsel for the plaintiffs, said:

> This misrepresentation of the state of the accounts was occasioned by a person of the name of Homer, who had been appointed superintendent of the affairs of the Company, and in whom great confidence had at one time been placed: he was afterwards found to have defrauded the Company.

An inquiry into the fraud headed by Lord St John, another investor, had examined the accounts and concluded that the company 'had been most grossly imposed upon' by Homer, who had no authority to receive money. Mr Warren added, 'The misfortune was, that Homer could not be procured to give evidence.' Lord Dundas won the case.

Homer's fraud had far-reaching consequences for the construction of the Regent's Canal, which was making slow progress, hampered by repeated problems and escalating costs. More capital was urgently needed but private investors were now reluctant to come forward. The company eventually managed to borrow money to complete the canal from a government unemployment relief scheme set up to create jobs for the poor.

Speculating on canals could bring enormous profits for those willing to invest, but it was a big gamble in a game with high stakes. John Sutcliffe, a civil engineer who had spent many years on waterways projects, made a scathing attack on the blatant profiteering he had witnessed and warned of the risks involved. He said, frankly, that the general public had been misled about the supposed rewards to be made, on schemes falsely:

> ... painted in the most glowing colours ... for trade without risk is a thing unknown to the mercantile world. I am sorry to say, that long experience has shewn me, that canal subscribers have generally been the dupes of all parties.

Sutcliffe still hoped more canals would be made, even though:

> They have already been so much disgraced by the improper designing and conducting of them, ... for public confidence is much sooner lost than regained. Canals are certainly of the greatest importance to trade and commerce; and no man admires the utility of them more than myself ... but I think there never was any scheme so much prostituted to the private interest of individuals and engineers as that of canals.

Most people who bought shares would never be paid a penny of interest. Some threw the dice and won, while others gambled and lost.

††††

The Regency era, for most of the population, was not the peaceful, clean and elegant world portrayed by Jane Austen in her novels, where genteel lives of country strolls, letter-writing and gossip were punctuated by fleeting excitement about a new sprigged muslin gown, a romantic engagement or an invitation to the county ball. Far from it. The vast majority experienced a very different reality in a precarious existence where cold, hunger, dirt and drudgery were all too familiar.

It was an unsettling period of rapid change and times were hard for many. While overseas the interminable war against Napoleonic France finally ended in 1815, it brought in its wake mass unemployment as thousands of soldiers returned home. Throughout Britain, there was a pervading mood of apprehension and unease. Frequent violent outbreaks of social unrest and rising crime levels fuelled this troubled sense of encroaching danger.

Crime was a particular concern and new efforts were made to try and understand the root cause of the problem. A lengthy report was produced by a special committee set up in 1815 'for investigating the causes of the alarming increase of juvenile delinquency in the metropolis'. A team of fifty public-spirited volunteers on the Alarming Increase Committee, as it was known, spent a year visiting convicted youths held in Newgate Prison and their friends on the outside in organised gangs. They found that all the lads lived in poverty, some were orphans, but others were sent out onto the streets by their parents.

The report was sympathetic to the boys and called for changes in the way they were treated, which could help reform them, noting that confinement in an adult prison only led them into a life of crime:

Dreadful, therefore, is the situation of the young offender: He becomes the victim of circumstances over which he has no control. The laws of this country operate not to restrain, but to punish him. The tendency of the police is to accelerate his career in crime.

It concluded that widespread poverty created by the shortage of jobs was to blame:

The want of employment, the degrading tendencies of the poor laws, and increased facilities for the consumption of spirituous liquors, have doubtless contributed much to deteriorate the moral character … of the lower classes of society. To an evil so general and extensive, it is impossible at once to apply a remedy.

Two such young offenders were 14-year-olds George Morris and Charles Showell, who were tried at the Old Bailey for stealing a saw valued at 5 shillings, belonging to a labourer working by the Regent's Canal. They were seen lurking near the yard in City Road, one December afternoon, before slipping under a gate to snatch the saw, but were caught as they ran off. Both were lucky to receive the lenient sentence of a whipping and were then discharged.

It could be hard to avoid trouble, given that even some harmless activities were deemed to be crimes. Several lads enjoying a swim one warm August evening were rounded up and taken before magistrates, charged with bathing after 8 p.m. in the Regent's Canal. They were severely reprimanded 'for the indecency of bathing at so late an hour of the day, when many females walk that way', but discharged with a warning that they would be convicted if caught a second time.

Youth crime in London was again examined by a special Parliamentary Committee on Policing and members of the Alarming Increase Committee were among those who gave evidence. Everyone agreed that the degenerate lower orders of society were the major source of crime, and their dreadful drinking habits only worsened natural criminal tendencies. Public houses came in for particularly heavy criticism as meeting places for rogues and prostitutes.

Drink-fuelled crime was, of course, not only taking place in the grimy streets and dockyards of the city. Work on the cut could often brew up violent incidents anywhere in the country that a new canal was being built. Many miles away in rural Lincolnshire, a mass protest erupted on the Witham Navigation in May 1815, when more than 500 navvies, who were digging out the riverbank, went on the rampage. The men decided to take the law into their own hands in retaliation against local shopkeepers and publicans, who had been ripping them off by overcharging for basic supplies. A huge crowd of angry labourers assembled in the village of Bardney, where one of the ringleaders produced a paper from his pocket and read out a statement, declaring that the prices of bread and other goods should be reduced.

As the terrified villagers cowered indoors, navvies converged on the Plough, where they tore down the pub sign, threw out the landlord and began drinking his beer, then marched on to the baker's shop to grab armfuls of loaves and bombard him with bread. By now the whole village was in uproar as mayhem spread through the streets and the riot seemed to take on a life of its own.

A gang of burly labourers broke into the Bottle and Glass public house to roll out casks of ale for the impromptu revels, cheering and shouting as they swilled as much free booze as they could get their hands on. Others marched around, knocking on doors and demanding money from householders. The Angel's innkeeper quickly rolled out his own barrels and locked the door before they could storm the premises.

Before long, the cavalry arrived to take back control of the besieged village, the Riot Act was read and some of the men were bundled roughly into carts and taken off to gaol. Nine were committed for trial, including William Buck, William Stringer and George White, who were all given a one-year prison sentence for rioting, committing diverse outrages and breaches of the peace. Two men received six-month sentences, but the others were acquitted, so most of the rioters escaped scot-free after a memorable pub crawl. It must have been a satisfying kind of revenge.

Many rungs higher up the social ladder, alcohol could also spark off aggressive behaviour, but wealthy men who lost their tempers were not likely to be arrested. A heated quarrel between Scottish landowner Lord Morton and Mr Moncrief, manager of the Edinburgh & Glasgow Union Canal Company, turned into a fist fight in July 1819. As the queen's former lord chamberlain, the earl was a public figure, but at 58 he was well past his prime. The undignified scuffle became a very public joke when a cartoon drawing by George Cruikshank, the best-known illustrator of the day, was published with the ironic title *Pugilism Extraordinary*.

Lord Morton evidently punched Moncrief on the nose before being knocked to the ground himself. The etching depicted the dishevelled earl lying on the floor of the canal offices, his nose bleeding, warding off further blows from Moncrief while a startled onlooker dropped a bottle of wine. A table was overturned, scattering papers, and on the wall a picture of the canal was flanked by portraits of boxers in the ring, with the inscription 'Boxing Extraordinary – or – a NOBLE fall!!!'.

Both men apparently made angry threats of legal action at the time but it's unlikely they ever did sue each other. The row about a canal scheme that was then under construction made an amusing topical subject for a satirical print, and it was sold on the streets that summer in one of the popular news-sheets called broadsides. Lord Morton no doubt soon shrugged off the embarrassment. The following year, he attracted more welcome publicity for his scientific interests in the field of evolutionary genetics by attempting to breed a quagga – an unusual animal that was part horse, part zebra.

†††

After eight long years and countless problems, the Regent's Canal finally opened on 1 August 1820. It was undoubtedly an impressive feat of engineering but had cost twice as much as originally estimated.

One of the many visitors who admired this latest improvement to the city described how the canal ran from a lock at the first bridge, through a short tunnel beneath the Edgware Road and entered Regent's Park, where it formed an ornamental sheet of water. It continued east by Hampstead and Highgate Roads, passed Kentish Town and crossed Mr Agar's grounds at the back of Pancras Church and Battle Bridge, where a large basin held the goods depot. The canal entered a tunnel under Islington, threading its way out to Hackney and finally going under the Mile-End Road into the River Thames.

Immense crowds gathered on the morning of the opening celebrations, jostling for a better view of the procession of barges decked with colourful flags and streamers, the boatmen dressed in their Sunday best of blue and white frocks with beribboned hats. On board were bands of musicians and invited dignitaries, carried triumphantly along the route into City Road Basin, where guns fired a salute.

There, the cheering spectators were crammed tightly together and made easy pickings for the many pickpockets unobtrusively working the crowds that day, slipping a furtive hand into pockets and bags while their unsuspecting victims were caught up in the noisy excitement of the occasion. Everyone watched a hotly contested boat race, as barges competed to land the first goods on the wharf. The crew of the *William* snatched victory from a close rival and unloaded a cask of ale, which was immediately drunk on the spot by navigators with loud huzzas toasting the canal's prosperity.

The grand procession of boats ended at Limehouse, where yet more people lined the canal banks to cheer them on, unaware of the lone thieves weaving in and out of the crush. But greater danger came from menacing gangs of twenty, fifty and even a hundred thugs, who milled about and robbed anyone who looked a soft target. Such rough trade was expected at any public event, but this time there were so many gangs roving about like packs of wolves in search of prey that constables on duty around the canal were afraid to take them on. The gang members worked in unison, some of them surrounding and hustling people, grabbing their arms or lashing out with a swift blow while others rifled pockets.

One helpless victim that day was John Aird, an infirm old gentleman from Hackney, who was knocked down and robbed by a gang as he walked slowly home from watching the celebrations. Many other bystanders were attacked and relieved of their watches or cash, and some who tried to fight back were thrown into the canal. A Mr Allen of Chapel Street, Pentonville, was badly beaten and robbed of his pocketbook containing a £100 note. A lock-keeper had his watch and money stolen after jumping down from a barge, while a youth who stopped to watch the boats entering the locks had his pocket-book full of banknotes snatched.

Most of the culprits ran off or simply melted into the crowd. Amid all the jollity, the sounds of happy cheers and animated chatter were punctuated with bursts of raucous laughter and sudden, terrified shrieks. Angry shouts echoed across the water as rowdy gangs surged through the crowds, dodging the scores of constables on duty that afternoon and well into the evening. It was chaos.

Soon after six o'clock, the last barge arrived at Limehouse and dropped off the final batch of VIPs. At the official dinner in the London Tavern that evening, almost 100 special guests raised their glasses and drank to the canal's success, applauding and toasting 'the commerce of England' and 'prosperity to London'. Charles Monro, the company chairman, rose to speak of the great undertaking and its many difficulties, which had:

... been overcome not only through great exertion, but through great expense. ... This is one of those great works which, though originating in the enterprising spirit of private individuals, was calculated to produce the greatest benefit to the public.

Monro added, with masterly understatement, 'In truth, the difficulties which have been surmounted are known only to those who have been engaged in superintending the work.' His remarks may have been oblique references to the disgraced Thomas Homer, who had come up with the original idea, though naturally he was not mentioned by name, and the architect John Nash was credited with the success of the whole scheme. Some things were best forgotten, as Monro may well have reflected wryly as he sat down to loud applause and cries of 'Hear, hear!'

Meanwhile, as the wealthy guests relaxed over dinner, the city's weary constables dealt with the aftermath of the crime spree and those few offenders they had managed to arrest. The daring spate of robberies was widely reported by a horrified press and *The Globe* noted:

On Tuesday thieves and pickpockets availed themselves of the opportunity to commit robberies, in consequence of the immense numbers attracted to view the ceremony ... The constables were very much maltreated in the execution of their duties; but they succeeded in securing about 14 very notorious characters.

Just like Thomas Homer, they too were exploiting the canal for their own ends, by literally taking money out of other people's pockets in brazen acts of daylight robbery.

Over the next few days, some of the thieves who had been caught were examined by magistrates, including Eliza Smith and two male accomplices charged with robbing a young gentleman of a silk handkerchief. At a separate hearing in Shadwell on 8 August, a crowd of ladies and gentlemen gathered and tried unsuccessfully to identify the men who had robbed them. But four gang members were committed for trial as reputed thieves at the next quarter sessions, when officers confirmed they were all known characters.

The ruffian who attacked elderly John Aird was 21-year-old weaver Joseph Ellinger, a member of the largest gang. On 18 September, he was convicted at the Old Bailey of highway robbery, assault and theft of £43 in banknotes. At the trial, Mr Aird described what happened:

As some barges were coming along, I stood by the handle of the lock; a crowd came round, and one put his hand to my throat and crushed me back; there was a great many people, I was quite surrounded and hustled about a long time, and saw my watch chain out, I took hold of it and the man who had hold of it made a severe pull at it, and broke the chain. I was then thrown on the ground, and all ran away.

Thomas Wells, a Hackney tailor, told the court how he helped Mr Aird to his feet, saying, 'I was within ten or fifteen yards when he was robbed, and went to his assistance. I picked him up. He was on the ground and several were pushing him with their knees to keep him down.'

Wells and other bystanders chased after Ellinger, who sprinted off. At Cambridge Heath Bridge, they were joined by carpenter William Lane, who recalled:

I heard the cry of 'Stop thief!' and immediately pursued and secured him, with his right hand in his breeches pocket. He made great resistance, and a man came up and said, 'If you do not let that man go, you will be murdered, for the gang are coming.' I said, let the consequence be what it might I would not let go.

The struggling Ellinger was pushed into a nearby house, where he was held until an officer arrived to take him to the lock-up.

Ellinger said he had found the banknotes and was running along the street to see the boats pass, but the jury found him guilty, and he was sentenced to death. Old Mr Aird, perhaps fearing retribution by the gang who would now know where he lived, made a request to the judge that Ellinger be recommended to mercy. However, Mr Justice Best said offences of that type had become so common, he did not think justice would be done to the public unless the law was allowed to take its course. Reporting the trial, the *Morning Chronicle* described it as 'one of the robberies committed on the opening of the Regent's Canal, which for atrocity has not been equalled by anything of a similar nature for many years'.

However, Regent's Canal witnessed yet more shocking scenes of violence two years later, when canal boatmen demanding higher wages started a riot. Spontaneous riots by angry mobs or workers with a grievance were regular occurrences at the time. This one, late at night on 24 July 1822, was planned well in advance. Pickfords was flourishing and had won a profitable government contract with the army, so boatmen employed by the company naturally felt they were entitled to a pay rise. Now was the time to press their claim, as 800 soldiers from the 3rd Battalion of the Grenadier Guards were assembled further along the canal at Paddington, waiting to board a convoy of twenty-six boats due to take them to Liverpool.

Pickfords needed 104 men to crew the boats, and just as they were due to leave their moorings in City Road basin at 11.30 p.m., there was a sudden loud cry of 'Now, my boys – this is your time!' from bargeman Edward Wray. Instantly, between seventy and eighty boatmen, who had been lying in ambush, sprang from their hiding places in the shadows yelling, 'Huzza! Edward Wray for ever!' and threatening that not a man or boat would leave the basin unless their wages were raised to 10 shillings a week.

In the darkness and tumult, some of the rioters ran over to the lock to stop the gates being opened as others cut towing ropes and two horses plunged into the water. Then they began searching barge cabins, shouting that they would knock out any man's brains who tried to move a boat and roughly grabbing those who refused to join the strike, tossing them into the canal. The ringleaders piled heaps of flint stones on the towpath and armed themselves with the sharp missiles.

At midnight, when police officers arrived to help the canal watchmen who were valiantly trying to restore order, 'a most desperate conflict ensued between the two parties, and several were desperately wounded in the rencontre'. Fighting continued until 4 a.m., when the police eventually dispersed the mob, capturing the ringleaders and taking them before the Hatton Garden magistrate. After a four-hour delay, the barge convoy finally set off to collect the waiting troops.

Two months later, on 21 September, ten bargemen including their leader Edward Wray appeared in court and were found guilty of conspiracy and riot. The men had no legal counsel and called no witnesses. Pickfords' clerk, John Wright, said they were paid 7 to 10 shillings a week, plus their victuals. Mr Walford, prosecuting, told the judge he was instructed by Pickfords to press for an exemplary punishment:

The men have sometime before struck for wages, and were forgiven on a promise of future good behaviour; and the return they made was to take advantage of their employers ... when they supposed their demands must be complied with.

The defeated boatmen were sentenced to imprisonment in the House of Correction for varying terms of between one and three months each.

6

DANGEROUS LIAISONS

It may all have started as a bit of harmless fun with some lively banter, joking and laughter aboard a barge, one winter's day in 1826. For young boatmen Daniel Osborne and John Cooke, who picked up two female passengers as they left Warwick at dawn, it was just an amusing diversion to break the monotony of another long, slow journey taking cargo up north.

But there are always two sides to every story. For Susannah Fell and her friend Elizabeth Fisher, a relaxed canal trip home turned into an entirely different experience. According to 20-year-old Elizabeth, she went to Warwick with Mrs Fell, and they decided to return home by canal, joining the boat at 4 a.m. on Monday, 21 November. They stayed on board all day, travelling up the Grand Junction through Birmingham and then on to Tipton in Staffordshire, where, at 5 p.m., the boatmen moored up in an isolated spot and went ashore. At 11 p.m. that night, they returned to the barge and later in court, Elizabeth described what happened next:

Osborne said he would drown me if I did not undress immediately, and he took me to the side of the boat to do so, I suppose. He laid hold of me, and forced me down stairs into the cabin, and again ordered me to undress. Osborne pulled off my boots by main force. I durst not cry out, because he threatened me. Osborne then made me get into Cooke's bed against my will. I had taken my gown off. I took it off myself, but Osborne made me do so. I had taken my stays off, and my under-petticoats. Cooke made an attack upon me. I was afraid for my life. I was obliged to submit, for fear worse should come of it. They threatened to murder me. While I was in Cooke's bed, Osborne was dragging Mrs Fell about the cabin floor. She was begging him to let her alone.

Before daylight, Cooke left the cabin and went out on deck to steer the boat along the canal. Elizabeth said Osborne then climbed into her bed and smacked her hard across the mouth as she fought him off, but eventually gave up his attack and left the boat. At 11 a.m. Cooke came back inside, grabbed hold of Mrs Fell and began to attack her. Eventually, the women escaped from the boat into a field where some men were working, but they did not make a complaint to them and instead walked the 2 or 3 miles to Mrs Fell's house at West Bromwich. Elizabeth then set off to Birmingham, where she lived with her father, but when she reached home two and a half hours later, she did not tell anyone about the incident.

In early December, Osborne (aged 21) and Cooke (23) were arrested and sent to Stafford Gaol. There they remained under lock and key, until at a brief court hearing on 20 March 1827, a charge of violating both women was dropped by the prosecution, for the reason that neither of the victims had expressed any wish to leave the boat, 'which they had the full power of doing'.

A few days later, the boatmen were brought up from the cells again for a trial before Mr Baron Vaughan, to face the lesser charge of assault on Elizabeth Fisher. She was called into the witness box to give her evidence, standing only 2 yards away from the accused men, and when asked to look round the court to point them out, she said she could not see them – clearly intimidated and too afraid to identify her attackers.

Under the silent scrutiny of the watching jurors, Elizabeth tried to explain that the barge was moored in the middle of the canal near Tipton, so they could not get off. During the assault, Osborne gave her a blow on the face:

My mouth was so much hurt, that I could not eat well for a week after. I went with Mrs Fell to her husband's at West Bromwich ...
On our way we met no one but boat folks, and I did not like to tell

them. I saw no women. When we got to Mrs Fell's her husband was out at work, and I went home to Birmingham. I met a great number of persons but I did not like to tell them a thing of this kind. I have a mother-in-law and a father, but I durst not tell them, because they keep me so strict. I thought they might be angry. I never mentioned what had happened to anybody till Mrs Fell came and told of it at our house a week after.

Cross-examined by defence counsel Mr Ludlow, she said that throughout the attack she had begged Cooke to let her alone, and Mrs Fell had struggled very hard with Osborne but did not actually cry out. Asked why she had not left the barge at Birmingham, Elizabeth said she didn't know where she was, although she admitted she had lived there for eleven years. Mrs Fell was not called to give evidence.

Mr Phillips, prosecuting, concluded:

I think I ought not longer to keep up this case. These women must have seen the town of Birmingham as they passed through it, and there is no satisfactory reason why they should not have got out of the boat and gone home, instead of going on further with the boat to the place where all this occurred.

The case raised many questions. Why didn't Elizabeth leave the boat at Birmingham? She said she did not realise where she was at the time, but perhaps she was simply waiting to reach West Bromwich, where Mrs Fell lived. What were the boatmen doing for those six hours from 5 p.m. to 11 p.m. that they were absent from the boat? There was no mention of alcohol during the trial, but it surely seems likely they went drinking. Did they attack the women on returning to the barge that night, inhibitions loosened by too much beer? And why didn't the women escape from the barge at Tipton when they had the chance – was the boat moored in the middle of the canal, as they said? The stark simplicity of Elizabeth's account undoubtedly rang true, but was it enough to convince the jury?

Courts demanded evidence of overwhelming violence and determined resistance in a rape case. And a woman who knowingly put herself in a potentially risky situation, alone with a man, was considered to have given her consent anyway. With no other witnesses at all, should the jury believe what the men said or the women? Who was really telling the truth about what happened?

The whole case hinged on the issue of consent. One newspaper reporter made his own opinion of the alleged offence clear, describing the accused as 'both exceedingly respectable looking young men', and noting unkindly that Elizabeth was 'a female who certainly had no pretensions to beauty'.

Summing up, the judge told the jury they must be satisfied that the prisoners had 'formed the horrible purpose of assisting each other in an attack' and if they had committed an offence by force or by threats equivalent to force, or whether there was consent. Mr Baron Vaughan pointed out that Elizabeth had given a different account of the incident before the magistrate and he said:

> The successful resistance made to Osborne went most strongly to negative the supposed resistance to Cooke, and besides that there was no recent complaint by the prosecutrix, even to her own family. One would suppose that there would have been an instant complaint, and an effort to have the prisoners apprehended on the spot. However, it turned out that the prosecutrix never complained at all; and but for a communication made by Mrs Fell a week after, the secret might for ever have remained in the prosecutrix's own bosom. Under all these circumstances, the Jury would say, whether they thought it could be inferred that this offence was committed against her will.

It was a clear direction to acquit the men, and after only a very short discussion the jury returned a verdict of not guilty – a regular outcome of rape cases at a time when attitudes to women, rules of evidence and the difficulties of disproving consent made it extremely unlikely that a prosecution would be successful. To have any chance of winning a case, a victim had to prove her screams had been heard by a witness, that she had made a complaint to someone immediately after the attack, brought charges very quickly and had her physical injuries confirmed by a surgeon's evidence. Above all, a victim had to be chaste and of good moral character. Even then, the outcome was far from certain.

But attitudes to sexual violence against women were, very slowly, beginning to change. In the 1820s, the number of prosecutions for rape and other sexual offences began to increase and there was more reporting of rape trials in newspapers. One case that attracted extensive press coverage was a brutal assault at Edgbaston in Birmingham, not far from the site of a new canal reservoir under construction.

Eighteen-year-old Ann Atkins was out walking in the fields with her sweetheart William Griffiths one evening in early May, enjoying some time off from her job as a servant to a button manufacturer. The young couple strolled arm in arm near Roach Pool, completely unaware they were being watched by a group of ruffians armed with bludgeons. As they reached a lonely spot a few yards from a barn, the men overpowered Griffiths and one of them, named James Pattern, grabbed Ann, who shrieked and clung on to a tree stump.

Desperate to save her, Griffiths hastily offered Pattern some cash to let her go. But it was no use. Cursing and swearing, he wrenched the terrified girl away from the tree, carried her into the barn and knocked her to the ground. Griffiths charged at the door, frantically trying to break it open, but the three other men forced him back, threatening to 'serve him out' if he tried to interfere. Inside, Ann was screaming and screaming. As she cried out, 'Murder!', Pattern clamped his hand down over her mouth and raped her. Afterwards Pattern wanted Ann to shake hands with him, but she escaped his grasp and fled outside, where the three men who had stood watch during the vicious attack were laughing at her distress. The gang then made off across the fields.

Next morning, Ann told her sister what had happened, then reported it to a constable, and Griffiths went to find her attacker. He knew exactly where to look. Among the hordes of navvies working on the canal reservoir he found James Pattern, a 20-year-old farmer's son from Norfolk, and easily identified him – 'a coarse made man, short, but remarkably thick and stout for his years'. He had been out drinking before the attack and had also been in a fight the previous evening, knocking down a man with his fist. Full of bravado in front of his workmates, Pattern insolently told Griffiths 'to fetch his dame again, and he would take her to the barn'. He refused to identify any of the other navvies as his accomplices.

Not long after that 'a stout man', presumably Pattern, sought out Ann and persuaded her to accept £3, which was a considerable sum at the time. Such casual payments to victims had long been common practice for felons wanting to hush up crimes and avoid a formal prosecution. Bribes had also been paid to witnesses to give false evidence since eighteenth-century 'straw men' blatantly advertised they were available for hire at the Old Bailey, by walking up and down outside the court wearing shoes packed with straw.

At Pattern's trial for rape, held at Warwick Assizes on 12 August, Ann told the court she had taken the £3 with her father's permission, but had never said she would suppress her evidence if the prisoner gave her money. The judge said it was evident someone 'had attempted to compromise a felony of a serious kind by the most corrupt and objectionable means' but the girl was not to be discredited on that account.

Two passers-by who heard the screams and saw Ann leave the barn looking very distressed appeared as witnesses to confirm the attack had taken place. Then a known prostitute, Ann Adams, who admitted she had been gaoled as a disorderly person, was called by the defence and swore the girl had been her companion in a life of common prostitution on the streets of Birmingham. She had obviously been paid for her lies, and they were indignantly denied by Ann. But such damning accusations, however unfounded, could often influence a jury. It was a clever defence tactic, deliberately calculated to cast doubts on the girl's character.

Summing up, the judge told the jury that if they were satisfied the prisoner's counsel had established the fact that the victim was an immodest woman, it would have weight as to the value of her testimony. But she was nevertheless entitled to the protection of the law. After a half an hour discussion, the jury brought in a guilty verdict. Pattern was sentenced to death and the judge warned him there was not the least hope of any mitigation.

However, that did not stop the condemned navvy, now being held in Warwick Gaol, from fighting for his life. His defence counsel claimed there was fresh evidence that had not been produced at the trial, sending someone to make further inquiries in Birmingham and then making an official application to have the death sentence commuted. On Friday, 2 September, a letter arrived from the Home Secretary refusing to grant mercy. The next morning, Pattern received the sacrament from the prison chaplain and mounted the steps of the gallows, and at ten o'clock, the drop fell.

Newspaper reports of the trial were sympathetic to Ann, describing her as 'an innocent-looking girl' and noting how she had been cross-examined at length deliberately to try and discredit her. But when Pattern was executed, he too was seen as a victim, and the local press was full of sympathy for 'the poor man', who was said to be of low intelligence and had struggled through a series of childhood misfortunes. They recounted how he lost his mother at the age of 8, and soon afterwards saw his father thrown into prison. At 12, he was apprenticed to a thatcher for only a few years until his employer had an accident. 'It seems, from his master's account of him, that he was a quiet man, obliging, and easily persuaded to anything.'

The crime was brutal, but so was the punishment. Media reports reflected a growing public unease about the death penalty, even for the most serious offences. The *Warwick and Warwickshire Advertiser* reflected on the moral tragedy of the case, blaming a lack of religious guidance by parents and masters for the alarming general increase in juvenile delinquency. It noted:

> Pattern appears to have been a hard-working, improvident man, but not notoriously vicious. It does not seem he was particularly addicted to drinking; but he was in liquor at the time he committed the offence, and this rendered him less aware of his crime, and the consequences of it, – an awful warning of the danger of taking a cup extraordinary.

†††

More than 200 criminal offences carried the death sentence in the early years of the nineteenth century, and many of these were property crimes that could involve theft of goods worth just a few shillings. But in the 1820s, the so-called Bloody Code was repealed, ending execution for almost all offences except murder, rape, aggravated robbery and treason.

This may well have been partly a response to changing attitudes and a more humane approach to punishment. Many criticised the public spectacle of the gallows, which actually encouraged crime by attracting pickpocket gangs to work the huge crowds who gathered to watch. However, the decision was probably also taken for far more practical reasons. As the population steadily grew, so did crime, and it was becoming problematic for the authorities to deal with the hanging of ever greater numbers of felons.

As prosecutions increased, the number of people sent for trial in England and Wales more than doubled from 1815 to 1830, although over two-thirds of them were charged with petty larceny. Previously, theft was punished by the death penalty, while even the worst cases of assault were not. Changing punishments now meant that convicted thieves faced transportation, while harsher maximum sentences were brought in for violence with the 1828 Offences Against the Person Act. It was a major shift in priorities for the criminal justice system, from protecting property to penalising all forms of personal injury.

Non-capital offences were dealt with at the quarter sessions, while more serious crimes were tried at the assizes, which were held four times a year in large towns throughout the country and at the Old Bailey in London. Most felons were from the working classes, while jurors were chosen on property-owning criteria and drawn from the wealthier ranks of society. Juries were, of course, all male and would remain so until 1919.

The right to a fair trial by a jury ostensibly made up of your peers was laudable in principle. In practice, though, it could be difficult for juries to weigh up all the conflicting evidence presented in court and the outcome of even apparently clear-cut cases was often unpredictable.

On Saturday, 26 July 1828, the *Lancaster Gazette* reported:

Dreadful Affair at Blackburn – A deep sensation was caused in Blackburn on Wednesday week, by the report of a young woman having been murdered near the town, and thrown into the canal, about three o'clock in the morning of that day. There were, of course, many contradictory rumours instantly afloat, respecting the circumstances of this melancholy case.

Ann Morris, an 18-year-old cotton factory worker, was a guest at a wedding reception held at the Castle Inn in Market Place, on Tuesday, 15 July. During the evening, people noticed Ann seemed very low spirited and guessed it was because her young man had refused to accompany her to Preston Races. She told one acquaintance that he would hear of something before breakfast, but he had no idea what she meant by this cryptic comment. The party went on all night, and when she left in the early hours, Ann agreed with her friends that they would go home to change into their work clothes, then straight on to the factory without going to bed.

As the two girls walked back along King Street, they were joined by soldier James Hughes, a bugleman of the 67th Regiment, who had been among the band of musicians playing at the wedding reception. Around 3.30 a.m., two men who were some distance away on the Bolton Road noticed Ann standing with Hughes on the canal bank near the aqueduct.

The soldier had his arm round her waist and suddenly grabbed her neck, while she appeared to be struggling to get away and escaped his grasp once or twice. He followed her along the towpath and again put an arm round her neck. One of the onlookers shouted at Hughes to let the woman alone, before continuing along the turnpike road, but looking back two minutes later, he saw Ann floating in the canal and Hughes at the water's edge.

Hughes swiftly ducked under the railings and, without raising the alarm or calling for help, he ran down the canal bank, under the aqueduct and along the road. As he reached some houses, he tore off his red coat, wrapped his bugle in it and sprinted off into Blackburn. A passing carter gave chase but could not catch him. The onlookers raced down to the canal, just as Ann's body sank beneath the surface. One of the men plunged in to try and save her, but the water was at least 9ft deep and he could not reach her.

It was not until 9 a.m. that the body was identified and inquiries made after the person supposed to have thrown her into the water. Realising there was no alternative, Hughes surrendered himself to the commanding officer of his regiment, Captain Harpour. He claimed the girl had run along the canal bank and when he next saw her she was floating in the water. Although he tried to get her out, he was unable to do so, then became confused and did not know what he was doing. He could not explain why he ran away without making the least effort to procure assistance. It was not a very convincing story, and he was immediately taken into custody.

Concluding its long report on the inquest, the *Lancaster Gazette* noted the whole incident remained a 'very great mystery; and the conduct of the prisoner was certainly very inconsistent with the story which he told'. The coroner's jury returned a verdict of wilful murder and the soldier was committed for trial. However, just a few weeks afterwards, the grand jury at the assizes court found him not guilty of murder. Hughes was discharged on the grounds that 'there could be little doubt that the unhappy young creature was the cause of her own destruction'. Two different juries could take entirely different views of the evidence, even in the same case.

In fact, Hughes was one of three indictments for murder dismissed by the jury at the court in Lancaster that day. Perhaps to avert potential criticism that they had been too hasty in order to be released early from jury service, Mr Justice Bayley commented that he was sure they 'had paid great attention to them, and exercised a prudent judgement in the decisions they had come to'. Jurors were becoming very reluctant to convict where offences carried the death penalty. Even for those found guilty of a capital offence, more than 80 per cent could now expect to be granted a reprieve, so public hangings were a rare treat for those who still enjoyed the whole grisly performance.

A vast crowd of more than 50,000 people packed the streets by the courthouse in Glasgow on Wednesday, 22 October 1828, to watch the execution of an Irish girl and her boyfriend, who were convicted of the assault and robbery of a Scottish boatman. Isabella 'Bell' McMenemy, 'a good-looking woman, about 23 years of age, fair complexion and red hair', had acted as decoy to lure Alexander McKinnon into the pub for a drink, then outside onto the banks of the Paisley Canal near Port Eglinton. There, she and her accomplice, Thomas Connor, 'cruelly maltreated their victim, and knocking him on the head with a stone, to the great effusion of his blood, they robbed him of 40s in silver, which the poor Highlander had secreted in one of his stockings'.

At the trial, their victim, McKinnon, whose broad Highland accent meant he had to be examined through an interpreter, said that on 20 May, he met the girl in Maxwell Street and they had a gill together in a public house. Promising to take him on for another drink at a house she was acquainted with, she led him towards the canal aqueduct bridge and asked him to sit down beneath the arch. Instantly, a man seized him by the neck-cloth and Bell struck him on the head. When McKinnon regained consciousness sometime later, he found his stockings were off and his shoes and the money were gone.

William Brown, a watchman in the Gorbals police district, had earlier that night seen the boatman with Bell, who was wearing a drab mantle lined with red silk. At 2.30 a.m., he accompanied McKinnon to the spot under the bridge, where he saw a pool of blood and a stone lying near it. He found a discarded stocking and 1 shilling on the ground about 5 yards away. Another police watchman set off to find the attackers, and at 3 a.m. saw Bell in Centre Street. He tried to grab hold of the fugitive, but she let her blood-stained cloak fall off and slipped free, dropping a man's shoe as she disappeared into a nearby house. The door was slammed in his face. When the two watchmen searched this building, where Connor and Bell had lodgings, they discovered a man in bed and Bell hiding inside a chest.

The jury found them both guilty and recommended Connor to mercy on account of his youth. Passing sentence, the judge, Lord Meadowbank, said McKinnon had not yet recovered from the dreadful attack and in all probability never would. Whatever his age, Connor was not young in crime and had appeared in court for a similar offence six years earlier, only escaping sentence by the intervention of Providence. Such offences were being committed so frequently that this time an example must be made. The judge told Bell he held her most guilty, as in this case she had been the principal in devising and carrying out the robbery.

There was wide coverage of the execution by many newspapers, including the *Aberdeen Press and Journal*, which reported the redhead from Tyrone had arrived in Scotland seven years earlier and was creditably employed at a steam loom factory. Bell had not been involved with crime until she met Connor, but was led astray by the charismatic Irishman, a depraved young man who had been 'a bad boy ever since he was able to crawl'. She dated all her wickedness and misfortunes to the day her friendship began with Connor and his mother. The *Journal* said that since being condemned to death, the couple had taken comfort from visits by Catholic priests and shown real penitence for their sins. Whether this was true or merely a creative ploy to embellish the emotive story of crime and punishment, newspaper readers had to decide for themselves.

On the morning of the execution, Bell and Connor were taken out to the scaffold accompanied by two bishops, who led the prayers as the ropes were adjusted and caps pulled down over the prisoners' heads, in the final minutes before the drop fell:

> Although some complaints were made amongst the spectators that the executioner did not give the female enough rope, her sufferings appeared to be as speedily at an end as those of her companion who received a much greater fall. After hanging the usual period, the bodies were taken down and conveyed to their respective relatives.

The *Journal* noted that the crowd, 'as might have been expected, was much greater than usual, on account of the execution of a female, which is fortunately a very rare occurrence in Glasgow'. Only four women had ever been executed in the city, the last one being hanged for murder, thirty-five years earlier.

†††

The network of watchmen and local parish constables which served as a basic system for keeping order in each neighbourhood during the eighteenth century had gradually evolved to deal with the larger number of offences being committed, especially in expanding urban areas. London's Bow Street Runners began work in 1751, the first trained and organised body of officers tasked with tackling crime.

This was followed in 1798 by the foundation of the Thames River Police, a small, independent police unit specifically for crime prevention on the river. The new plan for a preventive force of officers who would deter criminals by their regular presence on the Thames was spearheaded by pioneering magistrate Patrick Colquhoun, who had earlier pointed out the deficiency of laws, 'which have done enough to punish, but little to prevent criminal offences', and suggested that 'a remedy may be found in the improvement of the police system'.

Eventually, in 1829, after much opposition and years of heated public debate, the first large-scale unit of salaried professional officers was formed, known as the Metropolitan Police. The new force was established as part of Home Secretary Robert Peel's wider reforms of criminal justice and its aim was to prevent crime and maintain order. But the concept of a centralised, government-controlled police force was viewed with suspicion by large sections of society, who thought it was both an expensive burden on taxpayers and contrary to the cherished principles of English freedom. Others were more hopeful that it would at last improve policing, as the *Morning Herald* commented:

> Mr Peel is quite right in setting the New Police System to work in the city of Westminster; which at present as far as police is concerned, is the completest satire on the very term … Not only are crimes of every sort committed with impunity, but a sort of general hotbed and nursery is kept up, under the very nose of the Magistrates, for the supply of crime to the rest of the metropolis, as well as for the provinces. … we think there is now a chance of our having, what we never had even the semblance of, a thoroughly good police.

Respectable folk in Islington wanted stricter law enforcement on the Regent's Canal in their neighbourhood, where a correspondent to the *Morning Advertiser* in July 1829 complained that 'morality is daily offended by the most disgusting scenes, and is a further proof (if that, indeed, were required) of the very inefficient state of the police'.

The letter-writer protested that on every warm day, especially on Sundays, crowds of men and boys bathed and ran about quite naked by the canal, watched by women and girls of all ages, who congregated on the Britannia and Maiden Lane bridges. Although notices were posted on every bridge, warning that anyone found bathing in the canal would be fined £5, they were simply laughed at:

> Over these bridges gentlemen, with their wives and daughters, are compelled frequently to walk; what must be the feelings of a man of any delicacy! A good police should prevent crime, not wait until its commission, in order to get paid. … I hope the parish police may be called upon to exert itself, and stop scenes that ought not to be witnessed in any civilised country.

Policing such an innocuous pastime was not a high priority for hard-pressed officers dealing with far more serious offences.

Several thousand policemen in distinctive blue tailcoats and top hats were sent out to patrol the crime-ridden streets of London, day and night. The blue uniform was deliberately chosen to distinguish them from the military in their red coats. Nicknamed 'Peelers', 'Raw Lobsters' or 'Blue Devils', the officers were equipped with only wooden truncheons to defend themselves, even though trying to prevent crime could be risky work.

Five canal boatmen made a vicious attack on two police officers who intervened when they saw a horse being cruelly beaten as two barges travelled along the Paddington Canal. Sergeant John Collins, of No. 1 Division S, was doing his rounds with William Walters one Saturday morning in November 1829 and spotted a boatman named Atterbury beating one of the towing horses over the head with the butt-end of his whip. Collins warned him to stop, but Atterbury merely shouted the foulest abuse and continued to hit the animal.

When the policemen asked whom the horse belonged to, the barge captain, named George, swore at them and all five boatmen shouted (in language too obscene to be repeated), 'They are ***** policemen!' as they jumped ashore to attack. Collins was punched in the face and the point of a boat-hook was thrust into Walters' upper lip, before they were both thrown into the canal. As the injured officers thrashed about helplessly in the water, Rockingham, captain of the second barge, struck out at them with his boat-hook, while the crew cheered and exclaimed, 'Murder them – drown them!' Collins and Walters called out for mercy, but their cries were ignored, and the two boats carried on up the canal.

Bruised and bleeding, the officers managed to haul themselves out of the cut, their new uniforms sodden with cold, dirty water, and after recovering, they made for the nearest lock house to find out the names of their attackers. Before daybreak on Friday, Inspector Howells stationed ten of his men at the tunnel entrance to wait for the barges, which were due back on the return trip from Leicestershire. All the boatmen were promptly arrested.

When the case was heard by Marylebone magistrates, two gentlemen who witnessed the incident described it as one of the most brutal they had ever seen, but said they were 'fearful of assisting, from the well-known violence of the boatmen'. A solicitor appearing for George and Rockingham argued that the policemen had brought the attack on themselves by unnecessarily interfering with the horse, which was a vicious animal inclined to kick.

The magistrates ordered the two barge captains to pay a fine of £5 each, commenting that they should have controlled their men instead of helping them, and that such an aggravated offence deserved 'the highest penalty, as sending them to prison would not make them better men'. Atterbury was fined 40 shillings plus another 20 shillings for cruelty to the horse. The others were to pay 20 shillings each.

Whether on the canals or elsewhere, most violent offenders were men and most victims were women who, if they did report an assault, could expect to have their character and moral reputation openly attacked in court. To prosecute a case took a lot of courage. No wonder that most victims remained silent.

In Ireland, where a man accused of rape could often avoid a conviction by marrying his victim, a judge remarked to the jury at the start of the Summer 1829 Assizes sessions in Clare that, 'From the number charged with rape, he was of opinion that such a crime was the way of proposing for a girl in that part of the country, if the bachelor could not speak English.' The news snippet, headed 'Irish Proposals for Marriage', was reported widely by newspapers all over England, where such shocking attitudes were not tolerated and the traditional remedy of a private settlement for rape was seen as an unacceptable throwback to less civilised times.

It remained a highly contentious subject and the *Morning Chronicle* protested about the victimisation of increasing numbers of men unfairly charged with rape, who were kept in prison before trial and later acquitted. It commented sarcastically:

> Any girl who wishes a husband, and has no other means of obtaining one, is kindly invited to seek the aid of a Court of Justice, which will soften his heart by the fear of the rope which it suspends over his head.

A horrifying incident involving two Pickfords' boatmen took place in Staffordshire during March 1829, as 'a simple-looking country girl' of 22 called Matilda Parker set off along the road to visit her aunt. The road from her parents' house in Bromley ran beside the canal, and on her way, she was overtaken by a Pickfords' flyboat. The captain invited her aboard, promising to take her to Courton, near Tamworth, but when she was in the cabin, he threw her onto the bed where both he and his companion violated her.

They held her captive overnight and when, next day, she tried to jump from deck onto the shore, the two men pulled her back, tearing her gown, and then beat her severely. On Monday night, a few miles away from Paddington, the captain renewed his assault and Matilda scrambled out on deck to cry for help but was again knocked down. When the boat finally reached the wharf, she was put ashore and later went to lodge a complaint at Marlborough Street offices.

At the brief hearing, reported in the *Morning Chronicle*, Mr Dyer, the magistrate, 'who appeared quite astonished at the poor girl's statement, inquired if none of the men belonging to the boat offered to interfere on her behalf'. Matilda told him they did go into the cabin but took no notice of the brutal conduct of her assailants. Mr Nangle, assistant overseer of Saint Giles workhouse, said that unfortunately such incidents were a daily occurrence on canal boats. 'Every unprotected female who travelled by them was sure to meet with the same treatment; and the boatmen, instead of assisting them, were sworn to protect each other.' The magistrate issued warrants for the arrest of the two men and directed that Matilda should be taken care of in the workhouse.

Only a minority of boatmen were prosecuted for serious offence, but with attacks like this hitting the headlines, their reputation as a dangerous, closed brotherhood prone to appalling violence was steadily gaining ground. Assaults were committed by men from all walks of life, but boatmen had more opportunity to attack a lone woman, far from prying eyes on isolated stretches of canal, as Britain's most senior judge pointed out at the end of a trial in April 1829.

Boatman Edward Pearson, charged with raping Naomi MacDonald, and his crewman, William Parker, charged with aiding and abetting the crime, were both acquitted at Leicester Assizes but given a stark warning by the judge:

No man can doubt that your conduct, prisoners, has been most scandalous. You are boatmen, and I wish your fraternity to know from you, that should any boatman be brought before me convicted of the crime of rape, I shall most undoubtedly leave him for execution. You stand in such a situation as to have unprotected females frequently in your power, and that power, it is well known, you often use. I am therefore determined, to order for execution the first man of your calling convicted of such an offence as you have been tried for, and to add to the example, I shall order him to be executed on the banks of your canal.

The remarks perhaps reflected his frustration at the jury's verdict of not guilty, but as this presiding judge was the Lord Chief Justice (head of the judiciary under the Lord Chancellor), his words carried substantial weight and indicated he was well aware of a serious problem on the canal network with the number of assaults being made on women.

Two months later, a boatman driving his horse on the towpath attacked a woman near the wooden bridge at Paddington. Mrs Elizabeth Epples, described as 'a very decent middle-aged woman', was returning from Kensington gravel pits to her home in Mitcham Street, Marylebone, at about 10.30 p.m. on 9 June, when she was rudely accosted by Samuel Holdmoes and replied she had nothing to say to him. The boatman then seized hold of her, flung her on the ground and began violently assaulting her.

Another boat passed by during the attack but the bargeman merely urged him on, calling out in jaunty camaraderie, 'Curse you, go it!' Luckily, the woman's cries for help were heard by two watchmen on patrol, who rescued her just in time and took Holdmoes into custody. A stranger later called on Mrs Epples and forced her to accept a payment of 15 shillings in return for her silence, promising she could have another sovereign if her accusation was dismissed by the grand jury. Despite this attempt at bribery, Holdmoes was found guilty of assault.

7

THE CURSE OF BRITAIN

A deluge of beer flooded the country in 1830, when more than 24,000 new beer shops opened their doors to thirsty customers in just six months. Beer poured into foaming pint pots as fast as eager drinkers gulped it down, wiped the last stray droplets from their lips and, with a sigh of satisfaction, called for a refill.

This government-sanctioned binge was set off by the Beer Act, which was an attempt to get the labouring classes off gin and encourage beer drinking instead. It allowed anyone to run an alehouse for a small payment without applying to magistrates for a licence. Beer shops sprang up overnight, alongside the thousands of existing inns and public houses that were already doing a roaring trade. These new, unlicensed premises could be found in tiny front parlours and spare rooms, in villages, city streets and cottages alongside the waterways – everywhere that promised a steady flow of visitors.

Inside, you could expect to find only the most basic taproom with rough flagstone floors, bare whitewashed walls, a few stained wooden tables and rickety chairs clustered round a large, smoky fireplace, beneath grimy low ceilings hung with cobwebs. The worst places served only quarts of 'the thinnest and flattest beer' bought for a few pennies, with hunks of bread and cheese handed out from a grubby pantry hatch.

Beer shops like this, kept by enterprising blacksmiths, labourers or tradesmen seeking a profitable side-line, were widely condemned as being the unsavoury meeting places of thieves and poachers. But whatever their limitations, they had no shortage of custom.

Parliament passed the Beer Act because consumption of wine and spirits had soared, partly in response to worries that drinking water was unsafe. Conveniently for the government, brewing was also big business and a major contributor of tax revenue. However, while the sale of alcohol boosted the nation's coffers, there had long been concerns about the impact on society of alcohol abuse.

The origins of the 'gin craze', which gripped Britain in the first half of the eighteenth century, dated back to an earlier political decision to ban imported French alcohol and promote distilling of spirits from local grain. One of these was the potent Dutch 'Geneva', which soon became known as gin, and was such a favourite tipple that by the 1740s consumption in London reached an estimated 2 pints a week per person.

Not only was gin cheap and highly addictive but it could also be lethal, as unregulated spirits were often mixed with turpentine. Repeated efforts by the government to control production, through higher taxes and stricter regulations, only led to more illegal distilleries and an active network of smugglers. By the late eighteenth century, newly published studies on the mental and physical effects of intoxication were starting to widen understanding of addiction to alcohol – an insidious potion described by one doctor as 'this fascinating poison'.

Cheap gin was widely blamed for criminality and moral decay. It had been wreaking havoc among the poor for decades, as graphically illustrated in printmaker William Hogarth's iconic pair of engravings, *Gin Lane* and *Beer Street*, back in 1751. His vivid satirical portraits left no doubt that gin was a nasty, addictive foreign liquor, whereas beer was a wholesome and manly English beverage.

Hogarth's *Gin Lane*, set in London's notorious slums of St Giles, depicted in squalid detail the dreadful effects of gin drinking, with stark images of debauched and idle drunkards cavorting wildly in the streets, a pox-ridden prostitute dropping her baby, ragged mothers pouring gin down their children's throats and a starving boy fighting for a bone amid ruined buildings strewn with emaciated bodies. In contrast, *Beer Street* celebrated thriving scenes of merry England, where a prosperous crowd of healthy, jolly and productive labourers were shown relaxing beneath a traditional inn sign for the Barley Mow, enjoying well-earned tankards of ale and pipes of tobacco.

These striking twin prints continued to haunt the public imagination for years to come, stoking fears that a drunken and lawless underclass would threaten the whole fabric of society if allowed to go unchecked. *The Examiner* revealed the extent of the problem in London, where the number of gin drinkers charged at Bow Street, one Monday morning in 1830, with disturbing the tranquillity of the streets 'would almost exceed credibility'. Among them were several women with infants at their breasts. The magistrate observed it was hopeless to expect any police force to improve the state of the streets until something was done either to raise the price of gin or cut the number of dram-shops. The report also noted:

GIN-DRINKING – Several cases of vagrancy were brought before the Lord Mayor, in which it appeared that people who were out of employment, on receiving relief, often preferred gin to bread; so powerfully had the habit of gin-drinking taken hold of them, that they would snatch at the liquor first, even though they had not, during the previous twenty-four hours, eaten any food. One old woman was brought up by a constable charged with having disturbed the congregation at the Catholic Chapel in Moorfields. She said that gin relieved her distress of mind, and her mind stood as much in need of consolation as her body; she was a poor forlorn Irishwoman, without a friend in the world except 'the drop'.

It was becoming increasingly obvious that alcohol abuse caused poverty, and poverty caused alcohol abuse, trapping drinkers in a vicious circle that undermined health, corrupted morals and provoked disorder. Whatever the happy, romanticised picture of life in *Beer Street*, beer was not the benign liquid refreshment it portrayed. Brewers regularly adulterated pale ale with substances including opium, treacle, iron sulphate and liquorice to disguise it as more costly porter, the strong, dark beer made popular by London porters.

Even the finest ales were likely to create problems when drunk in excess, as opponents to the Beer Bill warned in Parliament, including an MP who nicknamed it 'A bill to increase drunkenness and immorality, and afford greater facilities to crime'. A proposed clause to the new Beer Act, imposing a 5-shilling fine for drunkenness in the street, was not passed. One speaker said it would be unjust for a labouring man to be penalised for tippling, while a knight or MP could indulge with impunity because he drank only claret and champagne.

Whether the new beer shops persuaded people to give up gin was debatable, but they were very successful at increasing beer sales; so much so that, within twelve months, serious concerns were being expressed. Alarmed campaigners began setting up anti-drink groups, including in 1831 the influential British and Foreign Temperance Society.

Heavy drinking was a fact of life everywhere and canals were no exception. Plenty of simple beer shops, plus the larger public houses offering a bar, taproom, parlour and stables for boat horses, could be found scattered along the waterways and clustered around locks or bustling wharfs.

Two such hostelries were the Black Star and the Bell Inn at Lower Mitton, which were both popular haunts for boatmen working the busy docks at Stourport. Set a short walk apart, alongside the Staffordshire & Worcestershire Canal where it meets the River Severn, they were usually packed with noisy drinkers on most nights of the week. There were always familiar faces to nod to and plenty of lively banter among the crowd of labourers gathered inside, but after a few pints, old grudges and petty rivalries could brew up trouble.

William Cooke and Francis Wassall spent the day loading a cargo of twenty packs of wool aboard a boat on Tuesday, 10 July 1832, and at 6 p.m. went to the Black Star for a drink. They eventually left the pub at around 10.30 p.m. and were returning to the boat at Heath's Wharf when they met Charles Hodgkiss coming out of the Bell Inn in Mark Lane, 100 yards from the canal basin. The three boatmen all came from Brockmore, in Staffordshire, and knew each other well.

As they walked along the street Hodgkiss, a tall, stout man with a broken nose, 'altogether of a most repulsive aspect', threatened to kill Wassall if he did not let him sleep on board his barge that night. Wassall refused, retaliating with the jibe, 'Go at it, then.' According to Cooke, Hodgkiss suddenly attacked Wassall, thumping him two or three times and, as they rounded the corner by the bridge, he struck the older man's head against the wall.

Postboy William Masefield had been out late on a job and was watering his horses in the Stour just as the clock struck twelve, when he heard a man cry out from the water by the bridge, 'Oh Lord!' and 'Murder!' He saw two men there talking together. His father, George Masefield, said he heard shouts from the direction of the Bell and sounds of a violent struggle.

Cooke said he was standing 40 yards away when the blows were struck and then saw Hodgkiss throw the body into the water. He spent the night at nearby lodgings and awoke at 4.15 a.m. next morning to go and help Wassall load a boat but found the cabin door shut. At 7 a.m. he met Hodgkiss on the bridge and the pair worked together unloading a cargo of pig iron. Hodgkiss admitted he was afraid Wassall was drowned and showed Cooke blood on the back of his hand.

Early on Saturday morning, Wassall, a widower known as Old Frank, was found dead floating in the canal basin, dressed in an old flannel smock. His hat, trimmed with two bands, was later found, sopping wet, hidden beneath the boards inside an old boat. Hodgkiss helped Stourport constable John Turner pull the body out of the water and carry it to a nearby stable.

At the coroner's inquest, Hodgkiss denied being with Wassall on the Tuesday and swore he was drunk at Kinver that night and did not go to Stourport until Wednesday morning. When challenged by a man who had seen him in the Bell Inn, he answered, 'Why, I was so drunk on Tuesday I did not know what time I came to Stourport.'

Both Hodgkiss and Cooke were charged with the murder. However, Cooke managed to avoid prosecution by turning King's Evidence and testifying against his workmate. In court Hodgkiss pleaded not guilty, saying he had no counsel to represent him and was a stranger with no friends in that part of the country. It was clear from the evidence given by witnesses that Hodgkiss had been fired up with liquor and looking for a fight.

Boatman Joseph Longmore told the court how, at Kinver on Monday afternoon, he had been accosted by Hodgkiss, who appeared drunk and, mistaking him for Wassall, said, 'Frankey Wassall I will pay your devil for you now.' Hodgkiss chased him along the canal about two boat lengths, stumbled and fell on his knees, then stood up and said, 'It is not you I want but Frank Wassall; I'll be his butcher before the week is out.'

On Tuesday, William Mann had seen Hodgkiss come out of the Bell by Gibbins' Bridge, nearly drunk, and challenge the best man on the river to fight him. 'I told him he had better leave that alone, as there were many good men on the Severn.' Another witness watching from her house window in Mark Lane saw four men quarrelling and roughly pushing each other about. Boatman John Sparrow saw Hodgkiss that night in the Black Star, where he was having a drink with his wife. The couple were asleep on a boat moored in the basin near Gibbins' Lock when, about midnight, they heard loud cries which seemed to come from a spot near the Bell.

Despite all this damning evidence, trial judge Mr Justice Bosanquet stopped the case, telling the jury there was insufficient testimony to establish Hodgkiss was guilty of murder, except that given by the accomplice Cooke, which should be viewed with great caution. He therefore felt it was not safe to proceed with the trial as Cooke's statements had been contradictory and his conduct throughout raised a suspicion that he knew more than he chose to disclose.

Hodgkiss was found not guilty and released. A lengthy report in the local *Worcester Herald* noted that throughout the trial, Hodgkiss had 'maintained the utmost self-possession, and frequently put very pertinent questions to the witnesses'.

What really happened that night was anyone's guess – Cooke may have delivered the knockout blow and thrown his victim into the canal, or perhaps it was simply an accident during a drunken brawl when Wassall toppled into the water. The quarrel may well have arisen because Wassall was hired for a job that Hodgkiss wanted. Boat owner George Elwell employed Wassall, who he believed was 'a respectable, decent, sober man', to take charge of a cargo at Kinver, but refused to take on Hodgkiss who had twice asked him for a job.

†††

Unsolved crimes were always a good read, and the public loved a real-life 'whodunit' mystery where a body was found floating in the canal. Cases like this provoked a heady cocktail of mixed emotions, from sympathy for the victim and horror at the terrible deed, to hatred for the culprit, perhaps a fearful shiver of relief that it had happened to someone else, and a natural desire for justice to be done.

Newspapers, always eager to attract extra readers, were now regularly printing longer and more detailed crime reports, particularly of the most unusual and intriguing incidents. Suspected murders were especially popular. It was not uncommon for cases to be left unresolved because there were no witnesses who had seen the offence being committed. Suspicions based on the strongest circumstantial evidence were not usually enough to secure a conviction.

Many national papers covered the case of James Irving in August 1833, who was charged on suspicion of murdering Elizabeth Sutton, the girl he had been courting, after her body was found in the Surrey Canal just five minutes away from where he lived. A crowd of curious local residents gathered for the hearing at the magistrate's office in Union Hall, to find out if gossip circulating in the neighbourhood was true. Rumour had it that Irving was pressurising the girl to marry him, and that a ring was found on her finger when she was pulled out of the water.

There were conflicting accounts of what took place, but Irving had apparently been drinking in his local pub, the Pilgrim, and was already the worse for liquor at 9 p.m. He was at home by 11 p.m. when Elizabeth called, asking him to escort her back to her house. She was not seen alive again. Walworth butcher Thomas Swanton saw the couple together at Camberwell Fair about 8 p.m. on the Tuesday before the incident, when Elizabeth was in high spirits and laughing with Irving's arm over her shoulder.

Irving denied he wanted to marry Elizabeth and tried to convince the magistrate she had committed suicide, saying she was 'a person of weak intellect'. His father backed him up, recounting a highly implausible scene when, on one occasion, Elizabeth 'became so outrageously violent as to tear all her clothes off in his presence, and appeared before him in a state of perfect nudity'. He swore that his son left the house only briefly, just before midnight, when he went to the Pilgrim for a swift half a pint of beer, before returning home to bed.

The most convincing witness was Mrs Hogden, who employed Elizabeth as a live-in domestic servant, and insisted she was a well-conducted, exemplary young woman who disliked going near the canal as she had often expressed a dread of approaching water. Mrs Hogden was certain she did not drown herself, saying that on the previous Sunday, Elizabeth had returned from an outing and complained of being held against her will by Irving until she promised to quit her place within a month to get married.

Several other rumours had emerged in the neighbourhood, 'which excited still stronger suspicions against the accused', but as they were only hearsay they could not be admitted in evidence. The magistrate, Mr Chambers, released Irving without charge and observed that, 'if a woman was induced to walk along the brink of a canal with a man who had a design upon her life it would be an easy task enough to shove her into the water'. A canal was the perfect place to dispose of an inconvenient living person or an unwanted dead body and then get off scot-free.

Another body shoved into the canal in London that same year sparked mass press coverage of a nasty case where a paedophile ring abducted 13-year-old Robert Paviour from home, held him captive for more than a week and then murdered him. Newspapers throughout the country ran in-depth reports of the murder, vying with each other to find words strong enough to express outrage at 'the most disgusting atrocity', which was 'the most revolting deed ever laid before the public'. It was a truly shocking crime, and one which must have given nightmares to anxious parents everywhere.

The boy's mother, Mrs Jane Paviour, had earlier on Shrove Tuesday prepared a dinner of hashed mutton and pancakes before going out to visit a sick friend and leaving Robert with instructions to boil potatoes for his father's supper. When she returned home after 8 p.m. to their lodgings in John Street, St Pancras, the fire had burnt down low in the hearth with a saucepan of potatoes on it, and Robert had gone, apparently wearing his indoor slippers. Alarmed, Mrs Paviour, with her husband and daughter Mary Ann, went out in search of him and they were quickly joined by neighbours, all running about the streets to make inquiries.

It was not until over a week later that two boatmen travelling along the Regent's Canal noticed something floating in the water and notified lock-keeper Daniel Williams, who hooked out a body wrapped in a bundle of canvas. Three men had been seen watching the Paviours' house on the evening Robert went missing, and police eventually arrested Frederick Marshall (an unemployed servant who had lost his job due to drink), furniture polisher George Evans and the Paviours' next-door neighbour, William Taylor.

At the inquest, held on 13 March 1833 at the York and Albany Tavern in Regent's Park, the Middlesex coroner said there was not the least shadow of doubt that the unfortunate child was forcibly taken from his home, probably stupefied with liquor, brutally treated and then destroyed to prevent him exposing the men, whom he knew.

The courtroom at the Old Bailey was crowded with spectators on 11 April, when Marshall, Evans and Taylor were brought into the dock charged with wilful murder. All three pleaded not guilty to the crime.

A long procession of witnesses appeared to give evidence, including several neighbours who reported seeing drunken men lurking outside Taylor's house.

Sailor John Ellen, who helped search for Robert at St Katharine's Docks, heard the accused men discussing the best way to make money from the boy, either by accepting the £5 reward being offered by the family or taking him to Portsmouth to sell for a pound or two. A couple who had been out walking in Hampstead one night described how they noticed two men leaning over the canal bridge near the York and Albany public house with a large parcel wrapped in canvas resting on the parapet. As they passed further on, they heard the loud splash of something being thrown into the water.

All the evidence seemed to indicate that Robert was held prisoner in Taylor's house, right next door to the Paviours' family home, where his parents endured an agonising wait for news. At the end of the trial, Lord Chief Justice Denman finished summing up the evidence at 5 p.m. and the jury retired. At 5.45 p.m. they returned a verdict of not guilty. No one was ever charged with the poor lad's murder.

Bargeman John Hughes, from Aylesbury, who was in the Albion public house at Battle Bridge one evening shortly after the abduction, said he was convinced the body had been thrown into the canal deliberately to excite suspicion that boatmen were responsible for the dreadful crime. Canvas was widely used to cover cargo on boats, so the choice of material to wrap the body may well have been a calculated ploy. In this case, the cunning tactics failed to cast the blame on boatmen. But they were well known throughout the country for rough behaviour and made useful scapegoats for crimes they had not committed.

You only had to take a brief stroll in the town centre of Stratford-upon-Avon to witness rowdy scenes and punch-ups among boatmen at one of the public houses by the canal basin – the Wheatsheaf, the Anchor, on the corner at the end of Bridge Street, and the Ship, which was a notorious 'disorderly house' frequented by prostitutes. The nearby Warwick Tavern, built by an enterprising lock-keeper next to a boat-builder's yard, had large stables where horses could be fed and sheltered overnight, so it was also popular with visiting boatmen.

And a visit to the pub often lasted for hours as time slipped away, pint by pint, in a haze of tobacco smoke and alcohol. On the second day of Leicester Fair, a group of boatmen went to the Magpie at 4 p.m. one autumn afternoon and spent over five hours there drinking together. Among them was John Gilbert, whose father kept Great Bowden Coal Wharf, and an acquaintance of his, 19-year-old William Barratt, who arrived at 6 p.m. with someone subtly described by the *Sporting Chronicle* as 'a woman of the town'. During the evening John Gilbert paid for some drinks, openly taking out a sovereign from his purse, which held £38 in gold. It was a big mistake.

Spotting an opportunity, Barratt persuaded him to go on to another pub called the Dublin Tavern at 9 p.m., in company with the woman, where the three continued drinking for another hour. When John Gilbert eventually decided it was time to leave, Barratt said he was hungry and would accompany him home to the boats at the wharf. When they reached High-cross, Barratt and the woman dropped back for a moment, and John Gilbert was suddenly tripped up and fell on his face. As he tried to get up, he was kicked in the head and left unconscious. He was found lying in the road by a passer-by, and when he recovered, he found that his watch and purse were missing, together with a pocket-book full of banknotes.

Barratt absconded from the town that night, not returning until seven months later, when he was apprehended at a beer house. He was found guilty at Leicester Assizes of highway robbery and sentenced to death.

†††

Despite its good intentions, the Beer Act only seemed to increase alcohol consumption, and concerns grew to such an extent that in 1834 a Parliamentary Select Committee on Drunkenness was set up to investigate the problem. It concluded that the higher classes of society were now drinking less, but among the labouring classes drunkenness was increasing. The Select Committee was in no doubt that alcohol and crime were inextricably linked, reporting:

> The spread of crime in every shape and form, from theft, fraud and prostitution in the young, to burnings, robberies and more hardened offences in the old; by which the gaols and prisons, hulks and convict transports are filled with inmates; and an enormous mass of human beings, who, under sober habits and moral training, would be sources

of wealth and strength to the country, are transformed, chiefly through the influence of Intoxicating Drinks, into excrescences of corruption.

A petition complaining of the evils caused by the Sale of Beer Act was signed by twenty-nine Sussex magistrates and presented to Parliament by MP Sir Charles Burrell. Speaking during the debate in the House of Commons in April 1834, he said that beer shops had proved to be 'a fruitful source of demoralisation in the country, encouraging drunkenness, gambling and all kinds of vice', forcing the county of Sussex to spend a huge sum on larger gaols to hold extra criminals. Other speakers agreed that habitual drunkenness among the lower classes had vastly increased during the past four years, and one magistrate said he was receiving repeated calls for advice from women whose husbands were now in the habit of spending their wages in beer shops, instead of bringing money home.

All sorts of facts and figures were quoted on the evils of alcohol, whether beer or spirits, resulting in what one MP described as 'the torrent of drunkenness that desolates the land'. An estimated £50 million was being spent annually on booze. The quantity of duty-paid spirits consumed had doubled within a few years, and that was in addition to millions of gallons known to be illicitly distilled or imported. Drink was cited as the chief cause of misdemeanours in the navy, and the Duke of Wellington confirmed that increased drunkenness was creating rising crime in the army.

There were no easy solutions to the alcohol problem, although plenty of creative suggestions were aired, including better education with museums, parish libraries and reading rooms providing cheaper, 'more innocent refreshments, than the liquid poison now consumed', and the idea that alehouses could have large, clear-glass front windows to try and shame the drinkers inside. The *Essex Standard* was indignant:

Lowering the duty upon tea and coffee and sugar [is] recommended, together with the establishment of parish libraries and *museums*! What on earth does this mean? If a man be thirsty, what avails showing him an alligator stuffed, a dried monkey, or a snake in a bottle? Museums, indeed, for the chimney-sweepers, and the canal-diggers, and the coal-heavers, and the dustmen, and all the rest of those who, tired with work, like a little comfort – What are alligators and snakes and monkies to them?

There was support in some quarters for stringent new laws to stop the 'further spread of so great a national evil', though others spoke up for the working man's right to drink. They understood the appeal of convivial company, a blazing fire and an easy chair in the pub taproom. The *Leamington Spa Courier* protested that men should be able to sit by the fireside of a beer house after long hours at work: 'Surely it might be pronounced harsh and rigorous, to rob the poor man of his glass of ale, taken when and where he pleased, after such excessive toil.' Although beer houses had been denounced as 'places where every species of crime was concocted', closing them would only force drinkers into public houses and 'those other more pernicious haunts of depravity', the gin shops.

London weekly *The News* ran a sarcastic critique on the absurd proposals of what it labelled the Drunkenness Committee: 'The nincompoops! Had not they better prescribe the number of ounces of bread each man is to consume, and the quantity of distilled water to be taken daily?' It was especially scathing about the committee's encouragement of new temperance societies – 'these meddling, impudent, humbug Societies for the diffusion of their low and malignant twopenny trash'.

In fact, more than 400 temperance societies had already been formed in England to tackle the evils of drink. But they were mere drops in the ocean of liquor swilling about the country. In London alone, according to the 1835 annual statement on metropolitan drunkenness, a total of 19,779 drunks had been apprehended by police in the past year, and of these 7,100 were women.

Most crimes were committed under the influence of liquor. The sub-sheriff of London said that nearly all those convicted of murder admitted they were intoxicated at the time they committed acts of atrocity. The *Bucks Gazette* reported the last words of one youth from the scaffold outside Maidstone Gaol, who addressed a crowd of 4,000 spectators waiting to see him hanged for rape, saying, 'I hope my fate will be a warning to all young men, and that you will refrain from going to public-houses.'

But despite all the warnings, hardened drinkers remained heedless of the consequences of spending too much time in the pub. It was easy enough to get hold of alcohol at any hour of the day, and the 40,000 beer shops trading by 1835 made it even easier to find a drink.

A five-hour drinking session at the White Hart landed bargeman John Dykes in serious trouble in October 1836. Young Dykes, 'a rough-looking athletic man' nicknamed Goosey, was employed on a barge called the *Susan*, moored in Maiden Lane Basin on the Regent's Canal. He was paid 4 shillings in wages on Sunday night and went straight down the pub with coal-heaver Thomas Lee, where they stayed drinking until midnight.

Everything probably seemed rather vague after that, but Dykes did remember they both left the premises full of liquor and returned to the barge to sleep. He heard a splash, which he thought was just a lump of coal rolling into the water, but realising Lee was gone, he tried looking for him and fell into the boat's hold, where he lay for some time – an excuse which may well have been true, given Goosey's state of inebriation. He eventually staggered to his feet and woke the barge captain, James Slaughter, and his wife, becoming so agitated that Mrs Slaughter urged her husband to find out what was the matter. Eventually, Goosey managed to tell them that a man had fallen in the water about an hour ago, but the captain decided it was no use making a search at that time of night as the man must be dead.

The next morning, several bargemen, including William Gobers, set about finding the body and eventually pulled it out of the canal with a boat-hook known as a hitcher. Rumours soon spread that Goosey had thrown Lee overboard and he was taken into custody at Hatton Garden Police Office by Sergeant William Millingnap, charged on suspicion of murder. However, during the inquest held at the Albion public house, it became clear that the whole incident was almost certainly an accident.

Mr Slaughter, proprietor of several barges in the employ of Mr Cubitt, the builder developing the city's Belgravia district, said Goosey was a hard worker but whenever he received his wages, 'he was in the habit of getting stupidly intoxicated, and knew not what he was about'. The jury returned a verdict of 'found drowned'.

The coroner said it appeared to be a case of an accident arising from intoxication of both parties, and commented with surprise that it was scarcely possible to account for the complete lack of feeling shown by all the boatmen. Did Goosey cut down on the booze after that? We will never know.

Beer was the cause of another death when two men who had been drinking in the Bell and Mackerel public house in Mile End, one July evening, started fighting outside on a bridge over Regent's Canal. The pub landlord saw Henry Nairey drunkenly dancing in the parlour, then sit down on a bench by the door, where he was approached by Thomas Whales, who was goading him to fight. The pair left about six o'clock, both stripped to the waist and went to fight on the bridge, where they were seen exchanging blows. A passer-by said Nairey at first seemed reluctant but finally said, 'If I must fight, I will', and then knocked Whales to the ground. The men shook hands and Whales admitted it was his own fault, no harm had been done and it was a fair stand-up fight. However, seventeen days later, he died from inflammation caused by a fractured leg. Nairey was charged with killing him but found not guilty by a court.

Alcohol regularly sparked off aggressive behaviour, but even when men were sober, violence was a normal part of everyday life for the labouring classes. A man took pride in his ability to stand up for himself and fight, whether it was simply an angry exchange of blows, a casual assault or a full-scale brawl. The traditional way for working men to settle disputes was in 'a fair fight' using their fists, but very often things turned nasty, and tools, bottles or chairs were grabbed as weapons. Manchester gangs inflicted injuries with their ornate metal-studded belts, while hob-nailed boots and heavy clogs could deliver a vicious kicking.

On any boat, a surprising number of objects could be used to inflict injury and some boatmen, anticipating trouble, kept offensive weapons on board. Thomas Blower, a boat captain employed by Pickfords' wharfingers in City Road, London, sprang ashore armed with a sword during a stand-off between rival boat crews in April 1837. Heated arguments often broke out in disputes over whose boat should go first through locks and tunnels, or who should pull over when several vessels were passing in opposite directions on a busy stretch of water. Always under pressure to deliver their cargo as quickly as possible, boaters were prepared to fight for precedence when time meant money.

At about noon on that Sunday, Paddington boatman William Rudd, alias Brentford Billy, was travelling along the canal headed for Liverpool when, 11 miles out of London, he saw four boats and a group of men quarrelling on the towpath. Billy passed them and leapt ashore to recover his rope, when he saw Blower wielding a sword, as his companions armed with pokers, tillers and a long shaft advanced on the opposing crews.

One man jumped in the canal to escape, and others sprang back onto their boats. Two boatmen then approached Brentford Billy and, without any provocation, Blower struck out. Billy warded off the blow with his boat tiller, but the next one levelled him to the ground, and while he lay there, Blower struck him twice on the head. Billy was taken to Uxbridge to have the bleeding wounds dressed, while Blower was later ordered by the Worship Street magistrate to find bail in the substantial sum of £50, together with two sureties of £40 each.

Another boatman who kept a lethal weapon for self-defence was Joseph Hodgetts, who had a loaded shotgun in his cabin. One Saturday afternoon, when he left the boat opposite a wharf at Tallow Hill in Worcester, it was fired at his 4-year-old son. People nearby heard a gunshot and ran out to find the little boy lying on his back in the boat, with blood pouring from a gaping wound in his chest. Within ten minutes, Mr Richard Hill, the surgeon, arrived but the child was dead, part of one rib blown away.

The gun was fully loaded with two pipe-bowls of shot and had been left in its usual place in the cabin on half-cock. It was found near the child's body, hung up against some boards, and had been recently discharged. Hodgetts arrived home to confront William Bishop, the young lad he had employed six weeks earlier to help on the boat, who denied he had touched the gun, saying he was in the stables. The coroner's jury took a different view and, at the inquest held in the New Inn next to the canal, returned a verdict of manslaughter against Bishop, but the frightened lad knew what was coming and had already absconded.

Ironically, public houses were both the source of much crime and where inquests commonly took place, right up to the end of the nineteenth century. After any suspicious death, the victim was taken to the nearest public place, which was usually a tavern or inn, for the postmortem to be carried out and inquiries made into the circumstances. Licensed premises were large enough to hold an official gathering with witnesses, a jury and interested members of the public, as well as conveniently offering the food and drink which must have been welcome during the grim proceedings.

†††

Solving the perennial problem of drunkenness was far easier said than done, despite what scores of earnest reformers believed was possible. One of these was confirmed teetotaller Reverend William Baker, who proudly boasted that he had not touched a drop of liquor for eighteen months, when he published *The Curse of Britain: An Essay on the Evils, Causes and Cure of Intemperance* in 1838. It described the dreadful effects of drinking on the poor and the wretched living conditions they were reduced to, with trembling alcoholics dressed in rags and their children wandering the streets picking up cabbage leaves to eat.

Reverend Baker was shocked at the estimated number of 600,000 drunkards in Britain, and he was particularly concerned about the amount of alcohol-related crime, noting a report to Lancaster magistrates that said 116 out of 189 offenders in the county gaol attributed their misfortunes to a passion for intoxicating liquor and:

> ... the temptations held out to them, by the alehouse and the beer shop ... an enormous amount of crime is the result of intemperance. It is this vice which fills our prisons, and which chiefly contributes to populate our penal settlements.

Promoting total abstinence was never going to be the answer to the nation's woes, but lesser measures to control drinking were also tried with some success, such as closing public houses from midnight on Saturday until Sunday lunchtime. A police inspector was quoted in *The Times* saying that many of London's principal streets, which had previously been crowded with drunks at weekends, were now almost deserted on Sundays from 1 a.m. to 6 a.m.

Of course, policemen were used to dealing with rough trade on the streets, but it took almost two hours and a squad of officers to subdue bargeman Thomas Townsend, who went berserk after a weekend of binge-drinking. One Saturday in September 1838, he had been out with friends, sharing 2 quarterns of gin and shrub (quarter pints of a popular cocktail mixed with fruit syrup and water), washed down with beer. On Sunday, he spent most of the day in the Noah's Ark pub at Limehouse, near his workplace on the Regent's Canal dock. At 5 p.m., after a skinful of liquor including at least five pots of beer, he went up to the bar and called for a pot of porter from the landlord, Mr Martin, stood there drinking it and refused to pay. After wrangling over the money, Townsend exclaimed, 'You ****, I'll serve you out', punched Mr Martin several times and sloshed beer over him.

The landlord managed to turf him out of the pub, still kicking and struggling, but minutes later Townsend returned to the parlour, lashed out at the barmaid and smashed two panes of glass in the bar window. By now, he was completely out of control, and other customers who tried to intervene were barely able to hold him down until Police Constable Pavitt arrived. But Townsend broke free, rushed to the fireplace and grabbed a kettle of boiling water, which he threw at one man, booted the policeman and hurled a quart pot. Soon, another officer came to help, and they pushed him outside, still kicking and cursing, but it took an hour to drag him 200 yards to London Street in Ratcliff. Here, Townsend pulled off his coat and said he would kill the first man that laid hold of him. Bruised and battered, the two constables were taking no chances and called in reinforcements to take the prisoner to the stationhouse, where he was finally locked up at 6.45 p.m.

When he was brought up before Thames Office magistrates, Townsend's solicitor said his client had been assaulted by the landlady, who demanded payment in a threatening manner and struck him with a quart pot. There was not a mark of violence on the publican or policeman, whereas Townsend had a cut on his head that was plain enough. The solicitor said Townsend could not afford to pay a heavy fine because he had a wife and family to support, and he would not have assaulted anyone if he had not been provoked.

The magistrate, Mr Greenwood, concluded that the landlord had simply asked for payment of a pot of beer:

> … and for that he was assaulted, his windows broken and the girl used in a most ruffianly manner. When the first policeman came he was kicked and knocked down two or three times, the second one

was served in the same manner, and scalding water was thrown at a person. Could anything be more outrageous than that?

He said the bench would put a stop to such outrages if it could, and ordered Townsend to pay a £5 fine or face imprisonment for two months.

†††

Alcohol mixed with testosterone was a highly toxic combination, which could inflame the blood and set off the most appalling acts of uncontrollable violence. A disturbing incident took place on the Staffordshire & Worcestershire Canal that same year, reported by the *Wolverhampton Chronicle* under the headline 'BRUTAL OUTRAGE'. Boatmen Thomas Giles and William Payton offered a lift to Mrs Elizabeth Thomas who, after a late-night row with her husband about him not seeking work, rose early next morning and was walking along the canal from Kidderminster to her brother in Bilston.

As she passed the boat Payton, who was steering, asked where she was off to and said he was going as far as Stourbridge, she could ride that far. At first, she declined, but when he asked a second time she accepted and took a seat in the cabin. After going about 100 yards the men came inside the boat. Payton poured something from a bottle in the cupboard and handed her a half-pint cup, which he told her contained port wine, saying, 'If you drink it all it will not hurt you.' Elizabeth swallowed about half and realised it was very strong brandy.

Soon afterwards, she became alarmed when Giles asked if she had any money. Fearing they would rob her, she carefully slipped 5 shillings from a pocket into her right stocking and asked to leave the boat, but Giles refused and threatened that, if she did not hold her tongue, he would drown her. Elizabeth tried to get out and was pushed back. Payton held her down while Giles removed her shoe, cut a hole in her stocking and took the coins.

She wept and entreated them to return the money, but they again threatened drowning if she did not hold her noise. Then Payton left the cabin and closed the door as Giles began viciously tearing off her clothes in a violent struggle. Ignoring her desperate cries, he raped her. Payton then returned and also assaulted her.

When the boat arrived at Kinver, both men leapt out and Elizabeth followed them, still determined to get her money back. But Giles had had enough. In one swift movement he grabbed her leg, fastened his other arm round her waist and tossed her into the canal. The Reverend Mr Wharton, who was walking some distance away, came to help when he saw her bob up in the water screaming and then was thrust under again by Giles. Elizabeth was finally rescued, 'stupefied and senseless, her clothes literally torn off her back'.

The *Wolverhampton Chronicle* reported cryptically, 'The conduct of a man of the name of Child, who keeps a beer-house at Kinver, was highly disgraceful and inhuman upon this occasion.' It was not explained what exactly Mr Child had done, but whatever it was had clearly made Elizabeth's ordeal even worse.

The men were gaoled until their trial at Worcester Assizes on counts of rape, robbery and attempted murder, where serious doubts were cast on Elizabeth's credibility. It emerged that after the assault she apparently went to a public house with the bargemen and, although she did ask for her 5 shillings to be returned, did not mention any other accusation. Unaccountably, she had used different names to make separate complaints, one to Worcestershire magistrates as Mrs Thomas, and another to Staffordshire justices calling herself Miss Jones.

Elizabeth herself failed to appear in court and the jury therefore dismissed the charges. Perhaps the men had paid for her silence, or Elizabeth may have felt too afraid to give evidence. Could there have been some other reason? It was another puzzling case and one reported in detail by local newspapers, which frequently ran lengthy crime reports with verbatim accounts of trials, enabling curious readers to piece together all the clues and mull over conflicting evidence to form their own judgement.

For the press and its avid readers, the more shocking a case was, the better. And when a severed head was found in a London canal, accounts of such a gruesome discovery filled many column inches on what was dubbed 'The Edgware Road Murder'. *The Times* reported that at 8.30 a.m. one January morning, lock-keeper Matthias Ralph was called over by a bargeman on the Regent's Canal near Mile End, where the lock gates were stuck. When he lowered his hitcher beneath the water, it caught on something and, to his surprise, he pulled up a human head, its long, brown hair tangled round the boat-hook. Two other men tried to help but backed off in alarm when they saw the head, one exclaiming, 'I cannot do it.'

Fishing out dead bodies was a familiar but unpleasant occupational hazard for lock-keepers. Ralph guessed it had been submerged for four or five days, but it was hard to tell, and later at the Old Bailey, he said:

> I pulled it straight up, I saw the ear first – that made me know it was the head of a human-being, the water was about five feet deep there ... Sometimes we pick bodies out of the canal – I have picked out several, and sometimes one that has been in the water three or four days will be a great deal worse than those which have been in ten days.

With remarkable composure, Matthias Ralph landed the head, untied the strands of hair from the hitcher and, as he carefully examined it, noticed the left jaw was broken, with bone protruding through the skin. He fetched a piece of old sack from his cottage to wrap it in, took it to the bone house, where bodies awaiting burial were kept, and locked the door.

Police were called in and the head was moved to premises in Stepney, where a vast crowd milled around outside, eager to catch a glimpse of the grisly remains. Inspector Feltham later carried it in a basket to Paddington poorhouse and the head was matched up with a torso that had been found in a bag hidden behind a flagstone on Edgware Road. A few weeks later, on 2 February, a pair of legs in a sack was discovered by a labourer working at a reedbed near Brixton.

It was not until 20 March that the dismembered corpse was eventually identified as Hannah Brown, a widowed washerwoman in her late forties. Police investigations soon led to the arrest of her fiancé, James Greenacre, for wilful murder, and his mistress, Sarah Gale, who was charged as an accessory. Public feeling ran high, inflamed by all the macabre details of the crime revealed in the press, and an angry mob chased the coach carrying the couple to Newgate and had to be fought off by police officers armed with staves.

Newspapers had a field day in the lead-up to the trial, running all sorts of nasty gossip about Greenacre that fuelled a growing hatred towards him. Rumours included speculation that he had murdered one or possibly two bastard children, conned an apprentice out of money and even been part of the infamous Cato Street plot to assassinate government ministers. Anything could be believed of such a diabolical murderer.

The trial at the Old Bailey received pages of in-depth coverage in all the papers, and no doubt the public relished every gory detail. Apparently, Greenacre was something of a fantasist. He worked as a cabinetmaker but boasted about his large farm of 1,000 acres in America and said he would be leaving for Hudson Bay after his marriage to Hannah Brown, due to take place on Christmas morning. The couple had arranged to meet friends at the Angel public house near St Giles' Church before the ceremony. But at 11 p.m. on Christmas Eve, Greenacre had turned up on their doorstep, very agitated, to say the wedding was off.

In court, Greenacre admitted he had been drinking on Christmas Eve and quarrelled with Hannah about money after discovering she did not own any property, contrary to what she had led him to believe. He lashed out at her, and Hannah fell off the chair, knocked her head and died. Greenacre panicked, decided to dispose of the body and cut it up into pieces. He wrapped the head in a sack and carried it with him on two omnibuses, sitting with the parcel unobtrusively on his lap, then took a lift in a cart part of the way to the canal in Edgware Road, where he dumped it in the water.

Greenacre was convicted of murder and sentenced to death, while Sarah Gale was sent for transportation. After the trial, the press continued to publish speculation and further revelations to cash in on the notorious crime which was boosting circulation figures. One newspaper joked that when the omnibus conductor told Greenacre the fare was sixpence a head, he paid for just one head instead of two. Thousands of people gathered for the finale of the riveting case to watch the execution, enjoying the thrilling spectacle and munching specially baked 'Greenacre tarts' on sale in the street.

8

'AN ATROCIOUS CRIME'

It was odd, very odd indeed, to see a woman sharpening a penknife on the steps of the lock cottage. John Tansley, assistant clerk on duty at Aston Lock that Sunday evening, noticed her at once – a small, determined figure intent on her task, the blade glinting in her hand. She was neatly dressed in a dark gown and blue-figured silk bonnet tied with pale ribbons. Oblivious to her surroundings, she thrust the knife with short, swift stabs, scraping it across the rough edge of the stone slab. Then a Pickfords' flyboat glided into the lock beside her, and the woman stepped lightly aboard.

It was not until next day that Mr Tansley was told the name of the lone female passenger with the weapon. And by then, it was too late.

Christina Collins had left her lodgings in Liverpool at about ten o'clock on Saturday, 15 June 1839, and set off on the long journey south with her few belongings carefully packed in two trunks, securely knotted with white cord. She bought a 16-shilling Pickfords' passenger ticket, and although a canal journey was not the quickest way to travel, it was the cheapest, and all she could afford. For weeks, she had been worried about her husband Robert and was impatient to reach him in London, where he had recently taken a job as an ostler.

Robert was clearly in a depressed and agitated state of mind when he had written in early June, asking her to join him and enclosing 1 sovereign to pay for the trip. Christina replied in a hasty letter, full of concern, posted from Liverpool on Wednesday, 12 June:

My dear Collins,

Sorry I am to read your wandering letter to me – do my dear strive against that misfortune which I fear awaits you; the loss of reason is dreadful. But I hope and trust that when I arrive in London you will be more reconciled. I set off on Saturday morning, in the Fly Boat, and shall be on the water six days and no bed, so how or when I shall reach home I know not, but the moment I land, to you I will hasten. I shall not write much in this, the post is going, but only hope and trust you will be better before I see you for the sake of all parties who know you; they are all sorry here, and myself I'll say nothing about; suffice it to say, that if you had not sent me that money, I should have been on the road without a penny perhaps, unless some one here lent me any thing; I have got a pound from you; I cannot bring very many of your things, but I can send for them ... I conclude my dear husband, with remaining your affectionate and unchanged wife,

CHRISTINA COLLINS

She knew only too well the consequences of depression, as her father, Robert Brown, was an inventor who had suffered from melancholy and tried to commit suicide, while the family struggled in poverty. A man 'highly respected for his talents and worth' in his hometown of Nottingham, he had spent years designing new machinery for the lace industry and took out three official patents. One of these, for making bobbin-nets, proved successful, but instead of bringing financial security it only led to a ruinously expensive dispute with two other men who claimed the invention was theirs.

Now 37 years old, Christina had bitter experience of life's changing fortunes. Despite a promising start with respectable parents and a good education, her childhood was blighted by hardship and by the age of 30 she was left a widow. Money had always been scarce and since marrying Robert Collins the previous year, she had been working as a dressmaker in Liverpool, barely able to make ends meet. At least their prospects seemed a little more hopeful since Robert had gone to London and found employment.

When her boat reached the busy canal junction at Preston Brook after the first leg of the journey, she transferred her baggage onto a Pickfords' flyboat, and at 7 p.m. she took a seat inside the cabin as it started out along the Trent & Mersey Canal. On board that evening were Captain James Owen, a married man of 39, boat hands George Thomas (alias Dobell) and William Ellis, both in their twenties, and a young lad called William Musson, who mostly led the horse.

The boat was fully laden for the trip to London with a cargo that included barrels of spirits. The four-man crew worked in shifts as usual, taking it in turns to sleep as the boat travelled non-stop through the night, then on through the dank and eerie Harecastle Tunnel, which was widely believed to be haunted, where Owen joined Christina to sit in the cabin.

They eventually arrived in Stoke-on-Trent at midday on Sunday, 16 June, where the boat moored at the wharf while the crew unloaded goods from the hold, heaving boxes and packages out onto the stone bays at the water's edge, flanked by warehouses. Here, Christina asked Pickfords' porter, William Brookes, if the boat would pass through Birmingham, and complained that Thomas had used threatening, indecent language. Mr Brookes thought the men had been drinking and heard Christina say to Thomas, 'Leave me alone. I'll not have anything to do with you.' But despite this, she was back on the boat when it left at 4 p.m., and Mrs Ann Brookes, who travelled with her for a mile or so, noticed Christina seemed troubled, saying the men wanted her to go into the cabin but she had refused.

By 8 p.m., when the boat pulled in at the market town of Stone, Christina had become seriously worried about the crew's behaviour. Hugh Cordwell, check clerk for the Trent & Mersey Canal Company, saw her tying up a bundle and told her not to get off until he had gauged the vessel. Once out on the canal bank, she complained to him that she was 'afraid the boatmen were getting drunk and would meddle with her'. Mr Cordwell had already noticed the intoxicated state the men were in, particularly Owen, but merely told her to report the matter officially at the end of the journey.

Alcohol was inflaming libido, Owen was becoming more insistent, and he followed Christina along the canal asking why she wouldn't go with him into town. She ignored his entreaties and walked away beneath the bridge. But despite this, she was on the boat again when it left at eleven minutes past eight, heading south past endless fields as the canal threaded its way through the Staffordshire countryside alongside the River Trent. There were few people about on that peaceful Sunday evening. Church service over and chores done, there was time for those who could to snatch a few hours rest after the week's labours.

The atmosphere on board was tense. As the men grew steadily more and more drunk, a simmering animosity between the captain and Thomas erupted into heated quarrelling. An ominous mood of aggressive bravado seemed to be taking hold. Now really alarmed, Christina left the boat and strode off down the towpath, walking for over a mile until she reached Aston Lock. Here she waited, sharpening a small knife on the cottage steps.

William Musson, the lad leading the horse, saw her there as Ellis steered the boat into the lock. Mr Tansley, the clerk, was also watching and he heard one of the boat hands curse her and say 'he wished she was in hell flames, for he hated the sight of her'. And yet, despite everything, Christina stepped aboard once more. Owen told her to get into the cabin and then handed her a cup to drink, as the boat slid smoothly out of the lock at 8.30 p.m.

Confident, assertive and described by the captain as 'a little fierce-talking woman', Christina was not just a simple country girl, unused to the ways of the world. In fact, in her twenties, she had toured venues all over the country as the wife of celebrated conjuror Thomas Ingleby, performing in his spectacular stage act. After one appearance at the Exchange Rooms in Nottingham, the local newspaper was full of praise, reporting, 'Mrs Ingleby's singing and recitations are of the first order, and her performance of the invisible hen, is the most curious specimen of art ever witnessed.' The act featured all kinds of intriguing magic by the self-proclaimed Emperor of all Conjurors, who boasted he had entertained audiences at the London Lyceum and later went on to thrill enraptured crowds at provincial assembly rooms and inns, who were only too willing to pay 2s 6d for a night out with front-row seats.

Among the 'wonderful deceptions by dexterity of hand' promised in adverts for the show, his tricks included cutting the head off a duck or goose, which 'by Ingleby blowing his magic breath upon it, shall rise and walk as well as ever'. He would also swallow two watches, a dozen knives and forks, and 'fetch three sets of child-bed linen out of one new laid egg, and a child out of another'. One night in London, he even demonstrated 'the method of Cutting the Head off a Man'. To consolidate his reputation, the magician published a book priced at 3 shillings, entitled *Ingleby's Whole Art of Legerdemain*, which revealed:

> All the Tricks and Deceptions performed by that Emperor of all Conjurors, with copious explanations, also several new and astonishing Philosophical and Mathematical Experiments, including directions for practising the Slight of Hand.

No wonder that Christina fell under his spell, leaving home for a glamorous and exciting theatrical career. It was not to last, however. Old enough to be her father, Ingleby was sufficiently well known to have his death in Ireland, in August 1832, widely reported in newspapers throughout Britain. The *Belfast Commercial Chronicle* noted:

> Death of a Conjuror – Doctor Ingleby, the Emperor of all Conjurors, who was so well known in Ireland some years back, departed this life on Saturday morning, the 11th instant, at his lodgings, Enniscorthy, much regretted by his friends and well wishers, leaving a young widow.

Christina had led a highly unusual life, and one which had already thrown up many challenges. A strong-minded woman, no doubt used to dealing with unwanted male attention, she knew how to look after herself.

Now, as dusk fell that Sunday, the flyboat passed a northbound pair near Sandon. One of them was a familiar Pickfords' vessel, the *Emma*, captained by Tom Bloor, who had taken on board a gallon of ale for his crew at Haywood Junction about 4 miles back. Bloor called out to Owen, 'How goes it?', and asked him to come over and join them for a glass of ale. Owen pointed to a woman sitting on the cabin and said, 'Will you have anything of this?' but Bloor replied, 'No – I have no inclination.'

Thomas jumped onto the *Emma*, eager for the beer, bragging that Jemmy had had concerns with the woman last night and he would too, 'or else he would Burke her'. Everyone knew exactly what that meant.

The phrase was commonplace at the time as a chilling reference to the infamous murderers, Burke (a former canal navvy) and his accomplice, Hare, who a decade earlier plied victims with alcohol before smothering them and selling the bodies to medical men for dissection.

The boat travelled on amid the deepening shadows, Owen by now completely intoxicated, and Thomas fairly tipsy. At about 10 p.m. that night, Robert Walker was steering a boat half a mile below Sandon Lock when he saw a woman walking alone on the hauling path near Salt Bridge and spoke to her, though she gave him no answer. She was 400–500 yards in front of Owen's vessel, and when it drew alongside, Owen asked Robert Walker whether he had seen their female passenger, saying in the most obscene and graphic terms what he wanted to do to her.

Two hours later, in the upstairs bedroom of remote Hoo Mill lock cottage, lock-keeper James Mills and his wife, Ann, were alarmed by the sound of shrill screams from somewhere outside in the darkness. Half-asleep, Mrs Mills thought at first it was a child crying in distress, but she got up to open the front window and, peering down into the gloom, she saw three men standing by a boat in the nearest lock just a few yards away. James Mills got out of bed to join his wife, looking over her shoulder at the boat below, and knew it was one of Pickfords' by the distinctive large white letters on the nameplate.

A woman in a dark gown was sitting on top of the cabin sobbing and cried out she had lost her shoe. She stooped as if putting the shoe on, then sat down again with her legs dangling over the edge and said, 'Don't attempt me; I'll not go into the cabin; I'll not go down there.' When Mrs Mills called out to ask what was wrong, one boatman replied, 'She's been in the cut', and a man stood on the lockside told him to 'mind her legs' as the boat went down in the lock chamber.

Mrs Mills called one of the men over to the cottage to inquire who the woman was and whether there was anybody with her. The boatman said it was a passenger whose husband was with her. Satisfied with this explanation, or perhaps deciding it was safer not to interfere, Mrs Mills closed the window and went back to bed.

In the early hours of the morning, sometime between one and two o'clock, a Bache & Company boat heading for London overtook the Pickfords' flyboat at Rugeley Wharf, about 5 miles south of Hoo Mill lock. William Hatton was leading the horse and recognised Owen on the towpath with Thomas, who he noticed was not wearing either jacket or waistcoat. They asked him three times if he had seen a woman anywhere between that spot and the bridge, but Hatton told them he had not.

Shortly after 5 a.m. on Monday, 17 June, Captain Tom Grant was travelling slowly along the Trent & Mersey near Rugeley, when he spotted something floating in the water, about 4ft away from the bank. He realised it was a dark gown, immediately stopped his boat and, grabbing a boat-hook, managed to pull it across the canal to the towing path. It was the body of a woman. She was lying face down in the water and had no bonnet or shoes on. He called over John Johnson of Bellamour Wharf to help, and between them, the two men dragged out the slight figure, still warm and dripping water from the sodden garments, and carried her up the steep sandstone steps at Brindley Bank to the Talbot Inn.

At 6 a.m., two hours later than scheduled, the ill-fated flyboat eventually arrived at Fradley Junction, where Pickfords' clerk, Charles Robotham, was at home milking a cow. While the horses were being changed, Owen came up to him and said, 'A very bad job has happened.' He believed that their passenger booked from Preston Brook had drowned herself, as she had attempted it once before and he had pulled her out of the cut.

Mr Robotham told him he should have taken more care of the woman and left her at the first place he came to. Owen said he thought 'she was off her head' because she kept on crying out to her absent husband, 'Collins – Collins – Collins'. The last place they saw her was at Colwich Lock and she had left her shoes and bonnet behind in the cabin with all her luggage.

Owen wanted her boxes taken off the boat but, suspecting something was amiss, the clerk told him it was useless to do that as they would find out who she was. When Owen refused to go back and see if they could find the lost passenger, Mr Robotham had a word with the lad, William Musson, and then decided he had to report the matter to his superiors.

He hurried off to the company's offices at Fazeley Junction, on the outskirts of Tamworth, and explained to the Pickfords & Company agent, William Kirk, what had happened. By the time the flyboat arrived, a police constable had been sent for and was waiting at the canal-side, while the boatmen were called into the office, one at a time, by Mr Kirk.

The three men insisted they had last seen the woman at Colwich Lock. Ellis was still intoxicated and when he handed in the boat's papers he began to curse and swear, saying, 'Damn and blast the woman; if she is drowned, I cannot help it.' Thomas was also very drunk and muttered, 'I hope the bloody whore is burning in hell.' Mr Kirk retorted, 'You are a drunk and a fool.' Owen said the passenger treated them to some ale at Stone, and the last time he saw anything of her, she was getting out of the boat at Colwich, 'saying she would ride no further'.

Meanwhile, Mr Robotham and Constable William Harrison together climbed on board the boat to search inside its cabin, where they soon found a pair of shoes, clogs and a battered, misshapen bonnet with the strings tied together, its crown crushed almost flat. The two boxes were tied up with white cord.

All three crew members were arrested and taken into custody at a public house in Fazeley, still drunk and cursing, together with the young lad. When Mr Robotham called in to see them later that evening, Owen took him over to the back door of the pub, saying he wanted to have the clerk as a witness at the inquest and he hoped he would do what he could for him. Then Owen swore he was innocent and burst into tears.

9

THE WHOLE TRUTH

Poor Robert Collins was grief-stricken at the inquest into Christina's death, which opened promptly at 10 a.m. on Monday, 24 June, at the Talbot Inn in Rugeley. It was painful to witness the depths of his despair as he confirmed to the coroner and assembled jury that he had seen the dead body and knew it was his wife from a mark on her ear.

All sorts of rumours had been circulating in the week since the victim was dragged from the canal, and the *Staffordshire Advertiser* ran a full report of 'the investigation of this melancholy and mysterious affair', headlined 'CHARGE OF THE MURDER OF A FEMALE, BY BOATMEN'. Rugeley surgeon Samuel Barnett, who examined the deceased, said he had observed two small bruises below the elbow and on the wrist of the right arm, but explained that the newspapers were wrong to quote him as being satisfied no illicit connection had taken place. In fact, he was of the opinion that there had been no *recent* sexual activity. He gave the cause of death as suffocation from drowning.

Many witnesses were called during the four-day hearing, including the Pickfords' crew being held in custody and the various boatmen who had seen them on the journey. It was difficult for those listening to try and piece together the events that led up to the tragedy and untangle the terse, factual descriptions from some more dubious hearsay accounts.

John Astley, a porter at Rugeley Wharf, recounted a conversation with Bedworth boatman John Barston, who claimed that when he met the accused boatmen on the Sunday night, one of them told him 'they tied a handkerchief about the woman's mouth to stop her screams, and when they untied it again she was dead'. Barston had added, 'You do not think I am such a damned fool as to mention it.' At the inquest, Barston would only admit that he had met one of Pickfords' boats at Haywood, but flatly denied ever saying anything else.

Finally, the coroner Robert Fowke, a Stafford attorney, gave an overview of all the statements made, and after a short discussion, the jury returned a verdict of wilful murder against Owen, Thomas, Ellis and Musson, who were committed for trial at the next assizes. Before the jurors left the room, jury foreman William Turner handed a paper to the coroner. It was a letter signed by all twelve men protesting against the iniquity of Sunday working:

Mr Coroner,

Now that this long and painful investigation has closed, we, the undersigned Jurors, who have attended your inquest on the body of Christina Collins, beg to state that we are not satisfied to separate without first strongly expressing our decided conviction of the great impropriety of the carrying business, both by land and water, being carried on upon Sunday, in the same manner as on other days.

The evidence before us has brought under our observation much of what appears to be the usual conversation and demeanour of boatmen, and the narration will not only excite the abhorrence of all respectable persons, but that it is highly disgraceful to the community at large, so long as that community has not done its utmost to stay the evil.

By this violation of the Sabbath not only boatmen, but great numbers of other persons who are engaged in the conveyance of goods, and also employed as clerks and porters, are entirely prevented from paying attention to religious duties on the day expressly set apart for that purpose. We beg further to state that we cannot but attribute the great demoralization that is proved to exist among boatmen principally to these causes, and we think it more than probable that had the unfortunate men been compelled to 'Keep holy the Sabbath-day,' the late deplorable event might not have occurred.

With these considerations, Sir, we feel that we should be failing in our duty were we not to remonstrate, as strongly as we can, against the continuance of the present system, and we beg of you, Sir, to make known these our sentiments in the proper quarter.

It was a highly unusual move by a jury, and the first sign that the Christina Collins case was destined to have far-reaching implications. The letter was printed in full by the *Staffordshire Advertiser* and confirmed to a shocked public that everything they might have suspected about boatmen was true.

All this negative publicity must have been highly damaging to Pickfords' reputation as one of the country's largest carriers. It had expanded steadily, investing in new wharfs and warehouses, and was now operating a fleet of 116 trading boats with 398 horses, to handle the ever-increasing demand for waterway transport. The company had also implemented strict new measures to protect cargo from theft, and each boat master was legally liable for all goods under his charge up to the time of delivery. If anything was missing, money to cover the loss was deducted from the captain's wages. As a goodwill gesture, and an attempt to dissociate itself from the actions of rogue employees, Pickfords decided to make a generous £30 donation towards the public expense of prosecuting the boatmen.

A month later, at the end of July 1839, the trial opened at Stafford Courthouse, an imposing neoclassical building fronted by four towering columns, with the stone figures of Justice and Mercy carved high on the pediment to remind anyone who chanced to look up of the lofty principles at stake here. Inside, the opposing lawyers deftly untied ribbons from bundles of papers as they prepared for battle.

A dozen men selected for the grand jury took their seats on the creaking oak benches, watched by the crowd of curious spectators who were squashed into the public gallery above. There was always a taut sense of anticipation in the most serious cases like this, where a guilty verdict meant the death penalty. And for the accused, it was a nerve-wracking experience to be brought up the steps from the holding cells below, to stand at the bar under the mass scrutiny of the assembled court.

James Owen, George Thomas (alias Dobell) and William Ellis (alias Lambert) were each charged with four offences. The first was the wilful murder of Christina Collins by throwing her into the canal, the second of rape, the third of common assault and the fourth of stealing property belonging to the unfortunate woman's husband. The prisoners pleaded not guilty to all the charges. The lad William Musson, from Chilvers

Coton in Warwickshire, who had originally been charged with the rest of the crew, was not named in the indictment and managed to avoid prosecution by agreeing to be a Crown witness.

Proceedings began with an unexpected opening gambit from Sergeant Ludlow, for the prosecution, who said he intended to offer no evidence against Owen on the charge of rape, whom he was willing to admit as a witness for the Crown. Owen's attorney, Mr Godson, said this was being done without his client's consent by means of a threat held over him. Defence counsel for Thomas and Ellis also objected that it would be most unfair to the prisoners.

The presiding judge, Mr Justice Williams, said he did not feel much difficulty on this point, but as the case was one 'of extreme importance', he would take the opinion of a learned colleague. He left the court briefly to confer and returned to say there was little doubt of the proper course to be taken as, in many instances, courts had allowed the prosecution to withhold evidence on behalf of the Crown. He would leave it to the discretion of counsel to do what 'would best promote the interests of public justice in this case'. It was clearly going to be a long-drawn-out chess match played between skilful opponents who could exploit every tactical advantage. The boatmen seemed like pawns in the game.

The facts of the case were outlined to the jury by Sergeant Ludlow, who described how Christina Collins set off on the boat journey and on several occasions appeared to apprehend some violence from the three boatmen. At one place, she was seen sharpening a knife and, though it was not for him to suggest the reason for this act, Sergeant Ludlow said one of the prisoners had a scar on his face and, extraordinarily enough, that knife was found inside one of the woman's trunks, which must have been uncorded and opened. He would be able to prove not only apprehension and alarm by the deceased, but also coarse, violent and threatening language by the prisoners.

There were many facts, comparatively trifling taken separately, which together formed a strong body of evidence against the men:

It will be shown that she was a woman of very decent and tidy appearance, remarkable for attention to her clothes. When her body was found, her clothes were considerably rent and torn, her drawers particularly were torn in such a way as to show that she had been used with great violence.

Sergeant Ludlow concluded by saying the case would stand or fall, in some degree, by the statement that Owen might give. But when the captain was asked to speak, he refused to give evidence for the prosecution. Sergeant Ludlow said he was not surprised, as he had observed the prisoners' attorney several times in conversation with Owen.

First into the witness box was Robert Collins, in a state of agitation and great distress, who 'wept aloud and seemed as if he could scarcely bear the sight of the prisoners', as he told how he had sent a sovereign for Christina to join him in London and later identified the body of his wife. He struggled to find the words to say that it was dreadfully disfigured and broke down again, sobbing, before he managed to regain his composure to confirm he recognised a mark on her ear.

After him came the dozen witnesses who had previously appeared at the inquest, all repeating what they had seen and heard. Then the lad William Musson was called to testify as a prosecution witness, but he was giving nothing away that could incriminate either himself or the rest of the crew. He said simply that he got out of bed and dressed at half-past one, about a mile from Colwich Lock, and went to work driving the horse down to Brindley Bank at Rugeley. He last saw the woman alive in the cabin at Colwich Lock, when it was the captain's turn to steer, and the other two men went to bed.

Between three and four o'clock in the morning, he asked the captain where the woman was, and Owen replied, 'He was affeared she was drowned.' Under cross-examination, Musson said the usual place for passengers was in the middle of the boat, called 'the hole'. There were blankets and counterpanes for the woman out there, but he frequently saw her in the cabin, and at Middlewich, she was lying down with her shoes, bonnet and shawl off.

Next to speak was John Bladen, employed by the Trent & Mersey Navigation Company at Rugeley, who explained that boat captains who lost a passenger or goods were duty-bound to report the loss at the next station on the route and the clerk would make a memorandum note on the bill. When Owen's boat passed the wharf on Monday, 17 June, no notice was given of any loss.

Police Constable William Harrison, who was called to the Fazeley canal offices to arrest the boatmen, recalled that Ellis began to damn and blast the woman, saying, 'What do I know about the woman; if she had a mind to drown herself, she might.' When he asked Owen what kind of person she was, he replied she was 'a little fierce-talking woman – a nice little woman'. While held in custody in an upstairs room at Rugeley, Owen also remarked, 'the woman wanted very little drowning', and said repeatedly that Thomas raped and murdered her. Constable Harrison showed the court Christina's shoes and battered bonnet.

Then Francis Jackson, a labourer from Drayton, was called into the witness box. He described how he had the charge of Owen in custody at the public house and was handcuffed to him on the Monday evening, when he heard Owen whisper to another labourer called Joseph Robinson:

> Owen said to Robinson, 'You go and tell the prisoners in the hole to say that we left the woman at Colwich lock.' Next morning Owen asked Robinson if he had told them, and Robinson said he had. Owen said: 'Go and tell them again, and be sure.'

Further hearsay evidence came from another labourer, Henry Sketchley, who was handcuffed to Thomas in an upper room at the Swan pub and slept beside him on the night of 22 June. Thomas had told him that the captain murdered the woman while Thomas and Ellis were asleep in the cabin this side of Colwich Lock. Owen was steering the boat and Musson was driving the horse. Thomas awoke to hear the woman cry, 'Oh my Collins! I will jump. Give me my shoes', and Owen saying, 'You bloody old cow, if you don't jump, I'll send you off.' Thomas added, 'The captain was a bloody rogue, for letting the boy take liberties with the woman.'

Another Rugeley constable, John Wood, produced for the court the penknife he had found when he searched one of Christina Collins' boxes, which had apparently been broken open. Two local women who were employed to take the clothes off the dead body next described the damaged state of the garments. Hannah Phillips said the gown was ripped at the back and cuff, and the left sleeve was ripped out of the gathers. A small chintz muslin handkerchief worn about the neck was also torn on each shoulder. They removed a white petticoat and Elizabeth Matthews particularly noticed that the fine calico drawers worn underneath were much torn. As the drawers were held up and shown to the courtroom, everyone saw they were torn completely across the front, from side to side. The two men who pulled the body out of the canal were recalled for further questioning and confirmed that they definitely had not torn the clothes with the boat-hook, or in any other way.

Finally, it was time for the jury to hear what the accused boatmen had to say, from their sworn depositions – Owen's signed with his name, Thomas and Ellis' statements with only a cross as, like many other boatmen, they were illiterate. Mr Godson, defence counsel for Owen, objected to the statements being read out because they had been taken under oath while the men were in custody and therefore were not legal evidence. He was overruled by the judge, and the depositions were read out by the court clerk.

George Thomas, aged 27, from Wombourne in Staffordshire, recounted the events of the voyage during which he claimed Christina Collins had been in the cabin on many occasions. With the boy, he had legged the boat through Barton Tunnel, for which the master paid him an extra sixpence. He steered to Change Bridge, and when he went to bed about ten o'clock, the woman was in the cabin. She went out while the men undressed, but soon returned and lay down on the side bench.

At Stoke, the woman went with them to a public house, where they took two or three quarts of porter, though she did not drink anything. About twenty minutes after Hoo Mill Lock, Thomas said, 'I looked into the cabin and saw her in bed with the captain; both the captain and the woman were dressed; the boy was undressed.' She remained there with the captain until they arrived at Colwich Lock, when Owen left to steer and the boy went to drive the horse. The woman was sitting inside the cabin as Thomas and Ellis lay down in their clothes and went to sleep. Thomas described vividly what happened next:

We were disturbed shortly afterwards by hearing words between the captain and the woman, and I heard the woman say – 'I'll jump, I'll jump.' And I heard the captain say – 'You bugger, if you don't I'll throw you off.' When we came to the stop place beyond the turn, I asked the captain if he was not ashamed to turn the woman out; he told me I might get out if I liked, and called the lad back to borrow some money to pay me. We were wrangling about it until we got close to Rugeley when he began to say the deceased was lost, she was

drowned, the boy was present. The captain and I went back to look
for the woman.

Twenty-eight-year-old William Ellis, a labourer's son from Brinklow
near Coventry, had a slightly different story. He had been engaged by
the captain only five weeks earlier in London, to work the boat up to
Preston Brook, and was setting off on the return trip to London when
the woman took her passage. He recalled the disagreement at Sandon
Lock, when he and Thomas argued with Owen, saying that the woman
ought not to go in the cabin, it was not a place for her. At Change
Bridge, when she was still in the cabin, another quarrel erupted and
Thomas said he would leave the boat, but the captain did not have the
money to pay him off. As they left Colwich Lock, the woman went out
on the boat hatches, while Ellis and Thomas went to sleep. An hour or
so later, the captain called and said the woman was gone. Several times
during the voyage she had threatened to destroy herself. Ellis said:

> I never saw anyone ill-treat her. She seemed very comfortable … she
> had half a pint of rum with her when she came on board at Preston,
> and she gave some to us. I did not see her drink anything herself. I got
> in at Colwich lock, and before I went to sleep, I heard Owen call her
> a whore and a cow. … As we were coming along the Fazeley pound,
> Owen asked us to say that the woman got out at Colwich lock.

The last and longest statement read out to the court was from James
Owen, a married man also from Brinklow, who said he first missed
Christina Collins at the watering place near Rugeley. He gave Thomas
sixpence to leg the boat through Barton Tunnel about 9 p.m., telling
the woman she might go into the cabin:

> She said it was very hard for her to have paid sixteen shillings and to
> have no straw. She said she was very short of money, and if I would
> find her victuals, she would satisfy me when we got to London.

When they passed the tunnel, she went into the cabin where the men
were in bed. Owen was steering and could see her sitting on the side bed:

She remained there for some time and then came out of the cabin and talked to me about plays. She said she belonged to Covent Garden Theatre, and would give me a ticket to go there when she got to London. She said she was married to a second husband who was in London.

At Middlewich, it was the boy and Owen's turn to get some sleep, so they undressed in the cabin. 'When I was in bed I told the woman she might come and lie down by me, which she did. The woman lay down with her clothes on.'

Next morning, Owen said he had breakfast with Christina, and at Stoke Lock, she followed him down the locks to a public house where they had half a pint of ale apiece. At Stoke Wharf, she sat on the steps at the office door while they unloaded cargo. At dinner time, between one and two o'clock, they ate bread and cheese then went to a public house kept by John Machie to drink three pots and a pint. Owen said the woman would not have any porter and sat by the back door while the men were in the pub for about an hour, before they loaded the boat, collected the invoices and started off. They had two hampers of wine for Atherstone. When they left Stoke, she seemed low and out of spirits, and Owen told her to have some chat with another female passenger, who rode with them a short way down to the Plume of Feathers at Darlaston.

When they reached Stone, Owen left the boat for fifteen minutes to buy some bread, admitting he was 'muddled' and did not know if the woman was on the boat or not when he returned. However, he did recall the disturbance that woke him between Haywood and Colwich lock at about midnight on Sunday, when he heard the noise of the woman and saw her in bed, with Thomas upon her:

I jumped out of bed and laid hold of her. She said, 'Oh captain! Oh my Collins! I'll drown myself before I get to London.' I asked if they had done anything to her, but she kept crying and sobbing very much and made no answer. I accused the men of having abused her; and they said they had not and were very saucy, and I threatened to dismiss Thomas. I borrowed six shillings from the boy to pay Thomas his wages … While I was quarrelling with the men, the woman attempted to jump from the hatches into the canal. I caught hold of her and pulled her into the boat. She said she would drown herself before she got to London. She was wet up to her knees.

Owen told her to go in the cabin, and he stayed in the hatches talking to her until they reached Colwich Lock, where Christina got off the boat on the opposite side to the towing path. Owen said, 'I was having words with the men and did not see anything of the woman again. I was jawing and differing with them and did not know she was missing.' Not surprisingly, given the amount of alcohol he had been knocking back, memories of that night were very confused and in a later separate statement Owen described a different scenario:

> When we came below Colwich lock, Ellis wanted to take the woman into the cabin and I would not let him. Thomas and I kept quarrelling about a mile. The last time I saw her alive was at Turnover Bridge, in the middle of the boat. … When I came to Fazeley pound I went to the hole and saw Ellis and Thomas with one of the passenger's boxes open. I told them I would not go any farther than Fazeley and they said: 'Go to hell with you. You are frightened about the woman. Tell them she got out at Colwich lock.'

The last witness called to give evidence was James Roscoe, agent for the Trent & Mersey Canal Company at Stoke. He had been in Rugeley for the inquest on 20 June, when he received a message from Owen, asking to see him at the public house where he was in custody. There, he agreed to write down Owen's version of events and read over the statement which the captain then signed.

Owen said that at Hoo Mill Lock, he could not help laughing at a conversation he overheard between Ellis and Thomas about 'cutting her trousers'. He claimed that at Colwich Lock, Ellis got hold of the woman and wanted to take her to bed but he would not let him. The woman complained they had been pulling her about. She did get out at Colwich Lock, but then returned to the boat. When they reached the stop place at Brindley Bank, he noticed her shoes and bonnet were in the cabin, and went to the middle of the boat to find her, but she was not there and he gave the alarm to his men.

That concluded all the evidence, and Sergeant Ludlow said, 'That is my case, my lord.'

Mr Godson, Owen's counsel, retorted, 'Then I contend that it is no case at all.'

The judge apparently agreed, saying that although he would have sat until midnight, or indeed for several nights, to patiently hear any evidence, there was 'not one particle of evidence' to show that any rape had been committed. While it was perfectly true there were suspicious circumstances in the case, there was no more evidence of rape than of murder, and there was not a case to go to the jury. Addressing the jurors, Mr Justice Williams said:

> Gentlemen, I in common with you, may suppose that foul play took place on board that boat. We may imagine that dreadful deeds were done that night with regard to this unhappy woman; but in this realm of England we do not go on mere suspicion ... where is the evidence this unhappy woman was ravished at all. You have not heard one word about the state of her person. There is no proof of any violence having been committed upon her. Whatever we may suspect, and whatever may be at the bottom of the hearts of those men, to accompany them to their latest day in life, and beyond it, I am bound to tell you there is no proof of them having committed the crime of which they stand charged in this indictment.

Sergeant Ludlow pointed out there was abundant evidence of assault – the state of her clothes, the prisoners' declarations, besides the fact disclosed that they were 'pulling her about'. But, quick as ever to respond in Owen's defence, Mr Godson insisted the only evidence, even of assault, would be from the crew's declarations against each other, which in fact were not legal evidence. The judge ruled against Sergeant Ludlow and directed the jury to bring in a verdict of not guilty on the charge of rape.

As they heard those two words spoken aloud by the jury foreman, the accused boatmen standing at the bar must surely have felt a flicker of hope that perhaps things were going their way after all. If so, it was soon extinguished. That was not the end of the matter, by any means. Sergeant Ludlow was a determined adversary on behalf of the Crown, and not to be put off by a comparatively minor setback. He stood up again now, to apply for the trial on the indictment of murder to be postponed until the next assizes, so a most material piece of evidence could be submitted. No one had expected this. What clever trick did the prosecution have up its sleeve?

After a short break, the court resumed and Sergeant Ludlow presented an affidavit revealing the existence of a new witness, a butcher named Joseph Orgill who had just been convicted of bigamy at the same assizes. It would not be safe to proceed to the murder trial without Orgill's evidence, but he was being held in the county gaol and could not be admitted as a witness. Sergeant Ludlow was therefore making an application to the Secretary of State for a free pardon for Orgill, and he asked for the trial to be postponed until then.

As usual, Mr Godson was on the attack at once and sprang to his feet, protesting there was nothing whatever to connect Orgill with the case:

If this course is adopted, convicted felons will think they have nothing to do but trump up some tale against a prisoner, still untried, in order to have a remission of punishment. It would be a bonus on falsehood and perjury … This is strange indeed. Upon the suggestion of a felon, of something that occurred in gaol, this extraordinary application is made.

Sergeant Ludlow replied that after the new facts were disclosed, he was sure the judge would think the ends of justice would be furthered by postponement of the trial.

Mr Justice Williams said it was impossible to separate in his mind the melancholy facts elicited in the investigation, and it could not be concealed that there was already a most serious case of suspicion against these men. With a view to the justice of the country, he therefore postponed the trial for murder until the next assizes. The ever-zealous Mr Godson rose swiftly to make one last move in Owen's defence, asking for the indictments of assault and theft to be dropped, but the judge ruled the charges must stand. The first round of the contest was over.

Meanwhile, as legal matters continued slowly and relentlessly in the background, news of the Christina Collins case was rapidly spreading in ripples of shock and horror, not only within Staffordshire but throughout the country, as people everywhere read and discussed all the lurid details in newspaper reports of the trial. There was naturally great sympathy for the victim in the local press, and the *Staffordshire Gazette* printed Christina Collins' touching last letter to her husband, commenting:

> She appears to have been a woman of strong mind, and devotedly attached to her husband; her conduct during the journey which proved so fatal to her, is stated by many respectable witnesses to have been both modest and prudent.

The *Nottingham Mercury* gave details of her family background as the daughter of inventor Robert Brown, saying that she had been well educated and was:

> ... well formed to move in a different sphere, but the unforeseen events that occurred in Mr Brown's family, when his children were young, blighted all their prospects. ... The deceased is described by one who well knew her to have been of a most amiable mind.

The *Mercury* went on to say that the distressing news of Christina's death had only recently been broken to her mother, who was now over 60 and working as a nurse.

For many people, it was just a fleeting topic of idle gossip; for others, it sparked curiosity and endless questions about this most intriguing of cases. But in some quarters, it prompted heated debates on serious moral issues and a resolution to take action. A national campaign to keep the Sabbath as a day for rest and worship, led by the Evangelical Church, had grown steadily more influential since the 1820s. There were proposals to ban Sunday activity everywhere, from public houses, coffee shops and cookshops to all forms of transport, including mail or stagecoaches, wagons and canal boats.

In 1835, the House of Commons had discussed the subject at length during readings of the Sunday Observance Bill, when some members argued that it would be unfair to poor men who needed to buy food and drink, and deserved innocent recreation after the week's labours. Others pointed out that the labouring classes would benefit by any law protecting them from compulsory employment on Sunday. During one debate, Sir Robert Peel said that although 'no one has a right to shock public feeling by desecrating the Sabbath-day', he seriously doubted whether legislation would be effective.

Plenty of canal boatmen who wanted Sundays off work had enthusiastically jumped on the bandwagon and were calling for improvements in working conditions. Among them were 616 men working on the River Severn and Worcester & Birmingham Canal, who signed a petition to Parliament pointing out they were compelled to work and violate the Sabbath by employers, and therefore could not attend church or have the benefit of rest from weekly toil. They asked the House to adopt measures which 'will entirely relieve us from such degradation and hardship'. Another group of 715 wharfingers and boatmen at Etruria Wharf in the Staffordshire Potteries petitioned Parliament for an end to all unnecessary travel on Sundays.

The brutal attack on Christina Collins, carried out on a Sunday by drunken working men, was now seized on by campaigners as proof they were right to demand far-reaching reform. Just days after the boatmen's trial, a group of twenty-two Chester clergymen in parishes alongside the Trent & Mersey held a meeting in Northwich to air their views and draw up a petition, which they presented to canal proprietors and carriers trading in the region, earnestly entreating them to stop boats working on the Sabbath. The clergy said they felt it was their duty to act, for the sake of watermen, 'whom we see around us perishing for lack of knowledge', and suggested that all canal locks were closed on Sundays so the rest day gave 'increased vigour and physical strength both to the men and the horses'.

The petition appeared in the *Chester Courant*, which commented:

The demoralized condition of the men employed on the navigations of this kingdom has long been notorious, though we fear not sufficiently deplored, or surely such a body of men, in a Christian country, would not have been left so long entirely destitute of all means of moral improvement. We rejoice that at length public attention has been directed to this useful, though wretchedly debased body of poor men.

The *Courant* declared that it hoped by printing the petition, influential residents and clergy living near navigations throughout the country would also lobby canal carriers and proprietors to end Sunday trading. It reminded readers of the Christina Collins case:

The horrible and atrocious occurrence … which has so justly and strongly excited the public feeling, is an affecting and deplorable proof, of the barbarous and lost condition of our inland watermen generally, to every moral principle. Surely such an awful and melancholy circumstance irresistibly appeals to every benevolent and Christian principle for amelioration of the poor and degraded, because long-neglected, watermen of England!

It was a powerful call to arms, reprinted by other newspapers, which fuelled much wider public debate on the contentious subject of Sunday working and rallied further support for change. A few weeks later, the *Staffordshire Gazette* ran a letter from George Hodson, Archdeacon of Stafford, who lived near Rugeley. He had support for a similar petition from the clergy and churchwardens of Stafford parishes, protesting that Sabbath desecration was responsible for:

The dreadful habit of swearing at their horses, and at each other, which so fearfully prevails amongst the boatmen, to the extreme annoyance and distress of those who live near canals, as well as the drunkenness and dishonesty which too frequently occur among them. And though we abstain from pronouncing judgement upon the unhappy men who have still to stand trial on a charge of wilful murder committed on the Trent and Mersey canal, near Rugeley, yet the horrid and disgusting details which came out in evidence against them, afford a melancholy proof of the moral degradation and debasement in which too many, we fear, of the class for which we plead are sunk.

The petitioners stressed they were motivated by compassion towards men working on canals, who were not only deprived of a weekly rest but 'reduced to the condition of a degraded class ... in which the bad are made worse, and confirmed in their evil habits'. The clergymen said they had the backing of many boatmen, lock-keepers and wharfingers, and hoped to see a speedy end to Sunday traffic. The campaign was rapidly gathering momentum.

The entrance into the great Tunnel, from Blisworth. Northamptonshire.

Blisworth Tunnel in Northamptonshire, where fourteen navvies were killed during construction in 1796 when the roof caved in. (© Chronicle/Alamy)

The traditional method of 'legging' through a tunnel was exhausting work for boatmen, such as these on the Cromford Canal in Derbyshire. (© National Railway Museum/Science Museum Group)

Boatmen worked long hours through hot summer days and chilly winter nights, walking many miles each day to lead their horses along the towpath. (© The Japics Historic Photography Collection/Mary Evans Picture Library)

The Mitre Tavern on the Paddington Canal, where George Foster and his wife Jane had a last drink together in 1802. (© London Metropolitan Archives/Heritage Images/Alamy)

The condemned cell in London's Newgate Prison, *c.* 1800, where felons awaiting the gallows were held. (© Mary Evans Picture Library)

A trial in progress at the Old Bailey in London, *c.* 1808. (© Classic Image/Alamy)

The bustling streets outside Newgate Prison, where huge crowds would gather to watch at public executions. (© Mary Evans Picture Library/Peter & Dawn Cope Collection)

Thomas Homer's bold scheme for the new Regent's Canal was hit by countless problems but finally opened in 1820. This 1827 illustration by Thomas Shepherd shows locks at the east entrance to Islington Tunnel. (© Alamy)

Industrial canals could be murky and desolate places, like this one at Dudley in Staffordshire pictured on an 1840 engraving. (© Mary Evans Picture Library/Mapseeker Publishing)

Drink-related crime was a growing problem and police ineptitude was blamed when the culprits were never caught. Here, two drunks slip away unnoticed by a patrolling constable. (© World History Archive/Alamy)

This iconic engraving of *Beer Street* by William Hogarth celebrates the innocent pleasures of drinking wholesome English beer. (© Classic Image/Alamy)

A London pub full of brawling drunks in an illustration by George Cruikshank. Public houses were criticised for encouraging drunkenness and depravity among the labouring classes. (© World History Archive/Alamy)

The stone figures of Justice and Mercy look down from the façade of Stafford Courthouse, where three Pickfords' boatmen were tried in March 1840. (© Nick Scott/Alamy)

A caricature of Sir John Gurney, one of Britain's most senior judges, who presided at the Christina Collins murder trial. (© Chronicle/Alamy)

Manchester was known as Cottonopolis, for its booming textile industry. This etching by Edward Goodall shows the smoky cityscape from Kersal Moor in 1857. (© Classic Image/Alamy)

Domestic violence is depicted in Plate VI of George Cruikshank's *The Bottle*: 'Fearful Quarrels, and Brutal Violence, are the Natural Consequences of the Frequent Use of the Bottle'. The popular series of eight etchings was published in 1847 to promote the temperance cause. (© Chronicle/Alamy)

Paddington Canal in west London, where the body of a young lady known only as J.S.M. was found floating in the water in June 1872. (© Mary Evans Picture Library/Peter & Dawn Cope Collection)

The scene of destruction on the Regent's Canal after an explosion on the barge *Tilbury* blew up part of central London in October 1874. (© Illustrated London News Ltd/Mary Evans Picture Library)

This 1874 illustration of a boatman smoking a pipe aboard his lethal cargo of gunpowder was published in support of a campaign to tighten safety regulations. (© World History Archive/Alamy)

Horses towing canal boats for over twelve hours a day were often led by children. (© Mary Evans Picture Library)

A cosy teatime inside a boat cabin is shown in this 1874 engraving by W.B. Murray, but many canal-boat families endured grim conditions. (© Illustrated London News Ltd/Mary Evans Picture Library)

Police Constable William Hine went missing on his way home from the Wharf Inn, Fenny Compton in Warwickshire, on 15 February 1886. (© Warwickshire County Record Office, PH 165/7-8)

Opponents of the temperance movement spoke out for the working man's right to drink. Here, a bargeman is moored outside the Cape of Good Hope public house on the Grand Junction Canal at Warwick. (© Warwickshire County Record Office, CR 2902/82)

Navvies take a rare break during excavation works on the Manchester Ship Canal, where the union claimed there were more than 1,000 fatal accidents. (© National Maritime Museum, Greenwich, London)

Gang warfare on London's backstreets spilled over onto the towpath of the Regent's Canal. This 1885 illustration from *Harper's Monthly* shows Maida Hill Tunnel in Little Venice. (© Mary Evans Picture Library)

10

BEYOND ALL REASONABLE DOUBT?

The Christina Collins case had not only revealed the appalling experiences of one woman on a flyboat – it had uncovered disturbing facts about the behaviour of working men which could not be ignored. And it was against this highly emotive backdrop of public debate that the second trial opened at the Spring Assizes in Stafford on Monday, 16 March 1840. Since early morning, the streets around the court had been crowded with eager onlookers, all hoping to secure a seat inside and watch the action unfold.

The last few minutes ticked by on the clock. All eyes were fixed on the accused men. The vast high-ceilinged courtroom in Shire Hall could be very intimidating, but if they felt a shiver of apprehension, the boatmen did not show it. Wearing the same clothes and traditional sleeve waistcoats, after more than seven months confined in grim prison conditions, they must have looked grubby and dishevelled to the smartly dressed onlookers, fresh from their morning toilette and a hearty breakfast. One newspaper reporter present that day noted:

> The prisoners were rather rough-looking men, and their dress and appearance completely indicated the class to which they belonged. They took their places at the bar with some degree of readiness and manifested great composure during the trial.

The benches up in the public gallery were half-empty, as presiding judge Baron Gurney had strictly forbidden admission of the excited hordes of spectators waiting outside. But a large group of visiting barristers had gathered in court to watch proceedings in this ground-breaking case, which was set to go ahead, contrary to the fundamental legal principle known as double jeopardy, which prevented anyone acquitted of a crime from being prosecuted a second time on the same facts.

One of the country's most senior judges, Sir John Gurney had earlier made his name as a barrister in many high-profile trials, including the prosecution of the Cato Street conspirators, and in 1832, he was knighted and appointed a Baron of the Exchequer (a role since abolished but equivalent to a present-day High Court judge). Now aged 72 and highly experienced, he was the right man to direct proceedings in this complex legal battle where the outcome could hinge on a technicality.

This time, Owen, Thomas and Ellis were charged with wilful murder by casting, pushing or throwing Christina Collins into the canal, by which means she was suffocated, choked and drowned. They each pleaded not guilty, and the jury was sworn in.

Sergeant Ludlow rose to his feet for the prosecution and warned the jurors that the prisoners had a right to fair, unbiased consideration of the evidence, urging them to ignore any unfavourable impressions they might have gained from widespread public discussion of the events. During a brief outline of the case, he remarked that part of the boat's cargo consisted of spirits, which he believed the men had drunk freely and 'lost part of their usual restraint over themselves, which was at the very best feeble'.

Sergeant Ludlow described the fateful boat journey, tracing its progress to Stone, where the men were seen to be intoxicated and the deceased expressed fears that she would be ill-treated by them. Then near Sandon, where two boatmen made disgusting allusions to Mrs Collins, one threatening what he would do to her. And at Hoo Mill, where the lock-keeper's wife was disturbed by cries of distress and saw a female crying on a Pickfords' boat with three men. He ended by observing that the deceased might have fallen into the water accidently, she might have thrown herself in, or might have been thrown in by one or all of the prisoners. The jury must decide from the evidence by which of these means Mrs Collins met her death. But he stressed that if there was any reasonable doubt in their minds, the prisoners were entitled to an acquittal.

One by one, the same witnesses were called into court to repeat for the third time what they had seen and heard. James Willday, captain of one of Bache & Company's boats, said when he passed the Pickfords' flyboat in the early hours of Monday morning, he warned Musson they had a kicking mare, saying, 'Hello my lad, tell your master to look out.' Musson briefly put his head in the cabin, then quickly closed the doors.

Captain Willday described the sharp turn in the canal at Brindley Bank, like an elbow, where someone sitting on a boat would very likely be thrown off. 'That is what we call a drop or lurch. Even boatmen are liable to be thrown off when a boat lurches. There is a pretty strong current for a canal, but you cannot perceive the water flow.'

Under further close questioning, however, he admitted that, in fact, he had never known a single instance of anyone being thrown off a boat at Brindley Bank. Flyboats travelled about 3 miles an hour and the canal was generally 40ft wide, shallow towards the banks with deep water only in the middle.

The lad William Musson was sticking to his original story that he last saw the woman at Colwich Lock. Under cross-examination, he admitted that when the woman went missing, they did not try to stop the horse. Ellis was asleep at Brindley Bank – he knew that because he heard him snore.

Ann Leigh, the lock-keeper's wife at Wood End Lock, told the court how Owen turned up at their house about 5.30 a.m. on Monday, 17 June, and said he was afraid they had a woman passenger drowned:

I said, 'I hope not.' He said he was afraid they had. He could not tell what had become of her, for she was like she was deranged. She had been in the canal once up to her knees, and he fetched her out and put her into the cabin. Owen appeared to be all in a confusion at that time; he did not appear to be sober.

When defence counsel Mr Godson asked her if Owen appeared to be in confusion from liquor, she said he was visibly trembling. Here, the *Staffordshire Gazette* reporter noticed one of the jurors turned to another and made a significant gesture that seemed to say, 'I told you so.' Owen had told Mrs Leigh he thought the woman had gone for a little walk and 'he thought she must be deranged for she kept crying out, "Collins, Collins, Collins."'

Other witnesses also testified that the boatmen were clearly very drunk and abusive. Pickfords' agent William Kirk, who dealt with such men every day, said boatmen generally used very disgusting language, particularly when in liquor. The judge interrupted at this point to say he could not refrain from remarking that no men in the country were so destitute of all moral conduct as boatmen. They were continually wandering about, they knew no Sabbath and had no means of religious instruction. Many in the court shared those sentiments, and as the day wore on, the atmosphere seemed to be hardening against the defendants.

Sergeant Ludlow then wanted to put forward the prisoners' statements made under oath before the coroner, but Mr Godson sprang up, protesting vigorously, and the judge ruled they were inadmissible, being the evidence of prisoners against themselves. The last few witnesses were questioned before Robert Collins was called, forced yet again to relive the awful experience of identifying his wife's body, and the *Gazette* reporter noted that a deadly pallor spread over Thomas' face. Robert Collins' eyes were filled with tears during the short examination, and as he left the witness box, he shook his head at the prisoners 'in a very mournful, but still revengeful manner'.

At last, it was the moment everyone had been waiting for and the reason the whole trial had been postponed at the original hearing. Joseph Orgill, the butcher convicted of bigamy and then pardoned by the Secretary of State, stepped into the box for his big moment. There was an expectant hush. Reporters noted he was very respectably dressed and spoke in a clear, straightforward manner without any hesitation.

His voice rang out across the silent courtroom as he recounted a conversation with Owen during the last assizes, while they were both locked up in a cell, lying awake one night talking about their trials:

I said, 'Mine is a bad job' and he said, 'So is mine. I can't think why they have taken the boy away from the other two men. Perhaps he will be a witness against us … if he is going to, it is for other things, not the woman. He did not know anything about her, the other two committed the rape and mauled her to death. I'm afraid it will be a hanging job. I will tell you about it.

His voice trembling with emotion, Owen had then described how the crew drank whisky stolen from the boat's cargo and began to get rough with the woman passenger. Thomas and Ellis followed her along the towpath, mauling her all the way, and when they were near a house, they raped her:

> The woman had a pair of trowsers on. One held her down while the other took a knife out of his pocket, and cut the trowsers out of the way, the woman screamed out.

If anyone in the house heard, he could not say, but supposed they had gone to bed. They put the woman in the boat again, she was in bed, and Owen confessed he 'tried to have to do with her but could not'. While the men kept drinking steadily from a bottle of whisky, the woman tried to escape but they pulled her into the cabin again, raped her and completely mauled her to death. According to Owen, 'what made them do it was, they knew what they had been doing with her, and she would tell'.

At Fradley Junction they wanted to unload the passenger's boxes but the Pickfords' clerk would not allow it. Owen said he warned Thomas and Ellis to leave the luggage alone, when he saw them taking a piece of cotton print material from one box, because they would be in enough trouble anyway. The men replied they would all be right about the woman, 'if he held his noise, for nobody ever saw them do anything to her'. That was the captain's story, and at the end of this frank night-time confession, as they lay in the darkness of their cell, Owen said to Joseph Orgill:

> I hope they will not hang us, but we will get off with transportation, and then I don't care. We have made a bad job of it altogether. If we had stopped the boat at Rugeley, and made an alarm to the people there, they would have had no suspicion; or even if we had taken the woman and left her in the middle of the boat in the place for passengers, nobody could have sworn we had done it, and Pickfords would have been fined a sovereign for not finding straw. If Thomas and Ellis had left her alone, she would have been alive and well enough.

Joseph Orgill certainly seemed to be a plausible enough witness, with an impressive memory for the details of a conversation that took place many months earlier. But of course, as a convicted bigamist, he had the one undeniable flaw of being an exceptional and practised liar. And he had been granted an official pardon for his crime (escaping an eighteen-month prison sentence) in exchange for agreement to testify against the boatmen.

Defence counsel Mr Godson did his best to discredit the butcher who, under forceful cross-examination, coolly admitted he was a married man with four children, had abandoned his family in England and lived for six weeks with another woman he had wed in Ireland, adding, 'I cannot say whether I left her in the family way.' Adamant that he first mentioned Owen's words with no thought of giving evidence or of receiving a pardon, Joseph Orgill insisted, 'I told the same story now that I did then.'

Mr Godson kept up his attack, firing questions at Orgill, who flatly denied robbing his second 'wife'. No, he had not taken her money or any property. 'I had a watch of hers, she gave it to me in Ireland. She followed me to England, and I gave it to her again.' It was a confident performance in being economical with the truth, but what else would you expect from such a disreputable character as a bigamist?

The trial was drawing to a close and Mr Samuel Barnett, the Rugeley surgeon who examined Christina Collins' body, was the last person to be called as a witness. He detailed the injuries and said, in his opinion, with twenty-one years of experience, the cause of death was suffocation from drowning, and she was alive when she went into the water. However, 'the symptoms of death by drowning are not always decisive, they are sometimes uncertain'.

Mr Godson rose to begin his lengthy closing speech for the defence and told the jurors they were being called on to perform a duty which had never before fallen to the lot of a British jury. They were trying three men for the second time, on precisely the same facts as those on which they had been acquitted at the last assizes. 'It is one of the first principles of criminal justice that a man should not be put in jeopardy of his life for a second time on the same facts for two offences.'

The crowd of visiting barristers, who had come to court specifically to hear exactly how the law could be manipulated in this unprecedented trial, were all listening carefully as Mr Godson continued, 'The prisoners are now being tried on an indictment found at the last assizes, on the same evidence with the addition of the statement of Orgill.' The indictment alleged cause of death to be drowning, but Orgill's statement showed the woman was not drowned. The question for the jury was, did the prisoners drown her? It was not whether she ceased to breathe under their brutal embraces.

Mr Godson feared the jury would find it extremely difficult to empty their minds of prejudice against these men, as they must have seen all the accounts of this extraordinary case which everybody had been talking about:

> Men read and heard with horror these exaggerated reports, so it was next to impossible for anyone to come to the consideration of the facts without a decided leaning against the prisoners. ... If their treatment, however brutal, induced her to throw herself into the water in a state of excitement, shame and remorse, or had weakened her to such a degree that she fell in, that was not a throwing and pushing into the canal by these men.

Orgill was a man they should be disinclined to believe, and Mr Godson said the evidence was far from satisfactory; even that of the surgeon raised a doubt whether the woman was drowned at all. The case was left in a state of doubt, and under such circumstances, Mr Godson expected the jury to acquit the prisoners.

The judge, Baron Gurney, began his summing up to the jury by saying he had never met with such a case in the whole course of his experience. Learned counsel had very properly cautioned them against press reports which must have been seen throughout the country on this melancholy case:

> By the publicity given to reports and rumours, the minds of jurymen were no doubt liable to be influenced, and all that could be done was to entreat them to dismiss anything they might have heard or read, and apply their minds to the evidence alone.

Before they could find a verdict of guilty, they must be fully satisfied the prisoners threw Christina Collins into the water and caused her death that way and no other. Although the evidence given by Joseph Orgill must be viewed with caution, the jury should give it due attention and decide from the demeanour of the witness how much credit he was entitled to.

His lordship said that in many cases of circumstantial evidence, the facts were so decisive it was possible to give an opinion with certainty. In this case, however, a great deal of careful consideration was needed, and an intelligent jury must not allow themselves to be misled by their feelings. He went on to say, 'The conviction of crime is not the first object of British courts of justice. It is far better that guilty men should escape punishment, than that one man should suffer unjustly.' If the jury were convinced the prisoners committed murder by drowning the woman, and not by any other means, they would find them guilty. If they entertained a fair and reasonable doubt, however much they felt disgusted at their conduct, and however great might be the suspicions, they would find them not guilty. Baron Gurney concluded, 'We should always take care that the disgust and abhorrence justly excited by the crime should not allow us to be satisfied with less, but rather to require stronger proof of the accused being its perpetrators.'

Now the jury had to decide.

The case was both disturbing and puzzling. Christina Collins knew she was in danger. Many other people could see she was in danger from the drunken boatmen. But still she kept returning to the boat, and no one else intervened to help. Surely, she could have transferred onto another Pickfords' boat, but the clerk merely told her to report the complaint when she arrived in London. The female passenger who joined her on board for a few locks must have noticed something was wrong but did not help. Not one of the passing boatmen, the lock-keepers, company clerks or wharfingers did anything to help. Even the lock-keeper's wife at isolated Hoo Mill did nothing more than ask what was going on.

Perhaps some of them resented this smartly dressed woman making a fuss about rough boatmen, whom they accepted as a little boisterous perhaps, but nothing to worry about. When there was trouble, no one wanted to get involved, and the canal community closed ranks against an outsider who ventured into their world. Faced with a crew of three aggressive drunks, it was safer to ignore the problem and not grass on your workmates or there could be repercussions later.

Despite all the danger signals on the nightmare journey, Christina stayed on the canal boat. Why? Maybe she simply hoped for the best, believing she could defend herself if necessary. Or perhaps it was simply down to poverty – she had spent 16 shillings of her precious sovereign on the boat ticket and was reluctant to waste her husband's hard-earned money or abandon the trunks with all her belongings. It proved to be a fatal mistake.

What really took place on the flyboat? After all the different accounts from witnesses and the conflicting stories of three men who were far too drunk to remember clearly, the stark truth was that no one could ever be certain. Christina was dead and could never reveal the truth about that terrible night.

Was there proof beyond all reasonable doubt that murder had been committed? And if so, who was responsible for the crime? Owen accused Thomas and Ellis. Thomas accused Owen. And if the boy Musson knew any more, he was keeping silent.

There were the incontrovertible facts of bruises on the body, torn clothing and drawers ripped across the front. Many witnesses heard the repeated threats of the boatmen and Christina's own desperate protests about their behaviour, but there was no physical evidence of assault. It remained a confused picture and much of the detail was, after all, from questionable hearsay evidence and confessions. From the surgeon's evidence, Christina was almost certainly alive when she hit the water, though even Mr Barnett said he could not be absolutely certain. She may have tried to escape and jumped into the canal, or accidentally fallen in. She may have been thrown in by one or more of the boatmen, but there were no witnesses and no other firm evidence to prove it.

After nearly three-quarters of an hour, the jurors had made up their minds. It was a tense moment as they filed back into the courtroom and 'every person in court appeared to await with breathless anxiety their verdict'. Jury foreman, Mr Edward Walley, announced they were all agreed and found the three prisoners guilty. There was a short pause as the black cap was placed on the judge's head. Mr Bellamy, the court clerk, asked the prisoners if they had anything to say but the men made no comment at all. The call for silence was made, and Baron Gurney addressed the three boatmen standing before him:

James Owen, George Thomas, William Ellis, after a long and patient hearing of the circumstances of this case, you have been found guilty of a foul murder – of murder committed on a helpless woman who was under your protection, and who there is reason to believe, was first the object of your lust, and then to prevent detection for that crime was the object of your cruelty! Look not for pardon in this world. Look only to the God of mercy, who has promised to pardon all penitent sinners, and prepare yourselves for the ignominious death that awaits you.

The case is one of the most painful, most disgusting and most shocking that ever came under my knowledge. It remains only for me to pronounce the sentence of the law – That you be taken to the place from whence you came, and thence to a place of execution, and there be hanged by the neck until you are dead, and that your bodies afterwards be buried within the precincts of the prison. And may the Lord have mercy on your souls.

One of the watching newsmen was surprised to see that:

The prisoners were wholly unmoved during delivery of this awful sentence, although the learned judge himself was evidently so much affected as to be able with difficulty to proceed, and the most solemn feeling pervaded all present.

The *Gazette* reporter noted:

The prisoners heard the sentence with the same stolid composure as they had evinced during the trial. They left the bar without saying a word. Owen's countenance slightly changed – in the others there was no perceptible difference, except that Ellis slightly smiled.

The three condemned boatmen were taken down to the cells. As the court dispersed and everyone else escaped outside into the fresh air of the spring afternoon, the reclining stone figures of Justice and Mercy gazed down inscrutably from the portico of the courthouse.

In many ways, it had been a show trial, designed to diffuse public feeling about the horrific crime and demonstrate that justice had been done. Yet there was the question of whether the butcher's evidence should have been allowed at all, and unease that the double jeopardy principle had been neatly side-stepped in this case.

The game was not yet over for the defence team, who refused to give up the fight to save the boatmen from the rope. They immediately set to work on an appeal, which was delivered to the Home Secretary on Monday, 6 April.

Meanwhile, incarcerated within the forbidding red-brick walls of Stafford County Gaol, Owen, Thomas and Ellis waited for the day of execution, which had been delayed for a week. The local press was receiving regular news bulletins on the case from long-serving prison governor Thomas Brutton, and these were reprinted in many other newspapers all over Britain.

The *Staffordshire Advertiser* informed readers that hostility between Owen and Thomas had reached such a pitch that they were being kept apart in separate cells to prevent them attacking each other. Both men angrily accused the other of the crime. Owen still denied ill-treating Christina Collins in any way, though he now claimed she had twice 'submitted to his embraces' without any objections early in the boat journey, while Thomas 'had connection with her against her will'. Thomas took refuge behind a hard front of reckless bravado, stubbornly denying any guilt.

On Thursday, 9 April, the Home Secretary, Lord Normanby, refused the appeal, saying there were not sufficient grounds to justify a recommendation to mercy and the law must take its course. Mr Brutton informed the boatmen there was not the slightest hope that they would be saved.

However, the defence lawyers remained determined to make one last move to win a reprieve, and on Friday morning, a delegation arrived at the gaol to interview the boatmen – the magistrate who chaired the quarter sessions, the deputy under-sheriff and two barristers. Significantly, one of the attorneys was Mr Lee, the prosecution counsel at both trials, who now agreed that Ellis' conviction on such flimsy evidence was unsafe. It was worth a try, as more than 90 per cent of those sentenced to death could expect to be reprieved.

Time was fast running out. Clutching the crucial signed legal documents, defence barrister Mr Gaunt dashed to catch the next train, setting off for London at 1.30 p.m. to seek a personal meeting with the Home Secretary.

The prison chaplain, Reverend Richard Buckeridge, spent the whole of that Friday with the boatmen. It was the day before their execution and, as he tried to prepare them for death, he pointed out the awful consequences of telling lies as they stood on the verge of the eternal world. Under the prolonged tension of the wait and these repeated religious entreaties, Thomas' defences finally crumbled. He wept bitterly and admitted 'he might have been steering at the time the woman was lost, he might have pushed her into the water, but he was so drunk he did not know what he did'. He exonerated Ellis, declaring his crewmate was asleep when it happened. Ellis continued to deny all knowledge of how the woman drowned.

Fevered speculation swept the country. The *Staffordshire Gazette* noted that the atrocity of the crime, the postponed execution and serious doubts being expressed about a verdict on such doubtful evidence 'had, we scarcely need inform our readers, given to this dreadful case a most unusual degree of notoriety, and created corresponding excitement'.

To satisfy avid curiosity about these men from a little known and apparently lawless community on the edge of society, the press published their confession to the prison chaplain, which revealed shocking scenes from daily life on the waterways. Thomas and Ellis confessed that 'their general habits had been of the most depraved and profligate nature', though not much different to other boatmen. The report went on:

> Thieving, it appears, is reckoned an accomplishment, and men are most sought after by captains of boats, who can pilfer cargoes most adroitly and to the greatest extent. They say there is no difficulty in disposing of stolen goods, receivers being on hand at all points of the canals. It is an invariable practice to abstract ale, spirits &c from casks, by means of syphon pumps which are in common use in the boats. Drunkenness is consequently habitual among boatmen to a dreadful extent; and as intemperance is the fruitful parent of crime, they are generally prepared for the worst offences.

Thomas and Ellis told the chaplain that fornication and adultery were prevalent, and as to religion, they paid no regard to it whatever and could not remember ever being in a church or place of worship. It was certainly a damning litany of sin. Whether this report was wholly true, or exaggerated for dramatic effect, it was up to readers to decide – with newspapers you could never be sure.

On Friday night, vast crowds of people from all over the country started arriving in Stafford, and beds in most of the public houses were full. That night, the scaffold was erected in front of the prison lodge and thousands more spectators poured into town. To avert potential trouble, extra special constables were sworn in by magistrates and barricades were placed at 20 yards from all three thoroughfares approaching the gaol to keep the crowds back. A reporter for the *Staffordshire Gazette* described the scene:

> From three o'clock on Saturday morning, gigs and spring carts, and humbler vehicles filled with men and women, were continually arriving. The railway trains also brought hundreds, and the road from the station to the town presented a living stream pushing on and, we fear we may say, eager to witness the scene of death!

At noon, the three boatmen were led from their cells into the prison chapel to take the sacrament. Prayer books were handed to Owen and Thomas, who knelt on the left of the communion table. Prison governor Mr Brutton knelt on the right, next to Ellis, who was not given a book as he couldn't read. The Reverend Buckeridge implored the men as sinners in the presence of Almighty God to confess the whole truth. Owen replied, 'I have no more to say.' Thomas answered, 'I have told all', and Ellis, who appeared very depressed, said nothing. As the chaplain conducted a short ceremony, Owen made his responses in a firm voice and, covering his eyes with one hand, seemed to be in prayer. Thomas was not so much moved, but Ellis was evidently wretched. As the solemn service ended, all three boatmen left the building.

Just a few minutes later, Ellis was called back into the chapel by Mr Brutton, who said that Her Majesty had granted a respite and his life would be spared. At this incredible last-minute reprieve, Ellis burst into tears. The chaplain urged him to thank God for his deliverance, and when Ellis asked to take his leave of the other two men, the governor accompanied him to break the news.

It was an emotional parting, as Ellis broke down again and wept, taking each boatman by the hand, kissing them affectionately and exclaiming, 'God bless you dear boys.' Owen began sobbing bitterly and as Ellis bade them a final tearful farewell, Thomas said, 'Bill, if you get off, let this be a warning to you for ever.'

By this point, the highly charged atmosphere had affected everyone present, and even Mr Brutton had difficulty restraining his feelings. Owen and Thomas were apparently reconciled and shook hands cordially.

Then the deputy sheriff arrived with final official confirmation that he had received the Home Secretary's letter granting respite for Ellis. For Owen and Thomas, the law must take its course. The solemn tolling of the prison bell rang out to announce that the long-delayed execution was imminent. There were now no more moves left to play on behalf of the other two boatmen. After all the many twists and turns in this nail-biting human chess game, it was finally checkmate to the Crown.

One o'clock was the appointed time. As the hour of execution drew near, all the streets around the prison were packed with noisy onlookers, and thousands more assembled on the road leading out to Stone. Newsmen estimated that almost 10,000 people had gathered, the majority from the lowest classes, and among them were numerous women. 'Walls, trees, windows, and gardens, and in fact almost every spot from which a view of the dreadful event could be anticipated, was occupied.' Some even perched precariously on house roofs for a better view.

Owen and Thomas were led from their cell and walked in silence through the vaulted passageway in a procession of officials led by the chaplain. As they reached the door, Reverend Buckeridge began reading aloud the church burial service and the men filed outside through the prison lodge to the foot of the gallows.

A low cry went up from women in the watching crowd as the boatmen appeared. Owen was the first to mount the platform, and as he took his place beneath one of the halters, he glanced up for a moment at the crossbeam. The executioner quickly placed the rope round his neck. Then Thomas went up the steps, stumbling slightly when his foot caught on the top plank. The executioner put the noose round his neck and shook hands with both men, who stood in silence and seemed to be saying a last prayer.

The chaplain read the final part of the service and as he concluded with the words, 'in the midst of life we are in death', the bolt was withdrawn and the platform fell with a resounding thud. The two bodies jerked in violent convulsions for several seconds and Owen's hand raised slightly two or three times. It was over.

The crowds began to disperse quietly, leaving the two corpses still hanging there. An hour later, they were cut down from the scaffold and buried near the prison chapel. Printed broadsides, hot off the press, went on sale in the town headlined 'THE LIVES, TRIAL & EXECUTION OF PICKFORD'S TWO BOATMEN'. They included pictures of the hanging, and the scene at Hoo Mill when the boatmen attacked Christina while the lock-keeper's wife peered down from the window. There was also a ballad recounting the whole tragic tale in rhyming verse.

Bill Ellis' sentence was commuted to transportation for life to Australia. By this time, fewer convicts were being sent abroad because of growing opposition to transportation. Critics argued it was not an effective deterrent to crime and complained that conditions in the colonies were inhumane. The Stafford prison chaplain and governor both sent letters to visiting magistrates asking for Ellis' sentence to be reviewed.

In October 1841, Mr Brutton recommended Ellis be considered for clemency and requested that the Court of Quarter Sessions apply for a royal pardon. He wrote:

> It is now nearly two years and a half since he was committed for trial, at which period he was an ignorant man and not capable of reading or writing, but since his conviction he has applied himself so strenuously of his own free will and desire to improve himself, that for some time past he has been able to read well, and write tolerably so, and his general conduct during the whole of his imprisonment has been most exemplary.

Shortly afterwards, Ellis had his sentence cut to fourteen years' transportation.

The boatmen eventually took their place in crime history as notorious felons, featuring in a volume of the best-selling book *The Chronicles of Crime, or The New Newgate Calendar*, which gave five pages to the trial and described the murder as one which 'scarcely excelled in brutal atrocity' any other case.

The question remained – had justice been done? Was this justice, either for Christina Collins or for any of the four boatmen? Was the outcome, in fact, nothing to do with justice at all but purely down to who had played the cleverest game? It was a sobering thought, and one which lingered on for many years afterwards. In Rugeley churchyard, where Christina's body was finally laid to rest, local residents put up a stone memorial engraved with the words:

> To the memory of Christina Collins, wife of Robert Collins, London, who having been most barbarously treated was found dead in the canal in this parish on June 17th 1839, aged 37 years. This stone is erected by some individuals of the parish of Rugeley in commiseration of the end of this unhappy woman.

Memories of what became known as the Bloody Steps Murder lived on in the area, to be passed down through the generations in stories of ghostly appearances and dark bloodstains on the flight of sandstone steps at Brindley Bank, where Christina's lifeless body had been dragged from the water.

11

INTOXICATING LIQUOR

Any lingering doubts there might have been about canal boatmen were wiped out by the damning revelations of the Christina Collins case. After years of whispered suspicions, they were now openly condemned as lawless outsiders by respectable citizens and vilified by a hostile press. Their already dubious reputation had sunk to an all-time low.

That same spring of 1840, fresh evidence of depravity was revealed in newspapers up and down the country, with banner headlines proclaiming, 'DIABOLICAL MURDER IN A BOAT ON THE ROCHDALE CANAL'.

Once again, it was drink that led to violence. After a hard morning's work, boat hand James Hanson and Captain John Clayton left their boat to be loaded on a wharf at Brown's Fields in the centre of Manchester and went for a bite to eat before heading off to a beer house in Port Street for a quart of ale.

Later on, finding that the cargo had still not been taken aboard, they walked round the corner to a public house in Beaver Street. It was a grimy thoroughfare, leading up from the canal which serviced the booming textile industry in Manchester, known as Cottonopolis, where dozens of tall chimneys belched out plumes of filthy smoke from the cotton mills.

Inside the Brownsfield Tavern, a popular haunt of boatmen, they met William Cheetham, who was a workmate on the same boat, and they sat drinking beer together all afternoon. Between six and seven o'clock, Thomas Hammersley, a labourer who had helped unload their boat that morning, was in the pub to collect his wages when a quarrel erupted, with Hanson swearing, calling Cheetham names and threatening to kill him, until the captain pushed him aside, saying, 'Nay, thou will not.' The boatmen, who had all had a skinful of liquor, eventually left the pub, Captain Clayton saying he was off to Mills Hill on the Leeds Railway and would be back next morning in time for their boat.

Just after 7 p.m., a cry of 'Murder!' was heard by George Rose, a private watchman on duty in a factory on the opposite side of the canal at Brown's Fields. He opened the engine-house window and saw Hanson jump out of a boat, go into Mr Bridge's slate yard and start picking up stones. He hurled the missiles at the boat cabin and, with an oath, shouted, 'I'll cut thy bloody head off. If I could find a stone, I'd make thee remember throttling me.' Cheetham poked his head out of the hatchway, calling for the Watch and shouting, 'Go away, go away, I'll have no more to do with thee!'

Hanson took no notice, angrily pelting the cabin with stones and threatening, 'Damn thee, I'll murder thee. I don't care a damn for thee or the boat. I can have another tomorrow if I like.' By this time, it was dark as Hanson climbed on board and aimed a vicious kick at Cheetham, who disappeared below. There was a heavy thud, then silence. Watchman George Rose later said he did not interfere because such rows were common among the boatmen, who were always fighting, and he was afraid they would throw stones at him and break the factory windows.

James Bold, a boatman employed by Messrs Thomas, Boothman & Company, also witnessed the drunken attack as he was winding up a paddle at Brown's Fields lock and called out, 'Let him alone. I think thou's done enough to him.' He saw Hanson kick Cheetham, then immediately jump into the hatchway to throw stones out of the boat onto the canal bank, which Bold thought was a curious thing to do.

About 9 p.m., Hanson called across to Jem Howarth, on the boat lying alongside in the cut, asking for matches. He was out of luck and both men walked up to the lockhouse to fetch a light from Mrs Jackson's. When they returned and entered the cabin, Cheetham was sitting on the bed, leaning forward over his knees. He raised his head and said, 'It was done in the cabin.' Hanson retorted, 'Nay, it was done in the street.' Jem Howarth helped to kindle the fire, then went back to his own boat.

Next morning, Captain Clayton was on his way to work when he saw Hanson standing outside the tavern door. He said Cheetham had been robbed by four men and a woman after they followed him on board, beat him and pummelled his head. They had stolen a sack of corn and some bread, and taken the ropes. Hanson said, 'He's not dead, but he has such a face as I never seed.'

In the boat's cabin, they found Cheetham on his knees on the floor, slumped forward over the bed. The captain called his name, shook him and when there was still no response, seized Cheetham's hair and, pulling back his head, saw the face was bruised, with a swollen upper lip, cuts to the left cheek and two black eyes. On the floor were blood marks and a broken slate. A wooden mallet they used to break coals was found under the bottom step, one corner still wet with blood. The captain went to find a policeman, and Hanson was arrested and later charged with wilful murder.

During the subsequent trial at Liverpool Assizes, witnesses identified Hanson (known on the cut as Giles) from his distinctive clothing of light-coloured fustian trousers, green waistcoat with sleeves and a low-crowned hat. Despite all the detailed witness accounts, no one had seen Hanson strike the fatal blow, which fractured the skull, and the prosecution case relied purely on circumstantial evidence.

The jury found Hanson guilty of manslaughter, and the judge remarked on the barbarity of the attack as he sentenced him to fifteen years' transportation. The case was reported at length in northern papers such as the *Manchester and Salford Advertiser*, the *Yorkshire Gazette* and *Leeds Times*, but with public feeling against boatmen already running high, it was also given extensive coverage further afield, from the *Dover Telegraph* and *Berkshire Chronicle* to London's *Morning Herald*, the *Morning Post* and the *Globe*.

Each new outrage hardened attitudes and added to the mounting pressure for something to be done. Concerned clergy, indignant townsfolk and local officials were all determined to put a stop to the unacceptable behaviour of this degraded underclass, who were apparently addicted to drink and violence. In July 1840, the government responded by hastily passing the Canal Police Act, which for the first time allowed canal companies to employ their own private constables to patrol the waterways and adjoining land half a mile each side of the banks, to keep the peace and 'prevent a recurrence of former outrages and depredations'.

The legislation included a specific clause to deal with the widespread theft of alcohol, bringing in a £5 penalty (or one month's imprisonment) for anyone found on a canal, river or dock with 'any tube or other instrument to carry away liquor in their possession, or anyone attempting to obtain goods unlawfully'. Assault of an officer was punishable by a £10 fine. At a time when the average weekly wage of a labourer was £1, these were substantial sums.

To reassure the public that crime prevention was being taken seriously, these private constables were given new powers to arrest without a warrant 'any loose, idle and disorderly person' disturbing the peace, or suspected of being about to commit an offence. And at night, from sunset to 8 a.m., they could detain anyone loitering on towpaths, wharfs, bridges, locks or banks who couldn't give a valid explanation for what they were doing there. It was a comprehensive effort to put a stop to canal crime, but enforcement was never going to be an easy task.

One private officer patrolling a canal basin in London at 1 a.m. was assaulted by a 'great raw-boned Lancashireman', who resented his interference in a domestic drama. Constable James Taylor heard a woman crying out for help and rowed his boat across to the spot where she was struggling in the water beside a barge. She was stripped down to her petticoat and he thought she must have been thrown overboard in a quarrel. Her husband, Samuel Candiliffe, was leaning over the side of their barge grasping her hand but did nothing to assist when the constable jumped on board and pulled her to safety. Candiliffe was obviously drunk, shouting abuse as he tried to push the constable off and threatening to run a boat-hook through him unless he decamped immediately.

Wet through and tipsy, Mrs Candiliffe wasn't offering any thanks for being rescued, but clearly sided with her husband and kept cursing Constable Taylor in the grossest language. He was forced to call for back-up, and it took three or four policemen to finally subdue the angry bargeman after a prolonged tussle. At Worship Street Police Court in Shoreditch, Candiliffe was charged with being drunk and assaulting a constable, but the magistrate accepted his story that Mrs Candiliffe had accidentally fallen into the water while drunk. However, for his abusive conduct to the officer, he was fined 40 shillings and locked up until he could find the money. Any trouble involving a boatman was certain to make news, this time with the headline, 'A DOMESTIC DUCKING'.

While the reputation of boatmen was being submerged in a flood of criticism, at Brentford in the freezing winter of January 1841, a flood of a far more deadly nature swept away narrowboats moored alongside the canal wharfs. Shortly after midnight, Police Constable Smith, who was on duty near the bridge, noticed the water level rising and roused families sleeping in their boats to warn them of the danger. A few minutes before 4 a.m., a loud roaring sound was heard as the narrow stream of the River Brent began to thaw after the big freeze, burst its banks and poured into the already swollen waters of the Grand Junction Canal, tearing boats from their moorings and surging through the town.

Men, women and children dressed only in their nightclothes ran in all directions, frantically seeking shelter from the icy torrent, while boats were driven onwards by the current and through the bridge towards the Thames. An onlooker described to the *Chelmsford Chronicle* how 'the roaring of the water and the screams of the wretched inhabitants of the monkey-boats, borne along on the stream, were most appalling'. Giant blocks of ice, 1ft thick, lay in the streets.

Local people were quick to help, and all seven children in the Tolley family were dragged to safety through a cottage window as their boat passed Boar's Head Yard. At the cottage next door, the Foster sisters took in youngsters rescued from another vessel. Other families had a miraculous escape by jumping off their boats to climb a wall bordering the Duke of Northumberland's estate, where a resourceful boy named John Jones tied a rope to a tree so they could all get over into the grounds. As the last lad leapt down, the wall tottered and fell under the force of the floodwater, but all twenty-one refugees were safe. They were later discovered by the gardener, who gave them food and shelter.

In all, nine boats were sunk, many badly damaged and their cargoes ruined, leaving dozens of people destitute. Two rooms of the Butts Infant School were opened to take in the homeless boatmen that evening, while throughout Brentford inhabitants had been glad to offer small acts of kindness to families in distress. Despite what they may have read in the press, and whatever society's prejudices about boat people as a whole, many folk grateful for the security of home felt only sympathy when confronted with a calamity like this.

†††

It was the itinerant lifestyle of boatmen which set them apart and created mistrust among others living a more conventional, rooted existence. Plenty of people who were stuck in the same village they were born in probably envied the freedom to come and go at will. Of course, having 'no fixed abode' could be useful and there is no doubt that many shady characters were engaged in nefarious activities. Some boatmen were literally outlaws, taking casual work on canal boats to evade justice and using aliases to disguise their real identity.

In the tight-knit floating community, many people had bye-names, or nicknames, like the Manchester boatman William Hatton, known to everyone as Moucher, who had been a witness in the Collins case. Most boatmen, however, were simply straightforward, hard-working men struggling to eke out a meagre living, and probably no better or worse than the rest of the labouring classes. But unfairly, they were all tainted with the same ill repute.

One letter writer to the *Staffordshire Advertiser* pointed out that after press coverage of the Christina Collins murder, anyone would draw the conclusion that:

> The inland watermen of England, without exception, were addicted to murder, lust and rapine; that they were never to be approached but with feelings of horror and never to have anything entrusted to their care but with a certainty of being plundered.

He said individual crimes should not be taken as proof of general depravity, and it was an act of justice to declare that, despite their acknowledged vices, their honesty and morality were not inferior to any other class of men in the same sphere of life. The letter went on:

> That their manners and deportment are rough and unpolished everyone will admit, but morality and good manners are not synonymous terms, and experience has shown that a person of rough exterior is

quite as likely to possess an honest and kind heart as one whose manners are better polished.

It was a perceptive view and one rarely expressed. Like many others working punishing hours in all weathers, boatmen did whatever it took to survive, and sometimes found comfort in hard drinking as a welcome refuge from harsh reality. They were not all hardened sinners.

Meanwhile, the long-running campaign to stop Sunday working on canals was gathering pace. Back in the early days, all locks had been closed on the Sabbath to prevent travel on the official day of rest, but pressure of trade gradually took over until seven-day working became the norm. Because manufacturers dispatched goods at the end of each week, flyboats usually set out on Saturday night or early Sunday, carrying cargoes from the northern counties and Midlands down to London.

Trade demanded an efficient round-the-clock delivery system. It was clear to many people that constant labour with no prospect of a day off was liable to lead to trouble among men denied any outlet for recreation. Others felt that a lack of religious teaching was at the root of the problem, and it was vital that everyone could attend church or Sunday school for a sound moral education.

In April 1841, the government at last decided to act on this contentious issue, and the House of Lords appointed a select committee to consider Sunday trafficking on canals. Putting forward the motion in Parliament, the Home Secretary said the law at present subjected boatmen to compulsory labour seven days a week, contrary to their own wishes. As a result, many smaller crimes, such as pilfering:

... principally arose from these boatmen, who being perpetually in transit – having no fixed locality – constantly moving up and down the canals, on which they all but entirely lived, were not easily followed or detected.

The Home Secretary acknowledged that it would be unfair to charge the crimes of individuals on all boatmen:

But an atrocious crime committed last year on one of these canals, and for which three men had been tried at Stafford, proved not only that the unfortunate men engaged in that transaction, but their fellow-labourers ... in fact, the whole class of these canal boatmen were alike deprived of religious and secular instruction. This proved there was an evil in the system.

Speaking in support of the inquiry, the Bishop of Lichfield said:

Men of all parties, and of various classes, joined in a unanimous wish for the abolition of the law sanctioning Sunday traffic on canals. ... The moral evil caused by it was painful to be considered. Almost outcasts from the very pale of humanity – aliens from the Church of Christ – the boatmen grew up from boyhood to manhood in the grossest ignorance, and hence the atrocious crimes to which the noble Marquess had alluded.

Lord Hatherton, a keen social reformer and Staffordshire landowner with extensive coalmines, told Parliament that several canals flowed through his own estates, and he had made it a habit to ask boatmen if they desired to work on Sunday. All of them gave the same answer, saying they only worked from compulsion, and all were unanimous in wanting the day off. He believed abolishing Sunday traffic would greatly benefit boatmen, whose interests had been neglected. Although canal proprietors were also in favour, none could afford to act alone and incur individual losses because of the strong competition between them.

Dozens of witnesses were called to give evidence before the select committee, chaired by the Home Secretary and Lord Hatherton, which, that autumn, produced a thorough 100-page report revealing the true picture of working life, not only on canals, but also on navigable rivers and railways. As expected, it was largely on the canals where a shocking state of affairs existed.

Questioned by the committee as to whether boatmen themselves wanted an end to Sunday traffic, former MP Sir George Chetwynd, who had been a proprietor of the Trent & Mersey Canal for twenty-five years, assured them that the men would be very glad of one day in seven to rest. He had taken the time to interview Bill Ellis, who was still being held in Stafford Prison awaiting transportation to Australia over a year after his conviction for the murder of Christina Collins. Ellis made 'such disclosures as beggar description, on the abominations that are committed on canals, and the habits of boatmen, their pilfering and horrid depravity', and agreed that abolition of Sunday traffic and receiving houses would help to improve matters. Ellis had never been in any place of worship. 'He is quite uneducated, not having the least idea of God, a Saviour, or a future state, in short having no idea of religion whatever until he came to Stafford gaol.'

Sir George said he believed a great number of boatmen were in a similar situation, 'extremely illiterate, uninstructed and depraved, more so than any other class ... I think their impression now is, that they are a degraded Class of Beings; that they are separated from Society'. Asked about the extent of crimes committed on canals, he replied:

Ellis told me that during the twenty-five years he has been a boatman there was scarcely a single cargo of liquors, wines or spirits, that had not been plundered. He described where I might purchase the different implements: hammers in the handles of which were turn-screws, and everything requisite for breaking open casks. There are syphons, and different sized pumps, some made of tin. The best are made from copper and screw together, so if found in a boatman's pocket you would not know what it was.

Although canal carriers seemed to want an end to Sunday trade, there was the question of what extra measures were needed to protect valuable cargoes of silks, wines, spirits, linen and other merchandise. And unless boatmen had access to a place of worship, what would they do on a Sunday? Sir George explained that, from his long experience in Staffordshire, 'wherever stoppages have been accidental, the boatmen have been found trespassing and plundering, and the greatest possible nuisance to the neighbourhood'. Canal companies were obliged to swear in special constables and local farmers had to watch their property.

Also appearing before the select committee was Francis Twemlow, a shareholder in the Trent & Mersey, who confirmed the opinions of other witnesses on the demoralised state of boatmen and the need for remedial measures. However, he thought fewer offences were being committed than in the past, saying that in six years as Chairman of

Staffordshire Quarter Sessions, he did not know of any cases of murder by boatmen except that of Christina Collins, nor aggravated assaults, and perhaps only half a dozen offences of robbing their cargoes.

Mr Twemlow highlighted the problem of canal beer houses, as did John Crowley of Wolverhampton canal carriers, Crowley, Hicklin & Company, who reported the difficulty they had 'to keep our Men to sober and orderly Conduct in consequence of the Beer shops that are established by the Locks'. Crowley described many of the men as 'trustworthy, honest, moral and sober', but said 'many of them are very much the reverse'. Richard Heath of Stourport carriers, Matthew Heath & Sons, said he had noticed the moral character of boatmen was very much improved within the last ten years.

The Hon. Philip Bouverie, a wealthy London banker and long-serving chairman of the Grand Junction Canal Company, said because the volume of traffic was greater on that canal than any other, he did not think it was practical to stop trade on Sunday, although the subject had often been considered. Pickford & Company partner Joseph Baxendale, who since joining the firm over twenty years ago had transformed it from a small family business into a national carrier, was a man known for fastidious attention to detail. He was in favour of churches being built for boatmen, but considered the plan for stopping Sunday traffic was impractical unless legislation also covered railways, otherwise canal companies would be unfairly disadvantaged.

While it was simple enough for everyone to agree on idealistic aims to reform the lives of poor boatmen, it was far more difficult to surmount the practical problems and persuade carriers to relinquish even a fraction of profitable canal trade. Spurred on by the select committee's report, campaigners persisted in their efforts, including the tireless rector of St Clement's in Worcester, Reverend John Davies, who had for many years carried out pastoral duties among boatmen. He gave a well-attended evening lecture in April 1842 on the spiritual destitution of bargemen and the need to promote religious instruction. He claimed there were many reformed watermen, such as those on the Droitwich Canal, whose conduct was exemplary since their employers prohibited work on the Sabbath. At the end of the meeting, a unanimous resolution was passed, calling for Sunday closure of waterways.

Despite all the compelling evidence reported by the select committee, the government did not introduce legislation to end Sunday traffic,
and work continued seven days a week until much later in the century.
As ever, it was money that mattered.

†††

In the early years of Queen Victoria's reign, times were hard for the
labouring classes. The population was growing rapidly, and ever greater
numbers flocked into cities, crowding into the expanding slum districts
and snapping up jobs where they could at flourishing mills or manufacturers. Yet, despite the industrial boom, a series of economic slumps
and political unrest created a climate of anxiety and extra difficulties for
those already on the breadline.

Unemployment in 1842 reached probably its highest level in the
whole of the nineteenth century and industrial areas of the north were
badly hit, with thousands of people forced to pawn and sell off anything they owned to buy food or depend on soup kitchens and charity
handouts to survive. Agricultural labourers were also struggling to
make ends meet during the lean years. It was no coincidence that crime
levels also increased, and 1842 marked a peak in the number of people
committed for trial.

Theft remained endemic on the waterways, with a larger, more
sophisticated network of receivers available to dispose of ill-gotten
gains. And a steady stream of offenders was brought before the bench
at the Old Bailey in London, many of them hungry or out of work.
Anything that could be used or sold on was regularly snatched from
boat cabins and cargoes by boatmen themselves and opportunist thieves.
Tools, planks of wood and lengths of chain, sacks of potatoes, clothes
and household utensils – there was always someone willing to buy, and
pawnbrokers did a brisk trade in stolen goods.

The culprits were often young men hired as temporary boat hands,
like 18-year-old James Williams, a casual worker on the Grand Junction
Canal, who was convicted of stealing from a barge tied up at West
Drayton. While the boat owner was asleep, Williams grabbed trousers,
stockings, two handkerchiefs, a shirt and 9 sovereigns from a cupboard. When accosted by a police constable outside the Red Lion in the

Edgware Road, Williams tried unsuccessfully to buy his silence with 'a drop of beer' and a shilling. The bundle of loot was recovered and he was lucky to leave the court without punishment.

Attempting to bribe a policeman did not work either for John Sams, aged 18, when he was arrested for stealing the property of canal-boat captain Thomas Mullett, who had taken him on only a few days earlier. When Sams was left alone aboard the *Providence* at Brentford Lock one evening, he broke open a cupboard and made off with a valuable haul including a brand-new velveteen jacket, two waistcoats, trousers, a shirt, a watch and chain, a neckerchief, coins and a corkscrew.

After being taken into custody by Constable William Griggs, he offered to hand over £100 if he was let out of the cell. At the Old Bailey, where Sams claimed he had worked hard all day but was given little food and no wages, he was sentenced to transportation for seven years.

Thomas Barker was another boatman who regretted his decision to employ a stranger asking for work. Twenty-year-old James Norman joined a boat which was travelling from the Potteries to London on the Grand Junction, and he was lent a flannel smock frock and boots. Reaching Harefield near Uxbridge, he ran off, taking with him a second pair of boots and a knife. Soon after the theft was reported, Constable William Newland found Norman sitting before the fire in the Standard public house at Cowling, where he had already managed to sell the knife for sixpence and the boots for half a crown, saying he was 'on the tramp, and wanted food'. Sams was imprisoned for six months.

Further evidence revealing the ingenious methods of plundering canal-boat cargoes, known as 'breaking bulk', had come out in a report by the Constabulary Force Commissioners. Boatmen apparently took impressions of the seals on corks and carefully resealed bottles they had partly emptied, or used a borer to draw sugar and dry goods from boxes. An assortment of cord was kept on board so that packages could be retied with matching twine. Little holes could also be hacked into the corner of tea chests and a handful of tea taken out of each one.

One practised thief admitted:

As an honest labourer, for factory work I got seven shillings and thirteen a week; but while I was boating I made fifteen shillings in one trip, by taking goods out of packages. I have cleared five pounds in a week.

Another old hand said:

> When boating, I always took a little every journey. The highest sum
> I got was £25 one trip. The whole crew were engaged in depreda-
> tions, and I did as my companions did, and took all sorts of goods,
> which were sold to different receivers on the canal. If we had one
> half for it, we thought well; the captain was the salesman, and used
> to have two shares for his trouble and risk, he having to make all
> deficiencies good.

Petty thefts took place on inland waterways every day, but it was the
more unusual headline-grabbing crimes in the morning newspapers
that sent shudders of revulsion across the nation's neatly laid breakfast
tables, and reinforced hostility towards watermen.

Yet another rape on a Staffordshire canal was brought to the attention of an incredulous public in August 1843, when two young boatmen
were sentenced to death at Stafford Assizes. The court heard that Eli
Salmon, aged 20, and 18-year-old William Palin were working in their
boat on Congleton Wharf at 6 a.m. on 11 July, when Mrs Hannah
Sutton approached them and asked if she could have a ride to Red Bull
Aqueduct. One called out, 'Captain, will you let this woman go with
us?' and the other man replied, 'Oh yes, we never deny any woman
going with us.'

Mrs Sutton, a respectable married woman from Marple in Cheshire,
was on her way to the Potteries on business. Glad to have secured a lift,
she promptly took her place on board and the boat set off along the
Macclesfield Canal, but at the aqueduct the men said it would be better
for her to go further on to a bridge near Tunstall.

As the boat entered eerie Harecastle Tunnel on the Trent & Mersey
at Kidsgrove, Mrs Sutton was sitting in the stern when Palin went up to
her and began running his hands over her body. She told him sharply to
leave her alone, she was not a common woman and had six children at
home. As she kept begging him not to interfere with her, Palin walked
off, but Salmon appeared, saying he felt sleepy and would lie down,
then suddenly thrust out his legs, trapping her beneath their weight.

Protesting that she could not bear him, Mrs Sutton asked him to
think of her children and husband, but Salmon only retorted, 'Damn

your husband, what is he more than any other man?' He pushed her back onto the deck, shouting for Palin to help hold her down, and while Palin lay across her chest, Salmon raped her. Then they swapped places, so Salmon could prevent her struggling while Palin took his turn, ignoring her desperate cries and threatening to throw her into the water if she did not hold her peace.

After the brutal attack, they left her alone for a while, shaken and afraid, as the boat slid on through the echoing darkness of the tunnel which was almost 2 miles long. Salmon returned to the stern of the vessel half an hour later, asking if she had heard of the Kitcrew Boggart, and Mrs Sutton replied she had, it was a sort of ghost. Salmon grabbed her and warned there was always some accident, or someone killed, when this boggart was heard. She begged him to leave her alone, for God's sake, but, unmoved, he merely threatened to shove her into the water.

Now terrified of what he would do, and convinced there was absolutely no alternative, she said that if he would spare her life she would submit to their will. Both boatmen raped her again, treating her very roughly. Three-quarters of an hour later, the boat emerged from the tunnel and Mrs Sutton tried to attract the attention of a group of men working near the canal, but they did not notice her. At Tunstall Bridge, Palin helped her out onto the bank and Mrs Sutton went straight to a nearby house to report what had happened.

At their trial the boatmen did not deny they 'had connection' with Mrs Sutton and, despite a suggestion by the defence counsel that there had been partial consent by the woman, they were found guilty of rape. Although both were given the death sentence, punishment was commuted to transportation for life, and the following spring, the men left England with 200 other felons on board the convict ship *Blundell*, arriving in Van Diemen's Land, Australia, on 12 July 1844 to make the most of a new start on foreign shores.

Another nasty incident was reported a few months later, when two 'ruffianly-looking' canal boatmen named George Patmore and Robert Jerram appeared at Marylebone Magistrates' Court, charged with a seemingly random and savage assault on another innocent, middle-aged married woman. Mrs Mary Roddy lived not far from Paddington Basin, in Stephen Street, Lisson Grove, and answered her front door one afternoon to see Patmore standing outside, very drunk and 'exposing himself in a most disgusting manner'. She was remonstrating with him when he rushed into the house and hit her on the head, knocking her down in the hallway. He then kicked her, and after a prolonged tussle, Mrs Roddy managed to make her way into the parlour, where Patmore struck two more blows as she cried out, 'Murder!' and Jerram joined in the assault.

Hearing the disturbance, Mrs Roddy's son, Robert, ran into the passage and seized hold of Patmore, then tried to push the door shut and keep out a mob of their companions. The two assailants fought back, Patmore landing a heavy blow while Jerram grabbed Robert's hand and twisted it violently. When police arrived on the scene, Patmore punched one of the officers.

In court, the magistrate said it was necessary to make a strong example of the prisoners. Patmore was fined £5, Jerram 40 shillings, and both men were locked up until they were able to pay.

†††

Although some boatmen were obviously beyond redemption, a path to salvation was urgently needed for other lost souls on the waterways before they too were tempted into sin. And the mission to provide that salvation was one which attracted dozens of devout Christians, determined to do their duty and stamp out all evil – whether boatmen liked it or not. Newspapers went on printing protests about the impact of Sunday labour, and one report in *The Atlas* commented:

> The physical condition of these men is decidedly superior to the common class of agricultural labourer ... Their moral condition is, however, as a rule, so low as to render it a matter of surprise that such things can exist in a Christian country. A large proportion of them live and die in a state of heathen ignorance ... Their habits and language are brutal and hardened, and they furnish a large proportion of the most atrocious offences in the criminal calendar. This extreme demoralization can clearly be traced to the practice of working on Sundays which has originated in the greed for lucre.

Large-scale construction projects to improve inland waterways were ongoing in some parts of the country (such as the Caledonian Canal, where more than 1,500 men were employed), and *The Atlas* report also criticised navigators who worked every day of the week as being much the same:

> Roaming from place to place, without a settled home, under no moral restraint, in the prime of life and physical vigour, earning high wages by great exertions, they are a reckless and dissipated set, rude and brutal in their habits, and destitute of instruction.

Trying to save navvies was perhaps a bridge too far, even for the most zealous reformers, but there was wider sympathy for the plight of poor watermen.

The canal network, with its efficient seven-day working system, had cut prices and spread prosperity throughout Britain. Ledbury, on the Herefordshire & Gloucestershire Canal, was reckoned to have saved the enormous sum of £28,000 on coal by 1844 and profited from other big savings on the carriage of cider, apples and pears out to the cities, plus timber and building materials brought into the town. No one denied the benefits of thriving commerce, but what was the human cost?

Clergymen stepped up their efforts, delivering hard-hitting lectures about the spiritual welfare of wretched boatmen and how best to save them from themselves. Some of it may have been empty rhetoric, yet genuine efforts were made by all sorts of charitable organisations, including the Inland Navigation Society, which was formed specifically to promote religious instruction and raise the moral condition of an estimated 100,000 canal and river boatmen. At a meeting in London to mark the society's fifth anniversary, the chairman noted that members had already done much good in providing assistance to distressed boat families and appointing waterways missionaries. The society also co-ordinated an ambitious scheme with other religious groups to hand out free Bibles – a total of 3,988 copies were distributed to boatmen in 1846 and a further 3,604 in 1847.

A boatmen's chapel had already been built in an old coach house at Paddington, and in September 1840, the first floating chapel housed on a barge had opened at Preston Brook, financed by politician and wealthy philanthropist Lord Francis Egerton. He had inherited estates belonging to the 3rd Duke of Bridgewater (including the highly profitable Bridgewater Canal and Worsley Collieries) and went on to purchase Ellesmere Port with its vast expanse of docks and warehouses. Other chapels followed in various parts of the country, including Runcorn, Aylesbury, Oxford, and Chester, where the Shropshire Union Canal Company funded a barge topped with a spire.

At Worcester, the energetic Reverend John Davies of St Clement's raised money to fit up an old Severn barge named the *Albion* as a floating chapel, which was moored by the old churchyard. During more than thirty years serving his parish, Reverend Davies, known as 'the waterman's spiritual friend', had witnessed at first hand the demoralised condition of boat people: 'The pressure of Sunday trading weighs heavily on the conscience of many an honest boatman, who finds himself compelled to violate the laws of God and his country, or lose his situation'. Of the 302 boatmen committed to Worcester City Gaol in a ten-year period, just one man could read and write well. Others told him they only knew Sunday as the day after payday.

In December 1845, the *Liverpool Mail* ran a series of readers' letters on the hotly debated subject of floating chapels and Sunday traffic on canals. Though one correspondent was impressed that Preston Brook Chapel was often 'crowded to excess', another claimed its services were attended not by boatmen, but chiefly by canal agents, clerks, porters and people from the neighbourhood. One letter said that such places were 'surely a cruel mockery of their woe' and a bitter insult to those forced to work every Sunday. Another drew attention to the terrible state of these poor men, describing them as 'outcasts of society … Debased, degraded to the level of the beast of burden'.

Opinion remained divided on the issue, but more positive news came from an intrepid clergyman who had been actively involved with outreach work on his local canal near Liverpool and reported that, thanks to the floating chapel:

A gradual improvement is visible, less drunkenness, less swearing and quarrelling. I have found boatmen more susceptible to kindness than was anticipated. The generality of them will now thankfully accept a tract, and listen to a word of friendly advice judiciously offered.

It was a hopeful sign that, in one place at least, all these strenuous efforts were not in vain. Elsewhere, however, boatmen kept on getting into trouble.

On 23 September 1846, Joseph Oldham, a police officer employed by the Trent & Mersey Canal Company, thwarted a robbery involving a cargo of malt being transported from Nottingham to Manchester. Acting on a tip-off, Constable Oldham, together with two other men, hid outside the premises of maltster and publican Charles Limer at Barton-under-Needwood. When a pair of canal boats pulled up by the door at 5 p.m., warehouseman John Preston dragged a heavy bag from one boat into the malthouse. Limer had a few words in the yard with one of the boat captains before driving off in his gig.

It was clearly a well-planned and regular transaction between the boatmen and Limer. This time, however, it didn't work out as usual – the boat was impounded and all the men were arrested and taken away to be locked up at Fradley Junction.

At Burton-upon-Trent Petty Sessions, they were charged with stealing six bushels of malt valued at 50 shillings and remanded in custody until their trial. A report in the *Derbyshire Advertiser* commented:

> The activity and tact displayed by Oldham in this case, and his increasing exertions on all occasions deserve the highest praise, and are doubtless suitably estimated by his employers; he is indeed a terror to evil doers among the boatmen.

That same week, 100 miles or so further south, a row about opening a lock gate flared into violence between the crews of two boats going through Harefield Lock near Uxbridge. James Carpenter and William Norman went into a nearby field to settle the matter with their fists accompanied by the lock-keeper, and after slugging it out for fifteen minutes Norman fell to the ground and expired.

Another punch-up ended badly in May the following year, after a seven-hour drinking binge by two boatmen at a Brentford beer shop. Edward Thomas, the 26-year-old captain of a monkey-boat, moored 300 yards away on the Grand Junction Canal and arrived in the taproom with boat hand Joseph Dawson for a first pint at one o'clock. At 8 p.m., they were still there. Landlord Robinson Lambert said the men were regulars and had always been very good friends, but that evening they began quarrelling and Dawson pulled his jacket off to fight. Mr Lambert told Thomas not to take any notice, and he persuaded Dawson to leave the premises quietly.

Thomas left half an hour later to fetch his horse from the stable, but was confronted outside by Dawson, who was completely intoxicated and aggressively goading him to fight. Although Dawson was a stout, powerfully built man, known to be 'a desperate fighter', Thomas could take only so much aggravation. When Dawson seized his left shoulder and struck a violent blow, Thomas retaliated and kicked out. Dawson was found at 8.30 p.m., lying on the canal bank, by Joseph Watkins, who turned him over and, realising he was drunk and unable to move, went to fetch help.

Policeman Charles Blake arrived at 9.15 p.m. to find several men on the canal bridge with Dawson, who managed to stagger a few yards by himself before being led back to the boat by the others. Early next morning, Thomas returned to the stable at the beer house, now sober and full of regret, saying he was afraid Dawson was hurt; it was a very bad job. He asked the landlord to do everything he possibly could, and Mr Lambert hitched up the boat horse in a cart to take Dawson to St George's Hospital where, two days later, he died from a ruptured intestine.

Thomas was charged with manslaughter and appeared at the Old Bailey on a hot day in mid-June, before presiding judge Sir John Patteson, who took his seat and inquired why no learned counsel had been engaged to prosecute the list of manslaughter cases. A court officer said other judges frequently made the same complaint, and explained that no respectable solicitors were willing to conduct cases because the allowance paid was so niggardly.

Mr Justice Patteson, a vicar's son who had been knighted and later served on many government judicial bodies, said if low fees were the reason, then it was time the system was altered. The judge was not in the best of moods that morning. He complained about the stifling heat of the courtroom and a 'gentle dose of cold air was administered', pumped through an ice-cellar, before proceedings could begin. The hearing ascertained that no one had witnessed what happened, and if Thomas had inflicted the fatal injury, it was probably done in self-defence. The boatman was found not guilty.

†††

Often, crime was a result of too much alcohol triggering reckless behaviour. As a judge in Hampshire reflected at the conclusion of another trial, in nine out of ten cases, drink was the principal cause:

> Indeed in almost every case the cloven foot of a fondness of liquor appears. The crime was either perpetrated for the sake of liquor, committed under its influence or its proceeds expended in its purchase.

Not only was beer cheap, at tuppence a pint, but most people chose to drink it as a safer alternative to water, which was frequently contaminated. For many labourers in different occupations, it was the custom for wages to be paid partly in beer, and weekly pay packets were often handed out in the local public house, which played a central role in community life. The idea that hard physical work demanded hard drinking was so embedded in British culture that drunkenness among the working classes was taken for granted, and even admired as a mark of manhood.

The authorities were constantly trying to devise new ways to curb the troublesome antisocial habits of the lower orders, and their efforts were backed by religious groups who were in favour of strict rules to regulate behaviour. These campaigners influenced the government's decision in 1848 to enforce Sunday morning closure of all pubs throughout the country, by extending legislation already operating in London.

The move was welcomed at the annual licensing meeting in Bolton, Lancashire, in August 1849, where residents wanted to see even more stringent measures brought in. Apparently, half of the miscreants arrested in the area were found in a state of intoxication. The borough coroner, Mr Taylor, dramatically described the public house as 'a full-grown monster' and strongly objected to granting any extra licences for the sale of liquor. He represented many of the town's clergymen, merchants and tradesmen, who shared the same view, and presented a petition from local working men asking magistrates not to increase the number of drinking places. An angry heckler stood up to protest about a pub being called a monster and asked him to prove it, but he was swiftly silenced by the mayor.

Mr Taylor went on to say that Home Office statistics showed crimes were still on the increase, not only theft but also murder, manslaughter, shooting and stabbing. Above average crime levels existed in the cotton districts of Lancashire and Cheshire, the iron districts of the Midlands, and in metropolitan areas. He said that, in England generally, and Bolton particularly, the causes of crime, disease and death could be attributed almost entirely to drinking habits and public houses. At the end of the meeting, magistrates announced they had decided not to grant any new licences and would ideally like public houses closed all day on Sundays.

Similar feelings were regularly expressed elsewhere. At a public meeting in York, the Reverend Camidge said no vice was so degrading as drunkenness, which 'sunk man below the brutes' and led to crimes being committed which a man 'in his sober moments would shrink from with distaste and disgust'. A resolution was passed calling for the abolition of liquor sales on the Sabbath and restrictions on how many pubs were allowed to trade.

The number of pubs had been growing steadily, especially in expanding urban areas like Bolton, a prosperous centre of textile manufacturing which, in 1849, proudly boasted 117 inns and 191 beer houses for a population of 52,380 – or one alehouse to every 170 people. The cheap premises Crompton's Monument was one of a dozen beer houses in the densely populated working-class district of Mill Street. Licensed establishments such as the Bull and Wharf at the canal terminus (nicknamed the Boat House) catered to workers on the busy Manchester, Bolton & Bury Canal, which carried coal to dozens of cotton mills and salt from Cheshire to the many bleach and dye works in the town.

In fact, the amount of alcohol consumed per capita in 1851 was the same as twenty years earlier, but as the population increased there were more people drinking in more pubs than ever before. And more drinkers meant more crime.

A newspaper editorial commenting on a session of Liverpool Assizes pointed out how dangerous alcohol was to society:

Almost the whole of the cases of violence might be traced to the use of intoxicating liquors. When an ignorant man … becomes excited with liquor … his passions, hitherto uncontrolled by anything but instinct, burst forth with redoubled energy, and at last he is swallowed up the unhappy victim of his own fury.

In earlier Parliamentary debates on the Sale of Beer Act, there was unanimous agreement about the social cost of alcohol abuse. Members commented that cheap beer houses not only held out an irresistible temptation to the poor, but such places were actually set up by thieves to host illicit activities. One speaker had been inundated with complaints about beer shops in large manufacturing towns, 'where scenes were going on daily and nightly, which it was quite out of the power of police and magistrates to control'.

So, what could be done to remedy the alarming drink problem? One radical solution was teetotalism. The temperance movement had been growing for some time, and by the late 1840s, most towns had a group promoting total abstinence. The mission was both religious and political, aiming to educate the working classes and lobby for new laws restricting sales of alcohol.

The temperance ideal of personal salvation through self-discipline had such strong appeal that it became the biggest social movement of the nineteenth century. Abstinence advocates hammered home their message in fiery lectures to packed meeting houses across the country, urging rapt audiences to 'take the pledge' not to touch another drop. And reformed drunkards stood up to regale the listening crowds with inspirational stories of their own ruinous addiction and path to sobriety.

Education was the key to moral improvement, and at a meeting of the People's Instruction Society, held in Birmingham, one of the city's judges said he had seen much of the misery created by intemperance, because 'under the maddening influence of liquor, crimes are committed'. He emphasised the importance of societies such as theirs, if they 'simply turned the minds of the masses from this degrading vice'.

Not everyone could be persuaded to give up alcohol, of course, and in Inverness, where 100 public houses opened their doors each Sunday, a meeting of the Total Abstinence Society in April 1848 was very thinly attended.

Unlike most other occupations, the nature of canal work, with its irregular hours and lack of close supervision, gave boatmen more freedom than most workers to quench their thirst whenever they wanted to, every day of the week. Some employers had already decided it was time to take more stringent measures to clamp down on troublemakers. The Grand Junction Company introduced closer vetting for new landlords of canal-side pubs, and ordered its officials to record the name of any boatman who was seen to be drunk.

Alcohol did not turn everyone into a criminal, whatever the earnest do-gooders might imply. Sometimes, it just made drinkers easy prey. Unlucky Derbyshire boatman Leonard Thorpe often enjoyed a few pints after work, but while he relaxed one August evening at a pub in Tipton, his money was stolen by a woman named Sarah Parkes. He decided to seek legal redress and, on Saturday morning, prosecuted the thief at Handsworth Petty Sessions, where she was committed for trial. Thorpe then returned to his boat, which was being loaded with fire bricks, and that evening went to the Angel public house at Dudley, drinking steadily until late with other boatmen. Some Irish shoemakers also at the premises were twice refused more ale and the waitress overheard one say, 'Come on, we have given the old bastard enough.'

They all left at midnight and one of the boatmen, a well-known pugilist nicknamed Jim Crow, was trying to help a tipsy companion home when he was struck by one of the shoemakers with a wooden stave. As they reached the ruined castle wall, a violent scuffle broke out between the opposing groups, the Irishmen armed with sticks shouting, 'Come on, you English bastards!'

At 12.50 a.m., three shoemakers were seen beating Leonard Thorpe, who cried out, 'Oh Lord! Oh Lord!' and shortly afterwards was seen lying with his head in the gutter, bleeding profusely from a deep wound to the skull. The shouts alerted the police, but by the time officers reached the spot, the attackers had made off. No one paid much attention to the wounded boatman, who staggered about for an hour or more until the tunnel-keeper noticed him lying on a bridge and had him taken to a companion's boat. Thorpe somehow managed to return to his own vessel, where he was found dead in the cabin a few hours later.

Three Irish shoemakers were tried for manslaughter at Oxford Assizes, seven months later. Patrick Grady was acquitted, but John

Maloney and Thomas Cavannah each received an eighteen-month prison sentence. 'MURDER OF A CANAL BOATMAN – BRUTAL AFFAIR' was reported in many of the national newspapers, including the *Globe*, the *Sun*, and *Morning Post*, as yet another salutary warning about the perils of intoxicating liquor.

Each new incident added weight to the temperance cause, and in 1850 the *Leicestershire Mercury* printed a letter headed 'CRIME AND CRIMINALS' by one campaigner, who set out the latest evidence on drink-related offences from police, prison governors, judges and magistrates. He wrote:

> Criminal reformers are engaged in one of the noblest enterprises which can possibly employ the great faculties of man. But, Sir, many of them do not sufficiently recognise the palpable fact – that drunkenness is the chief source of crime ... every person anxious to see crime diminished, prevented, and destroyed, should ponder the facts, and to all such we would say – the temperance reformation is what we want.

12

GRUESOME FACTS

It was late afternoon, one Thursday in April, as Richard and Mary Ann Francis stood together in the cabin of their boat, moored by the locks at Runcorn. They had just returned from the public house with another couple, but it had not been much fun, and they quarrelled bitterly after she refused to pay for more drinks. Now Richard seemed willing to make it up, saying, 'Mary forgive me, and I will quarrel no more.' She replied, 'I have forgiven you before', but Richard simply asked for a kiss. He drew his wife close and then, with one swift movement of his right hand, cut her throat.

The knife came out of nowhere. Mary Ann did not even realise what had happened until, seconds later, she felt his fingers on her neck tearing open the wound and saw the blood streaming down. She pulled away, desperate to escape, as Richard grabbed hold of her clothes, trying to force her back, but she broke free, scrambled out on deck and screamed for help. Glancing into the cabin, she saw Richard slitting his own throat. With one final effort, she climbed onto another boat lying alongside, still pursued by Richard, where boat hand William Cox stepped in to bar his way and then supported Mary Ann as she passed out.

Dr Cooper, the local surgeon, was called in to stitch up the 7in gash across Mary Ann's neck, which was half an inch deep and haemorrhaging badly. Word of the incident spread quickly through the streets, and when Police Constable Clayton arrived on the scene shortly afterwards, he found a crowd gathered near Delph Bridge to stare at the grisly spectacle, where on top of one boat lay a man with his throat cut and bleeding, while on the other side lay his injured wife. The *Cheshire Observer* described how:

> On Thursday afternoon, the quiet town of Runcorn was thrown into a state of excitement by a report that a man had cut the throat of his wife, which turned out to be too true. No reason can be assigned for the rash act. The prisoner was not in drink at the time.

Richard Francis' wound was only slight, so he was immediately arrested and taken to the lock-up, blaming the boat captain for cutting his wife's throat. He also denied owning the knife, which was found at the cabin entrance covered in blood. It did not take long to establish the truth.

Incredibly, Mary Ann survived, and after several postponed hearings, she had recovered enough to give evidence in court a fortnight later, although still in a very weakened state. Francis was charged with attempted murder – he appeared to be much distressed and said he hoped his wife would soon recover.

At Cheshire Assizes held at Chester Castle that August, the whole story came out. Mary Ann was the first witness called and she explained that she was with her husband in Stellfox's public house, taking a glass of ale, when they met Phineas Veere, who was captaining the pair of working boats they were employed on. She said Francis, who 'was not quite drunk, though far from sober', wanted more liquor and the captain's wife paid for a noggin of rum (a quarter-pint measure), which they all shared. An argument then broke out about buying more drinks, Mary Ann's husband hit her, and Mrs Veere pulled him off. The captain told Francis he would be discharged if he didn't treat his wife better.

The row carried on after they returned to the canal and Mr Veere warned Francis that he would force him off the boat unless he kept quiet. When the captain had gone, Francis jumped on board and Mary Ann gave him another ultimatum, saying she would leave if he did not alter his behaviour. It was that threat which prompted the murderous attack. In his defence, Francis claimed they had seven or eight half-pints of rum and raspberry brandy at the pub and he was so drunk that he did not know what he was doing. The court was unconvinced by the feeble excuse and he was sentenced to death.

Shocking cases like this kept alive the legacy of boatmen's ill repute in the public imagination. Although by the 1850s, regular coverage of their exploits gradually faded away as the press moved on to different juicy stories, any crime featuring canals was guaranteed to make headlines. While most boatmen laboured on as usual, far from the limelight, the cut continued to attract other dubious characters with questionable motives.

Newspapers were now printing a greater number of dramatic crime reports about violent offences with all the gory details, which they knew would entertain their readers. A cartoon in *Punch* magazine satirised the apparently insatiable appetite of the masses for sensational crime news, depicting a father reading stories aloud to his family, with the caption, 'Useful Sunday Literature for the Masses; or, Murder Made Familiar'. Another *Punch* cartoon of 1850, 'The Trial-for-Murder Mania', also highlighted the popularity of real-life courtroom dramas, which certainly made compelling reading – especially when they were poignant cases featuring helpless female victims.

†††

On a bleak, foggy night at the end of January 1853, piano-maker Henry Wilson was drinking in the clubroom at the Regalia Tavern when, about 11 p.m., he needed to nip out into the garden. It backed onto the Regent's Canal in Camden Town, and from the direction of the water, he suddenly heard a woman's cries and footsteps running towards him. He called to landlord Mr Woolfe that something was the matter, and both men dashed into Augustus Street.

At the top of the passage leading to the towpath, they met a man walking fast who was carrying a small bundle and coolly said, 'I think a woman has thrown herself into the water.' Mr Woolfe replied, 'Then come and assist us to get her out', and all three men ran down to the canal where they heard a cry, followed by gurgling and splashing sounds, but the fog was so thick they could not see even the surface of the water. Mr Woolfe called out, 'Can you float, or can you speak?' but there was no answer, and he ran to fetch a light and rope. When he returned to the canal bank, he asked Henry Wilson where the stranger had gone to and exclaimed, 'I believe that vagabond has thrown her in.'

Mr Wilson hurried out into the street where he met a policeman and inquired if a man dressed like a bricklayer's labourer had been seen, but there was no sign of him. Two constables accompanied him back to the canal, where they pulled out the body of 26-year-old Eliza Lea. She had separated from her lover Thomas Mackett five months earlier, and when Constable Charles Bone found him at lodgings in High Street, Marylebone, Mackett claimed he had left Eliza at a friend's house the previous evening. He asked if she was dead, and said flatly, 'I can clear myself.'

At London's Central Criminal Court on 13 May, Mackett, a 30-year-old mason, pleaded not guilty to wilful murder. Mrs Mary Lea gave evidence that she had last seen her daughter on the morning of 31 January, when she gave her a half-sovereign to redeem a blue merino dress, pledged at a pawnbroker's on Tottenham Court Road for 3 shillings. She did not see her again, until being shown her body in St Pancras Workhouse.

Eliza had gone out to work ironing clothes and lived with Mackett for six years, although they had separated several times. Mary described her daughter as 'full of spirits and life, very cheerful and happy', and admitted that while she had never seen her intoxicated, Eliza was occasionally addicted to drink and Mackett had often beaten her – a fact confirmed by other witnesses.

Apparently, Eliza had collected the pawned dress, as her friend Sarah Hermitage saw her at 11.30 a.m. on 31 January with a brown-paper parcel containing some blue merino. According to Sarah, Eliza and Mackett were drinking together in a pub that evening about 6 p.m., when Mackett announced he had been married a week ago. Eliza said she would not believe it until she saw the certificate, and he swore, 'So help me God, I am.'

Mackett said he had no money, and Eliza replied, 'I'll stand a pot of beer Tom, if I never see you again.' After that, she paid for beer and gin in two other public houses, then they all went back to Sarah's house in Pratt Street for tea and another pot of beer. They left at about 10.15 p.m., Eliza carrying the parcel. The couple were last seen together at 10.30 p.m. in the Victoria pub on Mornington Road, where they drank a quartern of gin at the bar.

On the morning after Eliza's death, pawnbroker's shopman Alfred Gush served a customer pawning a piece of merino, who called herself Anne Marshall, but was in fact Mackett's new wife giving her maiden name. At 8.30 p.m., following a visit from the police inquiring about the missing parcel, she returned to the shop and redeemed the item in a hurried manner.

The Regalia publican, Mr Woolfe, told the court there was no railing by the canal where the deceased was found and on a foggy night it was a very dangerous place indeed for anyone to walk. As defence counsel Mr Parry pointed out, there was no motive for murder or any signs of a struggle. There was no doubt that death was caused by drowning, and he suggested Eliza may have committed suicide because she had spent all the money her mother had given her and was afraid to go home. The other likelihood was that the girl had fallen into the canal by accident. He emphasised to the jury the circumstantial nature of the evidence and the fearful responsibility they faced if convicting a fellow creature on the mere probability that he might have been guilty. The jurors obviously agreed they could not take that risk, and after retiring for just thirty minutes returned a verdict of not guilty.

The Times ran a series of lengthy reports on the Mackett murder, and then four months later in September 1853 covered another tragic case, where this time there seemed to be little doubt about the motive. Out-of-work factory worker Thomas Moore was seen walking with his two little stepsons along a road leading to the canal at Stockport on a rainy Friday afternoon. Mrs Elizabeth Evans, a porter's wife, noticed them in Chimney-hall Street at about 2 p.m. because 4-year-old James was lame and his 8-year-old brother John scarred with smallpox. The boys were not seen alive again.

According to Moore, his wife went to work as usual that morning at the factory where she was employed, and the boys went out to play at 9 a.m. Shortly after 10 a.m., he took an umbrella and left his father-in-law's house, saying he was going to Hempshaw Lane, but was seen later with the children going in a completely different direction, towards Manchester Road, which led to the canal.

Three days later, boatman John Watson noticed a large object partially submerged in the water, as he was travelling along the canal with a load of coals aboard. He continued to Stockport to seek help and returned to the spot with another boatman, where they pulled out the two small bodies. When the canal was emptied for a further search, an umbrella and a cape worn by one of the boys were found.

Police Constable John Lee was sent to arrest Moore with a warrant for neglect of his family. At the police office, Moore insisted he only took the children as far as the street corner, then sent the elder boy home with an umbrella to tell their mother to send dinner at 1 p.m. to McClure's Mill, where he was working. Moore returned home at 6 p.m., asking his wife why she had not sent the food, and she replied that there had been no message. Owing to differences, the couple lived separate lives under the same roof, and she did not know if he was in work or not.

At the inquest, held in the Navigation Inn, the truth was soon apparent to everyone there. One witness giving evidence was Benjamin Berresford, who recalled that a week before they drowned, he had seen Moore one night going towards the weir, holding the children's hands. Reaching a bridge over the canal which supplied a mill, Moore had stood looking into the water for over a minute, then moved towards the cut-side. Mr Berresford said:

> When he saw me he walked away with the children. I afterwards overtook him, stopped, stared at him, and went on home. I suspected he intended to do something with the children, being there so late.

The reason why Moore may have decided to get rid of his stepsons became clear when officials from two different benefit societies, known as burial clubs, gave evidence. The secretary of Middle Hillgate Benevolent Burial Society confirmed that James was enrolled in two branches of the society and John in one, their mother paying regular subscriptions. Mrs Moore's brother, the collector for the Temperance Burial Club, said Moore knew both boys were members of that scheme too and £6 each was payable at their deaths.

Such benefit societies to assist the poor with burial expenses were widely used by the working classes, and fees of perhaps a farthing per person would be collected each week, ensuring a reasonable payment in the event of their death. However, there were few checks made and many people enrolled their spouse or children in several clubs so they could fraudulently claim multiple benefits. For some families with too many hungry mouths to feed, the temptation to kill in order to claim the money proved overwhelming, and many murders like this came to court during the nineteenth century.

In Moore's case, the anticipated settlement due at the boys' deaths apparently totalled £19 or £20 – an enormous sum at a time when a year's wages for a live-in servant were £16. The inquest jury had no doubt what Moore intended, and they took only five minutes to give a verdict of wilful murder. However, when he stood trial at Liverpool Assizes in December, despite the discrepancies in Moore's version of events, there was no actual hard evidence put forward to prove he had committed a crime.

Moore was said to be very fond of his stepsons and often took them out. His defence counsel argued that the fact Moore was seen with the children on the day in question was no reason he should be charged with murder. There were no marks of violence on the bodies. The boys liked water and might have gone to play by the canal and fallen in. Or perhaps one fell in, and his brother tried to save him. It was possible. Yet, was it likely?

After a long discussion, the jury decided Moore was not guilty. Significantly, the judge remarked that there was a prejudicial feeling against the prisoner in the Stockport neighbourhood, and as he discharged Moore he made a point of cautioning him about his future conduct. Whether he eventually managed to collect the payout on the two dead boys is unknown.

The verdict must have come as a surprise to many onlookers at Moore's trial, and also at the trial for the murder of Eliza Lea, where in both cases the accused men were acquitted because evidence against them was purely circumstantial. Were Thomas Mackett and Thomas Moore innocent men? Or guilty? Pushing an unwanted person into the water gave the culprit a fair chance of getting away with murder – if he was lucky. The canals kept their secrets and no one else was ever going to know.

†††

The truly grim conditions endured by poor families living a hand-to-mouth existence in Victorian Britain were brought to the public's attention in a series of hard-hitting reports by the *Morning Chronicle*. Published over two years, the articles detailed everyday life at work and at home in filthy, overcrowded cities, manufacturing towns and rural backwaters.

At the end of another gruelling shift, those fortunate enough to be in work returned home along roughly paved streets to fetid basements or a few smoky, smelly rooms in the rows of back-to-back houses built for metal and textile workers. Free-range wildlife was a constant nuisance, from roaming dogs and scavenging rats, to flies, fleas and infestations of lice. Disease was rife, and the poor drew water from the same polluted canals and rivers where they slopped out reeking chamber pots – oblivious of the risks.

Casual labour was the norm, and for the unemployed, life was even worse – reports described wretched, half-starved creatures with sunken eyes and dirty, ragged clothing. Conditions could be just as squalid in deprived country areas, where agricultural labourers subsisted on a meagre dinner of perhaps a hunk of bread and an onion, trudging home at sunset to rest aching muscles in chilly, ramshackle cottages, dimly lit by guttering tallow candles.

The revelations in the *Morning Chronicle*, by journalist Henry Mayhew and a team of investigative reporters, had such an impact that the newspaper set up a special fund to distribute charitable donations that poured in from sympathetic middle-class readers wanting to help. The findings raised many uncomfortable questions about the previously unknown victims of industrial progress. Among these was the age-old problem of alcohol-related crime committed by the labouring poor, and Mayhew included figures showing the correlation between drunkenness and common offences like theft and assault.

Writer Charles Dickens drew attention to the human cost of greedy capitalism in his novel *Hard Times*, published in 1854, which was set in Coketown, a sinister fictional northern mill town reputedly inspired by a visit to Preston. It described the fractured skyline of menacing tall chimneys from which 'interminable serpents of smoke trailed themselves for ever and ever, and never got uncoiled. It had a black canal in it, and a river that ran purple with ill-smelling dye.'

Canals had underpinned profitable trade since the earliest days of the Industrial Revolution, but work had long ago been completed on the full 4,500-mile network of navigable waterways, and in the mid-1800s new investment was being poured into building railways, which offered faster, cheaper routes. Tons of goods were still carried by water, but the competition was gradually changing the nature of canal trade, with far fewer flyboats operating. Pickfords, which employed 500 boatmen and boys in its heyday, had by 1850 sold off all but a few flyboats and left the cut for road transport, where greater profits were to be made.

Slow boats would continue plying their trade well into the twentieth century, delivering all kinds of supplies – from basics like coal, iron, limestone or corn to luxuries including bananas, malt for breweries, sugar for jam or chocolate-makers and tomatoes for Birmingham's HP Sauce factory, and taking manufactured products to market. Some, known as 'Number Ones', were the single boats owned by one family, carrying lower-value cargo, such as manure or bricks. The most profitable canal trade went to companies owning substantial fleets, including the new Shropshire Union Railway & Canal Company, which went on to become the largest, with more than 400 narrowboats.

The future was steam-powered, and railway enthusiasts were already sneering at the bad old days when waterway carriers monopolised transport and six days were considered a reasonable time to convey merchandise from Manchester to London. Once again, the notorious wickedness of boatmen was dredged up, and the *Manchester Courier* reported a festive dinner for rail workers where speakers extolled the virtues of railways, which in just a few years had:

> … wrought great moral changes in the characters of those employed by inland carriers. A more fearfully demoralised class of men than canal boatmen could not be found in England. Their occupation was a nursery of vice.

Canal life was portrayed as outdated and brutal, where boat horses were cruelly whipped forward with terrible oaths accompanying every lash. Children born into boat families worked as soon as they had the strength to be useful, growing up in a state of moral darkness, with no one seeming to care about their welfare.

However, that was not quite true. In the mid-century, groups set up by well-meaning reformers were still going strong. At one meeting held in the Boatmen's Chapel at Paddington, 140 workers had supper and were told about the free self-improvement activities on offer, including Bible discussions, the penny bank, a library and a course of winter lectures due to start on 4 November with a topical talk on gunpowder.

Despite these best efforts, odd cases of boatmen behaving badly kept popping up in the news from time to time. The *Morning Advertiser* reported a 'MURDEROUS ATTACK ON THE POLICE' when officers tried to break up a fight between two boatmen, at City Road Wharf on London's Regent's Canal. Sergeant Higgins and Constable Chapman were on duty in Regent Street when they were called to the scene at midnight. As they moved in to stop the brawl, they were surrounded by twenty rowdy boatmen who hemmed them in shouting, 'Pitch them into the canal!'

Staffordshire boatman John Cope dragged Chapman to the edge of the wharf, and when Sergeant Higgins grabbed hold of his colleague, Cope struck a heavy blow on the back of the constable's head as the rest of the gang rushed forward to attack. In the violent struggle that followed, Cope grabbed a hefty wooden boat tiller with both hands and used it to beat Police Constable Chapman as he lay stretched out on the ground. Sergeant Higgins fought his way through the crowd to rescue Chapman, but he was confronted by John Cope brandishing the massive, curved tiller, who, with the thick end, aimed a deliberate blow at his skull.

Sergeant Higgins dodged the full force of the hefty makeshift weapon, which would otherwise have killed him on the spot, but received a severe gash on the side of his head which knocked him out. The crown of his hat was completely torn out and the collar of his police coat saturated with blood.

Sergeant Higgins regained consciousness to find the wharf deserted and two badly injured fellow officers lying nearby. All the boatmen had scarpered.

The sergeant eventually succeeded in tracking down and arresting Cope, who had moved his boat to another wharf and denied any involvement in the affray, saying he had been in his cabin since 7 p.m.

Another dramatic incident in the same neighbourhood, headlined 'CANAL BOATMEN RUNNING "A MUCK"', appeared in the *London Evening Standard* on 9 December 1854. The landlord of the City

Arms, a noted haunt of canal boatmen, had at about 1 a.m. turfed out a riotous group of drinkers, who then ran wild in the streets, indiscriminately knocking down everyone they met, including carpenter Richard Prouse, who was punched and kicked viciously. Constable Leather chased and caught two of the boatmen, but as he was taking them into custody, prostitute Elizabeth Chambers tried to intervene and rescue one of the prisoners by tugging him away.

At a hearing before Clerkenwell Magistrates, Chambers was fined 5 shillings and Derbyshire boatman George Johnson was fined 40 shillings for assault. John Jones (described as a heavy, brutish-looking young man) was charged with violent assault on an old man and grievously injuring the carpenter. The magistrate, Mr Tyrwhitt, condemned the frequent outbreaks of violence by canal men at the City Arms, saying:

> Your conduct in this assault is one quite peculiar to the brutal class of boatmen to which you belong. You come up to this place heavily charged with strong beer, and bring with you that stupid and most savage spirit, that is very early and easily engrafted on you. To teach you better conduct, you, Jones, must pay a fine of 40s for each assault, or, in default of that, six weeks' hard labour.

Up in Scotland, the *Fife Herald* printed a letter headed 'DISGRACEFUL CONDUCT OF CANAL BOATMEN', from a correspondent who was disgusted by an incident when several boatmen refused to rescue a respectable gentleman who fell into the Forth & Clyde Canal unless he told them if he had any money in his pockets. The victim scrambled to safety unaided and reported them to police.

In Cardiff, even the innocent fun of a family day out was spoilt one August, when 'three ruffians, who appeared to be canal boatmen' disrupted the amusements as crowds were enjoying a grand procession with Hengler's famed troop of equestrians, performing monkeys and wonderful ponies. The *Cardiff and Merthyr Guardian* noted that police and soldiers managed to restore order after a brief scuffle with the culprits.

†††

Meanwhile, for most ordinary boatmen life was far more mundane, with little excitement to break the monotony of the dull daily grind needed to make a living. At least, unlike workers imprisoned for interminable hours of hard labour inside mills and factories, they did have a certain freedom.

A highly romanticised view of canal life was depicted by writer John Hollingshead in a series of reports for Charles Dickens' weekly magazine, *Household Words*, describing a journey from London to Birmingham in August 1858. The trip was organised by the Grand Junction Canal Company, and he was a passenger on the 'scrupulously neat and clean' flyboat *Stourport*, brightly painted in red, yellow and blue. It was crewed by the affable Captain Thomas Randle and three boat hands, who loaded aboard 50lb of beef and a vast meat pie before they set off.

Despite some complaints about the food, Hollingshead waxed lyrical about his experiences among cheerful boatmen, whose favourite and only drink was tea:

> Beer and spirits were little used, and a pipe seemed to be a rare indulgence. Melancholy pictures of drunken brawls, improper language, constant fights, hordes of licensed ruffians beyond the pale of law and order … all proved shamefully false. We were inmates of a new home and friends of a new family, whose members were honest, industrious, simple, and natural.

At Stoke Bruerne, he described boatmen singing wistful ballads of thwarted love as they went through the delightfully cool Blisworth Tunnel (which had, of course, claimed the lives of fourteen navvies when the roof caved in on top of them during construction).

They passed a boatman's village at Braunston, 'the only place we had seen on our journey where the people on the land seemed to belong to the people on the water; where everybody knew everybody, and seemed glad to see everybody', and later stopped to drink ale in a tavern. Afterwards, Captain Randle took the tiller again, cap set at a jaunty angle, his face glowing from the unaccustomed liquor, as they 'glided on through more valleys, lighted by a golden moon that shone brightly upon the slopes of yellow corn'. Perfect.

This state of dreamy bliss ended abruptly when they reached dingy, smoke-blackened towns, heading on past coal heaps and roaring furnaces into Birmingham, 'past a dozen grimy boys bathing amongst the floating dead dogs and factory scum of the inky canal; past all this and more, we leave the romance and beauty of our three days' journey far behind us'.

The rose-tinted picture painted by Hollingsworth celebrated a slower, simpler way of life, with contented canal folk afloat on benign and peaceful waters. It was a compelling image, and exactly the sort of romantic fiction some readers of *Household Words* may well have wanted to believe, as they glanced up from the pages of the magazine to gaze through a window at familiar houses opposite, daydreaming of freedom and fresh air.

And yet, many people were understandably wary of canals. There were more than enough unexplained deaths and press reports of bodies found floating in the water to make anyone think twice before they risked venturing out near the waterways. Only the naïve or foolhardy would choose to walk alone on the towpath after dusk. The chances of being murdered were, of course, extremely slim, but it was only too easy to slip on muddy tracks churned up by boat horses' hooves and tumble into the cut.

Macabre murder mysteries made the best news stories, like the case reported in the *Derby Mercury* of a woman's body taken out of the Regent's Canal at St Pancras:

> The face of the deceased is shockingly cut and disfigured, seemingly for the purpose of preventing identification, and the hands also mutilated as if in a death struggle; the body was divested of anything likely to lead to its identity; murder is supposed to have been committed.

In March 1858, there were reports of a 'MURDER UNDER MYSTERIOUS CIRCUMSTANCES NEAR LIVERPOOL', after a shoemaker was dragged out of the canal at Litherland. He had been missing from his home in Sefton for a month, when he was found with a 4in gash beneath the jaw, severe bruising and finger marks on his left upper arm. His pockets had been turned inside out and were empty.

Who dunit? In the absence of any evidence, the inquest jury had no choice but to decide it was wilful murder by some person or persons unknown – a verdict that was all too common.

Then in May that year, another unsolved canal murder in London stirred up panic when dozens of newspapers reported that a manhunt was underway after a 'SUSPECTED MURDER IN THE REGENT'S CANAL', 'which has certainly thrown the inhabitants of the district into a state of extreme terror, more especially as several bodies have recently been found in this canal with suspicious marks of violence'. A few days later, there was still no news of an arrest, and on the following Sunday, crowds of curious sightseers visited the spot where the body had been found at Old Ford Lock in Victoria Park.

Police Commissioners at Great Scotland Yard tried to reassure the public they had matters in hand, drafting in extra officers to make inquiries, but no progress was made in the search to identify the killer. Meanwhile, the body was kept in the landlord's charge at the Horsford Arms Tavern in Bethnal Green, where it was examined by surgeon Edward Seppings, who felt certain there had been 'a foul and deliberate murder'. He was so concerned about the peculiar circumstances of the case that he wrote to the Home Secretary, disclosing that certain parties were trying to hush the matter up and he was determined to discover the true facts.

A coroner's jury had the unenviable task of viewing what the press called 'the mangled remains' of unemployed 62-year-old John Turner, 'the head being nearly cut off, both arms broken and other dreadful injuries' made by a heavy chopper or blunt instrument. There seemed to be no doubt he had been robbed and murdered, although a former workmate said Turner was in a depressed state of mind, often complaining of his troubles and the hard times, and had twice attempted suicide.

On the night he left his home in Commercial Road East, Turner borrowed 7 shillings from his former employer and was last seen drinking at the bar of a public house near the canal. Jurors agreed there was no legal proof of foul play, but in delivering the verdict emphasised their strong opinion that the wounds were inflicted before immersion in the water. It was a highly unsatisfactory outcome, which left the public feeling jittery.

Three months later, in August 1858, there was 'ANOTHER SUPPOSED MURDER AT CAMBERWELL'. The lifeless body of 12-year-old servant Hannah Read was found by a boy fishing for eels in the Grand Surrey Canal when his hook snagged on her clothing. The girl's mother had told her not to return to their home in York Street, Walworth, by way of the canal, but she ignored the warning and had apparently been violated and drowned.

In November 1858, there was more excited speculation when the press reported the 'MYSTERIOUS DEATH IN THE REGENT'S CANAL' of barman William Weekes, aged 34. The mark of a ligature was found round his neck, and a medical man giving evidence at the inquest thought it could indicate hanging as Weekes was probably dead before he went into the water. The inquest heard that he had recently been in low spirits and suffered from ill health but had never threatened to destroy himself. Even the family could not agree what had happened – Weekes' sister said he had latterly given way to drinking, and she believed it was suicide, while his brother was sure it was a case of murder. The jury reached a unanimous verdict of 'found dead in the Regent's Canal; but how, when, and by what means, deceased came into the water there was no evidence to prove'.

The Regent's Canal claimed another victim in 1862, when a respectably dressed young woman was found drowned at New Globe Bridge on the Mile End Road. Cries of 'Murder!' and 'Help!' were heard by residents living in Canal Road between 12 and 1 a.m. A policeman fetched a lantern and, on searching the bank, found footprints and signs of a ferocious struggle with ripped shreds of clothing strewn about. Thirty minutes later, the body of a dark-haired girl was pulled out, about 5ft tall, with marks on her face and arms indicating she had been brutally beaten. She was without a bonnet or shawl, and her crinoline frock had been torn off.

A full description was posted at local police offices, and she was later identified as 19-year-old Emma Williams, who had been seen late the previous evening wandering in fields near the canal with a young man. At the inquest, her mother said Emma had left her place as a domestic servant three weeks earlier, after being seduced, and had since kept company with a young man, although they had recently quarrelled. Regent's Canal night lockman Robert Rogers heard the screams and saw something in the water, but made only a cursory drag of the canal before giving up the search until daylight, not mentioning the incident to anyone and later saying defensively it was not his duty to raise an alarm. His conduct was strongly censured by the jury, who agreed there was no evidence to show how Emma came to be drowned. If it was murder, yet another killer had escaped punishment.

†††

It was no wonder that melodramatic news reports fuelled a growing fear of crime, which reached peak terror levels in the 1860s when a media-created 'garrotting panic' swept through the capital, after street robbers attacked an MP walking along Pall Mall, choking him with a knotted rope and stealing his watch. Reports of other similar incidents soon followed.

London was the largest city in Europe, and its population of 1 million inhabitants at the start of the century had more than doubled in fifty years. Naturally, Londoners felt a heightened awareness of the dangers that lay in wait beyond the solid security of their own front doors.

In fact, official figures showed violent crime was actually decreasing, while public concern grew, as headlines proclaiming a 'Horrible Murder' or 'Another Suspected Murder' cropped up with alarming regularity. A simmering sense of unease, especially among the prosperous middle classes, was fed by uncertainty in a rapidly changing world that seemed to be full of threatening strangers, and where expanding towns overflowed with troublesome and frequently drunken workers.

It was well known that 90 per cent of criminal offences were alcohol related. The government made intermittent, fruitless attempts to address the drink problem, wary of antagonising the labouring classes after an earlier bid to cut Sunday licensing hours had set off two days of rioting in Hyde Park by angry protesters defending their right to drink when they wanted to. Nevertheless, consumption of beer, wine and spirits kept rising steadily and by the late 1860s had soared to unprecedented levels.

At the bottom of the social scale, people were prepared to stick up for themselves, when necessary, even if that meant breaking the law. Unfortunately, too often alcohol made them dangerously reckless, as

Mr Justice Mellor pointed out in his opening remarks at the Spring Assizes in Liverpool, where it appeared that nearly every case of manslaughter could be traced to drunkenness. He said he had read the court depositions with horror, for he found persons who were probably honest in ordinary life, when under the influence of liquor using the most outrageous violence.

Seventeen-year-old Cleethorpes boatman Charles Mitchell was the worse for drink when he over-reacted to an incident at Leicester during the summer annual races week. His boat was passing along the canal by Abbey Meadow when some children on a school outing threw stones at him and persisted in their annoying behaviour until he grabbed a loaded gun and fired at them.

Teachers heard the gun go off, with shots rattling against nearby factory windows, and were shocked to find that four pupils had been wounded. Edwin Brown, aged 12, was peppered with shots, including one just below the right eye, nine in his cheeks and one which blasted out a front tooth. Emma Ford, aged 9, was hit in the face by a pellet, and two other boys were also injured. A passing doctor took the children in his carriage to a surgery for treatment, while a teacher pursued the boat and stopped it at Belgrave to detain Mitchell, who was arrested by the parish constable.

Many boatmen carried a loaded shotgun on board to defend themselves and their cargoes – usually it was enough 0000to frighten off an assailant, without any shots being fired. However, there were other shooting incidents on the waterways, such as a case in Manchester when a gang of rough lads hurled mud and missiles at a boatman leading his horse along the towpath in the Ancoats district of Manchester.

Goaded into retaliation, David Rushby fetched a gun from the cabin and fired at his tormentors, slightly injuring three lads with the pellets. One report, headlined 'SHOOTING ANCOATS ROUGHS', described the dramatic confrontation. Rushby claimed he did not realise the weapon was loaded and magistrates later dismissed the case, accepting that there had been considerable provocation. Rushby's employer gave him an excellent character and described the sort of0 abuse boatmen were regularly exposed to when passing through Ancoats, which would vindicate any response, except perhaps the extreme measure resorted to on that occasion.

The press deliberately selected news stories that were likely to provoke strong reactions. And every editor knew that violent crime reports, especially those with a sexual element, sold more copies because they satisfied readers' morbid curiosity, triggering powerful emotions of fear and outrage. The abolition of taxes on newspapers in mid-century, combined with advanced printing technology, made them much cheaper and more affordable to the lower classes at a time of improving literacy, when over three-quarters of the population could now read. To exploit this vast and lucrative readership, a whole new type of journalism was invented to appeal to the masses – it gave them simplified, punchy reports, written in a chatty style with easy-to-read, short sentences.

The traditional quality press, dominated by 'The Thunderer', as *The Times* was nicknamed, retained its influential position as society's fourth estate. Alongside these respected titles, other canny publishers were competing for the attention of working-class readers, who greedily devoured every column inch filled with the grisly facts and human drama of crime. The *Daily Telegraph* and *Lloyd's Weekly Newspaper*, among others, filled half their pages with crime coverage in 1866. The popular press certainly knew its market, and ruthlessly deployed sensational reports with startling headlines as weapons in the circulation wars – sometimes with very little regard for the truth.

A hideous tale of wife murder hit the headlines nationwide in late August 1865, when one succinct paragraph set off a media frenzy:

DREADFUL MURDER IN CHESHIRE – On Saturday night, a boatman in the employ of the Shropshire Union Canal Company, committed a most brutal murder on his wife at Calveley, six miles from Crewe. He severed her head with a razor, all but a ligament of the skin.

The report was pounced on immediately and carried by dozens of other papers, including the *Globe* and the *Leicester Journal*, which ran the story in a round-up of six murders, commenting wryly:

We appear to be passing through something like an epidemic stage of murder, attempted murder and suicide. The papers daily record the commission of some dreadful crime, either north or south, east or west, and it is impossible to take up any of the daily journals without being shocked at the tales of horror spread out in startling type, with all the zest and point of penny-a-lining.

There was, however, no truth in the rumour at all. The killer boatman was pure fiction. And when the true facts came to light, only a couple of newspapers bothered to print even the briefest correction to set the record straight. The *Cheshire Observer* explained how press rivalry was responsible for creating the whole drama:

> The lovers of terrible tragedies have been rather disappointed this week. According to reports a horrible murder was perpetrated at Calveley on Saturday night, a boatman on the Shropshire Union Canal having cut his wife's head off. This would have been good enough if it had been true, for there is something attractively sensational in a head being cut fairly off. But fortunately for the woman in question, she has not been sacrificed as an offering to the newspapers, and the affair turned out to be nothing more than a common assault, although at first a report was certainly widely spread that something serious had happened.

It went on to describe the chain of events, which originated with a small, obscure paragraph in the *London Star* on the supposed murder, which was snatched by 'that death-dealing paper', the *Liverpool Mercury*, 'the most murderous of all the sensational newspapers', and elevated to a prominent position with a big headline and bold typeface in its eagerness for a local tragedy. Other papers then copied the wildly exaggerated report. The *Cheshire Observer* added:

> It is curious how few people understand the law of sensation. It is a perfect truism that all the great murders take place between August and December. It is simply that Parliament is not sitting … in the absence of Parliamentary speeches, the daily newspapers have to fill up with the most exciting news they can obtain. A murderer who would have but a paragraph devoted to him, is honoured with a three-column report and a leader in the *Times* … people actually

get to believe that more murder and dreadful crimes are committed during the autumn than at any other time of the year.

The mass media certainly had a lot to answer for. So-called 'news' could be distorted for all kinds of reasons, and in a tense period when the public seemed to be gripped by an overwhelming fear of crime, facts easily became tangled with rumours to create complete myths. One London coroner was well aware how easily false reports could start, and in November 1867 ordered an officer not to dispose of a knife in the canal, which had been used by a debt-ridden shopkeeper to commit suicide, warning, 'Do not do that, or it will give rise to a sensational trial … we will have "A Blood-stained Knife Found in the Canal – Supposed Murder".'

Canals had become inextricably linked with crime, and killer boatman myths were whispered in many different places – often linked to spooky apparitions such as the Kidsgrove Boggart, a headless woman reputed to haunt Harecastle Tunnel on the Trent & Mersey. So terrifying was the shrieking phantom that working boatmen would even take long detours to avoid going through the tunnel. Ghost stories often had their roots in a real-life tragedy on the cut, and legend had it that a boatman had hacked off his wife's head with a piece of slate.

The origins of the Kidsgrove tale were recounted in the *Staffordshire Sentinel*, which explained that a connecting passage had been dug from one of the coalmines to the canal tunnel by the village of Ranscliff, where local boatmen lived in cottages:

> They were a set of men to whom all sorts of crimes were attributed, and who were believed to be capable of any deed, no matter how shocking or villainous … one of these boatmen, while passing under the tunnel quarrelled with his wife, and for some provoking words which the woman used, he cut her head off. Afterwards, to conceal the murder, he dragged the body into the colliery working.

The ghost was believed to herald some accident or fatality, making appearances not only in the tunnel and the locality but 'over the whole of the Potteries in one direction, and over parts of Cheshire'.

The Kidsgrove Boggart was sometimes known as Kit Crewbucket, a name that may have been a mishearing of the original phrase spoken in broad northern dialect. Other reports said the victim's head was found in a bucket, and the same headless ghost was also reported over 80 miles away in Crick Tunnel, on the Grand Junction Canal in Northamptonshire. It may be that the location of an actual crime became confused with repeated retelling of the story over several decades. Or was the bucket and its grisly contents dumped at Crick by the guilty boatman later in his journey down the canal network? Perhaps an entirely different woman was murdered at Crick – if so, the facts had been lost long ago in the mists of time.

Many cases of murder were never solved. There was just a dead body found and a confused set of rumours woven into creepy yarns told by the fireside on dark nights, or around a trestle table in the village pub. Such folklore was traditionally passed on by word of mouth, but with the advent of the sensation-seeking mass media, newspapers too played a part in making myths.

Victorians were fascinated by the supernatural, and this popular interest, shared by all social classes, was nurtured by regular reports of ghost sightings in the press. Spine-chilling tales of uncanny happenings could unnerve even the more sceptical readers.

Perhaps the first urban legend was of a strange creature, part-man, part-beast, with powerful springs on the soles of his boots, called Spring-Heeled Jack. He was first spotted in south London at the start of the Victorian era, and throughout the nineteenth century there were numerous accounts of him frightening women in various places. His unearthly figure was said to come out at night in Brentford, running across bridges and jumping onto the roofs of narrowboats moored on the Grand Junction. Haunting stories of ghostly encounters seemed to stick around the waterways and become part of canal folklore.

Not all otherworldly incidents were connected to suspected crimes, and many appeared to be the legacy of straightforward accidental deaths – though no one could be sure. Among them were the ghost of a 'legger' seen in Dudley Tunnel, and a drowned boatman reported desperately splashing about in Standedge Tunnel on the Huddersfield Narrow Canal, his low moans echoing in the eerie silence.

At Lapworth, where the Stratford-upon-Avon Canal meets the Grand Union, the sounds of ice cracking and shouts have been heard on winter nights near the place a man fell in on his way home from the village pub. Such accidents were commonplace, and the body of another young boatman named George Simonds was discovered in the canal near Lapworth early one Sunday morning towards the end of May. He was last seen alive at 11 p.m. the night before, coming from the New Inn at Rowington towards Austerton Lane, and he apparently fell into the water while searching for his boat. At an inquest held at the Boot Inn, Lapworth, the jury returned a verdict of 'found drowned'. The superstitious might well have felt a shiver of apprehension when passing the spot where the tragedy occurred.

The Shropshire Union Canal, known as 'the Shroppie', was believed to be the most haunted canal in Britain with at least five well-known resident ghosts. One, who could be heard screaming at Betton Cutting near Market Drayton, was thought to be a navvy crushed beneath a load of stones. Another apparition encountered at Bridge 39 was a weird, shadowy creature with enormous eyes, which leapt out from the undergrowth to terrorise passers-by and was said to be the spirit of a boatman who had drowned there.

†††

In June 1872, the body of a young lady in her mid-twenties was discovered floating in the slimy, filthy water of the canal at Paddington – a petite figure with a fair complexion, brown hair and eyes, her small, delicate hands plainly indicating that she had never needed to work. She was expensively dressed in black, with a jet brooch and one earring, a red petticoat, white stockings, leather boots and soft, black kid gloves. In her pocket was a bunch of eight keys and some silver and copper coins. The only clue to her identity was found on a cambric handkerchief and her underclothing, both marked in red with the letters 'J.S.M.'.

Who was she? No one seemed to know. She had obviously been brutally murdered as there was a severe fracture to her skull and wounds from a violent blow behind her right ear. The London newspapers were agog with the mystery and incredulous that neither the victim's name nor her murderer had been traced. The *Daily Telegraph* was scathing about the efforts of Scotland Yard:

> The intelligence of the Police is limited in its scope ... in cases at all out of the common track we are sure to find our helmeted and truncheoned protectors hopelessly at fault. The sole clue to the tragedy, are the letters J.S.M. upon the clothes. Are we to believe that these three little letters will not yet aid us to track the assassin? Did J.S.M. live so wholly alone – was she so utterly homeless in this great desert of London that no one has missed her?

It was a shocking case, but worse still, J.S.M. was the second respectable young woman found in the canal recently with a fractured skull, and speculation began to mount that a serial killer was at large. A few months earlier, another body, evidently that of a lady, was found in 'the green slime and muddy ooze' of the Regent's Canal and no one had ever come forward to identify her. According to the *Daily Telegraph*:

> The assassin had searched the body, and taken from it everything that might possibly give the clue to his crime. There were no letters, no cards, no marks upon the clothes. The inquest ended in an open verdict, and the matter was forgotten. Hardly six months have passed, and a second murder has been perpetrated, so like the first in all its circumstances as to lead us to believe that murder in London is a perfectly feasible crime and our Police are more active in the show than in the reality.

The *Telegraph* pulled out all the stops to reimagine the murder as vividly as possible, in a melodramatic passage that would not have been out of place in one of the sensation novels that were popular at the time:

> And so, too, whoever J.S.M. may be, her murderer is still among us, and free. He met his victim, possibly on the banks of the canal in the early twilight, when all London was wrapt in sleep. The crime, long planned, took but scant time in the doing. One stifled cry for mercy – one short, sharp, cruel blow behind the ear – and all was over. The slimy, fetid waters of the canal hold their horrible burden ... the long

hair floating wildly amid rank duckweed and other filth, the eyes star-
ing up to the blue summer sky; the thin, delicate hands that tell their
own history clenched in the agony of death.

In August 1872, 13-year-old Elizabeth Chipp, who had disappeared on
her way to visit an aunt, was fished out of the canal near Haggerston
Bridge at Hoxton. There were suspicions of foul play, and the *Pall Mall
Gazette* reported sardonically:

> The Regent's Canal, which is an object of disgust to all whose mis-
> fortune it is to live in its neighbourhood, may at least lay claim to
> the proud distinction for being the most popular depository for mur-
> dered persons in the metropolitan district. Scarcely a month now
> elapses without some dead body being found in it, and how many
> other bodies lie imbedded in its mud and hidden by its green slime it
> is impossible to say. The jury returned an open verdict, and this case
> must be added to the list of the Regent's Canal mysteries.

Sadly, little more than half a century after the proud celebrations
of engineering innovation at the opening of Regent's Canal, it was
now being condemned as a filthy, outdated relic of the olden days
– renowned as a hotspot for nefarious activities. But despite all
the bodies and potential horrors to be encountered in the Regent's
Canal, nothing deterred a group of local lads in Islington from
enjoying a swim that summer. Bathing in the canal was still an
offence, and the Clerkenwell magistrate imposed small fines on each
of the daring lawbreakers.

The London papers could hardly believe their luck during the
summer of 1872, printing regular follow-up stories to whip up public
anxiety about unsolved crime. It was also useful ammunition for the
press to indulge in one of its favourite pastimes of goading the authorities about their inadequacies – in this case, a failure to tackle crime
effectively. The *Pall Mall Gazette* commented that the dirty waters of
the Regent's Canal were so accustomed to having 'the dead bodies of
murdered persons flung into them' that 'no sober or sane person,
of however romantic a temperament, would select the towing path
for a moonlight walk'. The paper ridiculed police constables on duty,

plodding along at the rate of 1 mile in two hours, who were responsible for the slow pace of criminal justice.

Then, in early September 1873, came a new atrocity, the so-called Battersea Mystery, which only inflamed fears that a maniac was on the loose. The left-upper quarter of a female torso was discovered at Battersea, followed by her severed head at Limehouse, where the Regent's Canal enters the River Thames. Other segments were retrieved bit by bit – one forearm with tarred rope marks on it at Woolwich, a foot on the shore of the Surrey Canal at Rotherhithe, and the other arm was picked up from the Albert Embankment.

The whole dreadful case was a gift to the press, which revelled in all the horrors of the unfolding saga. The *Leicester Chronicle* headlined it, 'HORRIBLE MURDER IN LONDON. A WOMAN HACKED TO PIECES' and reported:

A discovery was made on Friday morning week of the mutilated parts of a woman's body, which gives rise to the belief that probably one of the most horrible crimes that have been committed since the time of Greenacre has just been perpetrated.

Older readers would recall that in 1836, James Greenacre had chopped up his fiancée and dumped the severed head in the Regent's Canal.

The case set off another angry tirade about police incompetence by the *Pall Mall Gazette*, which noted:

The discovery of the mutilated remains of a woman ... thrown piecemeal into the river is or ought to be something more than a mere 'sensation', to last nine days and then be forgotten. It is another symptom not only that crimes of this nature are often perpetrated in London, but that they are, as a rule, perpetrated with impunity. It is useless to recount the long list of murders which have of late years been committed by criminals who have 'baffled the ingenuity of the police' ... some very strenuous steps should be taken to solve these mysteries and bring the offenders to justice.

Initially, a Thames bargeman was suspected after rumours that his wife had gone missing, but it was only a 'red herring' in the murder mystery, and she was seen alive on board the boat shortly afterwards. The crime remained unsolved and was later linked to the infamous Thames Torso Murders of the 1880s.

By the autumn of 1873, press hysteria had dissolved into attempts at macabre black humour. One wit advised murderers that the river or canals were the safest places to deposit bodies so they should not resort to other means of hiding a crime:

> ... merely because they are too lazy to carry the remains of those they have killed to the towing-path of the Regent's Canal, or to one of the bridges, from whence they may be pitched into the water.

The *Pall Mall Gazette* even ran an anonymous letter from someone claiming to be 'a retired murderer', who complained about the practice of mutilating victims, which was clearly being done by young, inexperienced killers:

> ... and exciting in the public a disgust not generally awakened by a simple assassination artistically effected, without undue violence and with a proper regard for the feelings of survivors. I venture, therefore, on behalf of a growing and important class – the murderers of London, having spent some of the happiest days of my life in their society – to beg the public to believe they have no hand whatever in [it] ... So far from the London murderers approving this practice, they would willingly lend the police every assistance in bringing to justice the low scoundrels who disgrace the criminal classes.

13

A CRY FROM THE BOAT CABINS

A few minutes before 5 a.m. on Friday, 2 October 1874, Londoners were awakened by the sound of an enormous explosion so loud that they thought it was an earthquake. Windows shook, doors rattled, and furniture was hurled across rooms all over the city. The shock was felt as far away as Gravesend at the mouth of the River Thames. In Regent's Park Zoo, cages were blown open and exotic birds escaped, while the monkeys leapt to safety as shards of broken glass fell from the shattered roof and terrified giraffes huddled together in a corner.

Panic spread through the streets of north-west London as hundreds of residents jumped from their beds and rushed outside, some screaming that the end of the world had come. Patients at the Hospital for Diseases of the Nervous System in Portland Terrace had a terrible fright when the front windows were blown in, and all thirty beds were covered with splintered wood and bits of glass.

At Albany Barracks, the colonel of the guards reacted quickly to what he believed was a Fenian attack and sent out an armed troop of soldiers. At Enfield, people thought it must be a major incident in the rifle factory, and at Woolwich they guessed a load of ammunition had exploded in the marshes.

What none of them had witnessed was the ear-splitting blast at a bridge on the Regent's Canal, the column of flames roaring up into the sky and a great ball of smoke billowing above, as trees were uprooted, iron railings were wrenched out of stone walls, windows were smashed, buildings were damaged, and lumps of mortar rained down on the streets. In the confusion, fire engines set out in all directions across the city to try to find the scene of the disaster.

A blazing severed gas main lit up the scene of destruction with an eerie glow. As dawn broke, a huge crowd of stunned spectators gathered in the pouring rain to stare at a 10ft-high pile of tangled ironwork, bricks and muddy debris blocking the canal, and the jagged remnants of boats strewn everywhere.

Five tons of gunpowder had wreaked havoc. Police set up a cordon around the area to keep everyone back, while salvage workers and firemen used small boats and long grappling hooks to dredge the canal, searching for bodies and pulling out submerged cargo.

What caused the explosion? That was the question on everyone's lips. And it did not take long before enough fragments of information could be pieced together to explain what had happened that morning.

At about 3 a.m., a fleet of six barges owned by the Grand Junction Canal Company left City Road Basin heading for Nottingham, towed by the steam tug *Ready*. Behind it came the flyboat *Jane* and the *Dee*, followed by the *Tilbury*, which was carrying a cargo of sugar, nuts, straw boards, coffee, four barrels of petroleum and 5 tons of gunpowder. At the rear of the procession were the *Limehouse* and the *Hawkesbury*.

William White was a deckhand on the *Dee*, and as the boat passed North Gate Bridge he saw a flash, then smoke, and heard a noise like the report of a gun from the stern of the *Tilbury*. He called out to the young boatman steering it, asking what was up with the gunpowder on board, '"I thought they were having a bit of a game ...," he said. "It's nearly blown me out of the hatches already ... Stop her!".' The tug stopped, then immediately came the explosion and White was knocked out against the side of the cabin.

The *Tilbury* was instantly blown to pieces. Part of its keel crashed down onto the roof of a house 300 yards away and fell through three floors into the basement, though the occupants were unharmed.

Cumberland Terrace and Gloucester Terrace suffered the worst damage. Some local people sustained a few cuts and bruises but, remarkably, none were seriously hurt. The blast left a large crater in the canal, North Gate Bridge (also called Macclesfield Bridge) was completely demolished, and its massive cast-iron supporting piers were scattered as if they were matchsticks.

The *Limehouse* was lifted out of the water by the blast before it sank, and one man was blown onto the towpath, where he was found with only minor injuries. The *Dee* was totally wrecked. All the boatmen survived, except the three-man crew of the *Tilbury*, who were killed outright. They were steerer Charles Baxton (aged 35) from Loughborough, who was a married man with several children, boat hand William Taylor (aged 26) of Brierley Hill, and 18-year-old Jonathan Holloway, known as Birmingham Joe, who had left home in Oldbury a year earlier to find work.

Graphic descriptions of the calamity filled the press. There was speculation and fierce debate about the incident, but most of all, a furious indignation that something like that could happen in the middle of the capital city. If the blast had taken place inside Islington Tunnel, the consequences would have been unimaginable. The *Illustrated London News* commented:

> Explosive substances are carried through the heart of London every day ... Gunpowder, nitro-glycerine, and other materials of the like kind, are passed to and fro as articles of commerce under restrictions so loose that the wonder is, not that accidents sometimes happen, but that they should happen so rarely. Parliament must see to this.

Rumour had it that a barge carrying 30 tons of gunpowder was moored on the canal near Bromley Rice Mills in the East End during a recent fire, when burning embers were seen showering down onto its deck.

On Monday, 5 October, a meeting chaired by the local MP was held at the Eyre Arms in St John's Wood for residents whose properties had borne the worst of the devastation. They set up a subscription fund for donations to help those affected, and formed a committee to lobby ministers for urgent government legislation on the transit of explosives.

During the inquest held at Marylebone Workhouse, Braunston boatman Edward Hall, who was steering the *Limehouse*, recalled that he was in his cabin and had undressed for bed when the blast occurred. He thought they had been struck by lightning. 'My boat was knocked all to pieces and sank. I was thrown out of bed against the stove. I was stunned and was in the water when I came to.'

William White, the injured mate on the *Dee*, was out of hospital and able to give his crucial evidence about the final minutes before the explosion. He could not say for sure if anyone was smoking on the *Tilbury*, but acknowledged it was usual for boatmen to smoke. Often, they did not know what cargo they were carrying, though of course the contents could be guessed at.

Reporting on the inquest, the *Globe* put forward some of the suggested causes of the accident. These included a lightning strike, the possibility that one of the powder kegs was ignited by a spark from the tug's chimney, or that one of the *Tilbury*'s crew had started smoking under the tarpaulin, where he had gone to get out of the rain. As the *Globe* pointed out, it was doubtful if the truth would ever be known as all the men on board had perished.

The inquest went on for several days, but finally, on 20 October, the Grand Junction Canal Company was found guilty of gross negligence for failing to take proper precautions in the transport and stowage of cargo. Crews often lit candles in the cabin and smoked, but it seemed most likely that an oil lamp or the cabin fire used to boil a kettle had ignited benzoline vapour, which set off the explosion. Returning a verdict, the inquest jury formally stated their opinion that 'the existing statutory laws are inadequate to secure the public safety'.

A gang of 200 navvies worked around the clock to shift 500 tons of rubble, and the canal reopened to traffic four days later. The ill-fated bridge, known ever since as Blow-up Bridge, was eventually rebuilt, but the disaster spelt the end for the Grand Junction Canal Company, which for so many decades had been a powerhouse of the nation's longest and most lucrative waterway.

More than 1,000 buildings had been damaged. The proprietors fought the first claim for compensation, which was brought by Mr Jackson, whose house in Regent's Park was structurally damaged, and the case was heard at the Court of Common Pleas in May 1875. Summing up at the end of the trial, the judge, Lord Coleridge, said the case against the company was plain: 'Every child knew that gunpowder required extraordinary precautions [to be] used in dealing with it.' He told the jury to consider whether they would sleep soundly if they knew that such a barge was passing along a canal within 100 yards of their homes that night. The jurors didn't need to leave their box to decide immediately for the plaintiff, and the verdict was greeted with applause and clapping in court.

In June, the government passed the Explosives Act to tighten up regulations, but it was too late for the Grand Junction Canal Company. The initial court case paved the way for more than 800 further claims and almost £80,000 (roughly £4 million today) was paid out in compensation by the company, which had to be rescued with a loan from its bankers and finally gave up the carrying trade in July 1876.

†††

The *Tilbury* explosion was a dramatic reminder of just how dangerous working conditions could be in Victorian Britain. Health and safety was an emerging concern and some employers were making greater efforts to protect their workers, if not always for humane reasons, then certainly to avoid the financial liability incurred by accidents. As usual, it was money that counted.

The Trustees of the Bridgewater Canal were forced to pay compensation to boatman's wife Mrs Shoebottom for the loss of her husband, who fell through a hole in the middle of a dilapidated bridge. He had been returning to his boat late one December night and was crossing a bridge near Liverpool Road, Manchester, when he crashed down beneath the rotten planks and was found dead, stuck fast in the mud at the bottom of the canal with water up to his eyes. During the court action brought by his widow at Manchester Assizes, several witnesses said they had narrowly escaped falling through the old bridge themselves. The Bridgewater Trustees claimed it was private property and Shoebottom had no business crossing it anyway, and he was drunk at the time. However, they were held responsible for the accident and Mrs Shoebottom was awarded £400 in damages.

Canals were widely known to be miserable places of pitiful, unremitting toil for the boat families, and a poignant first-hand account was later given by novelist Arnold Bennett in *Clayhanger*, describing a scene on the Trent & Mersey he recalled from his youth in the Potteries:

Towards the bridge from the north came a long narrow canal-boat roofed with tarpaulin; and towards the bridge from the south came a similar craft, sluggishly creeping. The towing-path was a morass of sticky brown mud, for in the way of rain that year was breaking the records of a century and a half. Thirty yards in front of each boat an unhappy skeleton of a horse floundered its best in the quagmire.

Horses towing the boats for mile after mile every day some-times suffered appalling neglect, as the *Preston Herald* reported in September 1875:

CRUELTY TO A HORSE. Another charge of cruelty against a canal boatman – making the third within a month – was heard at the county petty sessions on Saturday.

William Walmsley from the canal boat *Ann* was fined 20 shillings for working a horse in an unfit state between Glasson Dock and Preston. The poor animal, which had raw wounds and one leg out of joint, was ordered to be destroyed.

Conditions could be equally bad for some youngsters on the cut, who were born into a way of life where they were expected to work from an early age. One onlooker watching family barges on the canals described the children as 'helpless little ones, dirty, ragged, and stunted in growth' who, at 5 or 6 years old, were entrusted with a whip and made to drive the horse by their thoughtless parents.

An inquest into the death of 14-year-old Margaret Evans, the daughter of a canal-boat master plying the Shropshire Union, heard that her daily task was to trudge wearily ahead of the horse and open the lock gates. At the village of Christleton, on the outskirts of Chester, she fell into the water and drowned. The jury could only record a verdict of accidental death, but they asked the deputy coroner to approach the canal company about the dangerous state of the locks and the impropriety of employing children. The *Illustrated Police News* commented:

It is no secret that children much younger than Margaret Evans, are compelled to walk thirty and even forty miles along the bank without going to bed throughout the whole journey. Many who have been subjected to this inhuman treatment have their ankles twisted through having been compelled to remain so long on their feet. The possibility of their enduring such fatigue seems almost incredible; but we are assured that there is no exaggeration in the statement.

There was no doubt that many families lived a grim existence crowded together on small, cramped boats, exhausted from long hours of labour and struggling to make ends meet. Living under constant strain created frustration and anger, which sometimes erupted into violent outbursts. On a boat moored in a pound at Wolverhampton, Joseph Mincher lost his temper after a few drinks and beat up his wife, one evening, because she was tipsy all day and had not even dressed the children. He then dragged her from the cabin, a rope fastened round her neck with a noose, one hand twisted in her hair.

Constable Thomas Smith, who was on duty in nearby Southampton Street, heard cries of 'Murder!' and children screaming. He ran down to the lock side, where Mincher was about to heave the woman overboard, saying, 'I'll drown you like a **** dog.' In the nick of time, Police Constable Smith managed to grab the boatman and pull him onto the wharf.

Mincher was charged with assaulting his wife, Martha, who appeared in court with her face shockingly disfigured from the beating but insisted that it was all her own fault. It emerged that she married at 16 and had ten children, though only five of them were still living. The magistrate said it must have struck everyone there as a terrible tale, and sentencing Mincher to six months in prison with hard labour, he told him:

> What your intention was is perfectly clear from your words ... and even if you did not intend to drown her, it would have been almost impossible for her to escape in her drunken state. Your wife, no doubt, ought not to have got drunk, but that's not the smallest excuse for your conduct.

Imprisonment may have been preferable to transportation (a sentence which it was designed to replace) but it was no easy option. The nine large convict prisons, including Pentonville in London and local gaols housing short-term inmates, imposed a harsh regime where silence and spells of solitary confinement were strictly enforced. Felons were incarcerated in gloomy cells measuring no more than 7ft by 13ft and existed on a meagre diet. Most were sentenced to penal servitude with hard labour, intended as a deterrent to crime, and could expect to spend their days in gruelling tasks like stone-breaking, walking a tread-mill, pulling apart filthy old ropes (known as picking oakum) or doing shot drill, where they repeatedly lifted a heavy cannon ball to chest level. An equally futile occupation was turning the crank handle of a machine, which prison warders – nicknamed 'screws' – could adjust by a screw to make the resistance harder. Any slackers were punished with a flogging.

Mary Spencer was another boatwoman who survived a violent attack by her husband. But she begged the magistrate not to gaol him or she would have to work the boat herself and care for their five children, who were all under 8 years old. Edward Spencer, who was employed carrying coal on the Bridgewater Canal, had to stop to help his brother rescue a horse from the cut, one Friday afternoon, and ordered Mary to take the boat and get some corn for their own horse at Monton Bridge. Later on, at Worsley, when she admitted that she had not done so he began to swear and threw a stone, which struck her on the temple with such force that it knocked her into the canal.

At the county police court, Mary explained that her husband was half-drunk at the time and had been drinking for three or four days. He earned at least £3 a week, although they had to keep the horse out of that, and as she had no other way of making a living, she would be con-tent if the bench would bind him over not to offend again, rather than imposing a prison sentence. The magistrate, Sir John Mantell, decided to take a pragmatic view, telling Spencer:

> I should like to see you go to penal servitude, which would serve you right; but if I send you to prison I shall reduce your wife and family to absolute poverty, because, wretch though you are, you seem to find them the means of living.

He was bound over to keep the peace for six months, in two sureties of £25 each.

Many boatmen were decent, law-abiding workers doing their best to make a living in hard times, but their reputation was tarnished by the brutality and appalling crimes of a rogue minority on the cut. Bad news sold newspapers, and it was these cases that grabbed the headlines, like an incident at Liverpool where unfortunately, this time, the killer boatman was no myth.

The *Manchester Evening News* was first to report the 'SHOCKING WIFE MURDER' on Thursday, 10 September 1874, followed the next day by other northern papers, including the *Huddersfield Chronicle* and *York Herald*. Within a week, the news had spread across the country, appearing in the *Birmingham Daily Post* and nationals such as the *Pall Mall Gazette*. The hot story was a harrowing account of a brutal assault on boatwoman Ann Worthington by her husband.

The couple had started quarrelling at a public house in Vauxhall Road, Liverpool, as they sat drinking glasses of ale. When they left about 10.30 p.m., they seemed to be friends again, but as they crossed the yard William Worthington asked his wife for money. When she gave him only a shilling, he became abusive and kicked out savagely, knocking her against a wall.

Carter's wife Susannah Daley heard screams coming from the backyard but ignored them at first. After fifteen minutes, when the noise continued as she was going upstairs to bed, she opened the window and yelled at the man to stop. Mrs Daley ran outside to find Ann clutching her ribs in pain, her face covered with blood, and their neighbour John Kerr quickly whistled for a policeman. When Constable James Flint arrived on the scene, however, he refused to take Worthington into custody because it was a matter between husband and wife, and he advised them to go back to their boat and settle it between themselves.

The Worthingtons returned to their boat *Ada*, moored at Boundary Bridge, and there the violence resumed. Inside the cabin, the boatman kicked Ann in the abdomen, his heavy boot landing with such force that it broke the central bone of her corset and knocked her off the bench where she sat. Ann's daughter Mary watched the attack helplessly before she slipped out to feed the horse, and when she returned she found Worthington asleep on the floor. Mary and Ann stayed awake most of the night.

At 7 a.m., Worthington woke up and, without a word, began viciously kicking Ann in the side, then seized a poker and smashed it down onto her hand before leaving the boat. He was back a few minutes later and, seeing the terrible state she was in, asked if she was ill.

Ann was taken into a house in Hopwood Street, her body 'covered from head to heel with fractures and bruises', and soon moved to Wigan, where a surgeon attended to the injuries. But the damage was done, and she died a few days afterwards. Ann left an 18-month-old baby and six children by her former husband.

When Worthington was arrested for murder, he was full of remorse, saying, 'It was a bad job, and I wouldn't have done it for a thousand pounds.' He was sorry now, but of course it was too late.

At the opening of Liverpool Assizes in December, the presiding judge, Mr Justice Mellor, remarked that the calendar of cases to be tried showed 'a melancholy picture of the results of ignorance, drunkenness and brutality – a state of things which, he regretted to say, was not exceptional in that part of the country'. He pointed out that there had been a great outcry about crimes of violence, which were believed to be on the increase, and new legislation was needed. While he had viewed with horror a return to the flogging system, he was now convinced it was necessary for cases, not only of robbery, but other crimes such as assaults on women or children, arson and stone-throwing by boys.

The courtroom was packed with hundreds of spectators on the day of Worthington's trial. The 33-year-old captain of a flat trading between Liverpool and Wigan, he was described by the *Liverpool Courier* reporter as a muscular man of medium height with a very manly type of countenance. Opening the prosecution case, Mr Samuell said the crime was one of the worst types of wilful murder because the person Worthington killed was his wife. 'He killed her in a brutal and cowardly manner – in fact, he kicked her to death.'

Among the witnesses called was Elizabeth Wright, who was working at the bar of her cousin's pub on the night in question. The couple had both been sober when they left the premises and William afterwards admitted to her that he was very sorry for what he had done. She had known the Worthingtons for a long time and never seen either of them tipsy. 'They were not drunken people.'

The darker side of the marriage was revealed by Mary Prescott, who described what she saw in the cabin that night. She said her stepfather was in the habit of beating her mother, but she did not dare to interfere in case he might ill-treat her even more severely.

Mr Justice Mellor asked Constable Flint why he had not taken Worthington into custody when he saw she was badly hurt. If he had done so, the woman might have been alive today. The officer replied, 'I thought it was merely a word between man and wife. I did not think it was so bad as it was.' The judge gave him a stern reprimand for making what proved to be a fatal mistake and told him that although slight disturbances ought not to be meddled with, it was the duty of police to interfere in cases of violence. 'A man has no right to beat his wife because she is his wife, and she has as much right to be protected as anybody else.'

Defence counsel, Mr Cottingham, told the jury that the prisoner felt great sympathy for his unfortunate victim and, listening from his place in the dock, Worthington twice dissolved in tears. Mr Cottingham said there was no intent to cause serious injuries, a fact proved by his client's anxiety that Ann should receive proper medical assistance. It was a pathetic excuse. Mr Justice Mellor saw no reason for the charge to be reduced to manslaughter and dismissed any mitigation on the grounds that Worthington had taken 'more stimulants than was proper or wise'. He said there appeared to be no provocation for the violence and it seemed to be a deliberate attack by the prisoner, who was therefore guilty of murder.

The judge concluded his remarks at 4.12 p.m. precisely, as one of the watching reporters noted, and when the jury left the box to consider their verdict, an excited buzz of conversation broke out among the crowd of onlookers, which included 'several well-dressed "ladies" whose morbid curiosity already anticipated the death sentence'. They were right. At 5 p.m. there was a call for 'Silence!' and the jurors returned to give the verdict – guilty of wilful murder. However, to the surprise of many in court, they added a strong recommendation to mercy. Perhaps they were moved by the prisoner's tears.

Hearing the foreman's words, Worthington looked bewildered then leant down from the dock and spoke to his counsel, who handed the judge references to his previous good character. After a cursory glance at the papers, the judge put on the black cap and, passing sentence of death, warned Worthington it was unlikely the jury's recommendation would have any effect:

I beseech you not to buoy yourself up with any false hope or delusion; but to prepare as if for death ... while you have time, by repentance and contrition, endeavour to obtain that pardon at the throne of grace which the human law denies you.

Worthington was led away looking completely dumbfounded, too surprised to make any exclamation or signal to friends in court. The *York Herald* report was headlined succinctly, 'A WIFE KICKER SENTENCED TO DEATH'.

On Saturday, 2 January 1875, the boatman was one of four condemned men being held in Kirkdale Gaol who were allowed visits from relatives to say goodbye. Worthington was still expecting to be granted a reprieve and was adamant he had not murdered his wife, saying, 'She was sick', over and over again. The *Manchester Evening News* commented:

Worthington was a type of the rough characters that are born and bred on the boats that navigate our inland rivers and canals, and 'as ignorant as the horse that drew his boat' ... in his opinion she had died, not from the effects of his brutality, but quite naturally.

When news of a reprieve came for one of the other convicts, Worthington asked eagerly if there was not one for him too, and insisted it was bound to come on Sunday.

At five o'clock on Monday morning, the three men due to be executed were called and, after attending a communion service in the chapel, were given breakfast – only Worthington had any appetite for the food. About 7.45 a.m., the prison bell began to toll, and the convicts were taken to a room where the hangman waited. That morning, he was Welshman Robert Anderson, a lawyer's son who had trained as a doctor and learnt the job of executioner by assisting well-known hangman William Calcraft.

The condemned men embraced and shook hands before their arms were pinioned. Then, ghastly pale, they took their places in a solemn procession led by the governor of the gaol, Captain Gibbs, followed by the deputy under-sheriff, chaplain and warders.

Outside in the prison yard stood fifteen news reporters, who had been admitted to watch the event. Parliament had abolished the death penalty for all offences except murder and treason in 1861, and the last public execution took place in 1868 (the problems of crowd-control considered to outweigh any potential deterrent of an open spectacle attracting jeering hordes). Now it was up to the press to record proceedings and reassure the public that justice had been done.

It was raw and foggy in the bleak enclosure, where three ropes swung ominously beneath the beam of the scaffold erected in one corner. Heaps of broken stones lay on the ground everywhere, covered in half-thawed mud and snow.

The prisoners were helped up the steps and Worthington was first to be led to the drop. The hangman fitted the noose, drew a white cap over his head and pinioned his legs. Then came John McCrave and Michael Mullen – members of Liverpool's notorious 'High Rip' street gang, found guilty of murdering a man who refused to hand over sixpence for beer. The chaplain loudly recited the litany, and the men's muffled voices could be heard praying fervently in the final moments as the hangman drew the bolt of the trapdoor.

It was a short drop of 2ft 6in and death was instant. Three bodies twisted slowly on the ropes, and as the black flag was hoisted above the walls, a dozen people who had gathered outside the prison walked away.

The Times commented that it was a long time since so many executions were recorded in one day, and these three cases would be remembered 'as marking the grievous degradation which the lower classes in Liverpool had reached'. It added:

> We hope this example will administer a decisive check to the violence which has lately disgraced some districts and classes of the country. Those who are liable to similar temptations may be assured that no amount of rigour which the law can exert will be spared, in order to repress the inhuman brutality of which these crimes are but the more conspicuous instances. It is a disease which can only be effectually encountered by sharp and unflinching remedies.

†††

One man was determined to do something to improve the lot of boat families. George Smith was a Staffordshire brickmaker's son whose early experiences of hard labour made him acutely aware of social injustice. From the age of 9, he worked thirteen-hour days in the brick trade but saved his wages to buy books and managed to educate himself, eventually becoming manager of a brickworks and campaigning relentlessly for better conditions. His efforts eventually paid off, with new legislation introduced to inspect brickyards and protect child workers, but the victory came at a price. Although he had made a name for himself as a philanthropist, his work roused hostility in the trade, and he lost his job.

Living in poverty with time on his hands, Smith decided to tackle the problems of another neglected group – canal boatmen and their families, who seemed to be trapped in a harsh way of life with no escape. He particularly wanted to help the children. Once again, it was his own vivid childhood memories which prompted this social crusade.

He began by writing a stream of letters to the press, drawing attention to the miseries of life afloat, and in 1875 published *Our Canal Population: A Cry from the Boat Cabins*, a book which revealed startling scenes he had watched as a boy on the canal near his home. 'I can never forget the scenes I witnessed. Drunkenness, filthiness, and cruelty, selfish idleness at the cost of children and animals, thieving, fighting and almost every other abomination prevailed among them.'

Some boat cabins were models of neatness, 'others are the most filthy holes imaginable, what with bugs and other vermin creeping up the sides, stinking mud finding its way through leaky joints to the bottom of the cabin'. Many boats were towed by worn-out horses only fit for the knacker's yard.

Smith's aim was 'to write a dark chapter in the annals of the poor' and draw attention to the worst excesses of this self-perpetuating lifestyle, which he believed could only be ended by compulsory education for boat children, and new laws to improve sanitary conditions on board.

Unlike many other Victorian reformers, Smith was not a rich and powerful man, but what he lacked in social position, he made up for in boundless energy and passion for his cause. Considered by some to be an eccentric, he believed himself to be chosen by God for great work, but this earnest self-belief helped him persevere despite the hatred and abuse he encountered from opponents. They thought the proposed reforms were disruptive, costly and unnecessary. After all, tens of thousands lived in city slum conditions probably no worse than those on the waterways.

But Smith had already learnt that publicity was the most effective way of lobbying for change, and he made enormous efforts to ensure his canal campaign won the backing of the mass media, which he referred to gratefully as the 'all-powerful Press'. Hungry as ever for sensation, newspapers throughout Britain pounced on the shocking revelations of Smith's book, filling pages with a steady stream of articles, commentary and letters which immediately grabbed public attention.

The *Daily Telegraph* ran a leader on the boaters who 'form a race apart', but it tried to give a balanced view, acknowledging that large numbers who leased their barges were thoroughly respectable and some, in time, became substantial men. The real nomads who travelled longer routes into the Midland counties and the north had a reputation for using foul language, and from an early age grew familiar with drunkenness and fighting. 'They are, however, the most honest of all waterside characters, and that is about the best that can be said for them.'

The *Coventry Herald* praised the graphic power of Smith's writing, and his fervid zeal in describing the wretched conditions of those living on narrowboats, in cabins only 8ft 6in long and 6ft 6in wide. In his book, Smith claimed 95 per cent could not read or write, 90 per cent were drunkards and 60 per cent of couples living together were unmarried.

The very worst conditions were to be found on leaky old boats carrying loads of ironstone from Warwickshire and Staffordshire, worked by boatmen whom Smith called 'the lowest in the social scale of any I have ever met; idle, profligate, and brutal to a degree you can scarcely believe'. They lived on board with a wife and five or six children. 'How they are packed to sleep is a mystery ... But I am credibly informed that some of the smaller ones actually sleep in a cupboard.'

Satirical magazine *The Hornet* was a keen supporter of Smith's battle, blaming boatmen's carelessness for the catastrophic *Tilbury* gunpowder explosion, and noting:

For many years the name of Bargee has been synonymous with ignorance, coarse vulgarity, and even murderous brutality. Country magistrates have learned something of the savage ways of the bargee. They know too often he is a low, brutal fellow, without the least particle of humane feeling, and so ignorant that he rarely knows his own name.

The medical journal *The Lancet* ran an article on the dangers of disease in filthy, overcrowded cabins. And the *Globe* commented that bargemen and their families were:

> … about the most degraded people in England … It is horrible that in these days there should be living in our midst a very large class who are, so far as the rest of the world knows, practically outside the pale of civilisation.

Smith even sent a copy of his book to Queen Victoria, and made sure the *Star* and other papers published her letter, which replied graciously, 'Her Majesty takes much interest in the endeavours which you make to ameliorate the condition of this class of the labouring population.'

Smith said the boatmen themselves told him that nine out of ten were drunkards, some buying pints of rum and drinking it like water. He thought men spent so much time in the pub to escape from cabins crammed with children and to hear the newspaper read aloud. They frequented the numerous canal-side public houses to be found 'hiding modestly in a corner of a dark wall'. Such places usually had dirty little windows and a tatty sign with uneven lettering to advertise the ale, porter, cider and tobacco on sale within.

Venturing inside one of these dodgy premises, Smith was disgusted to find:

> The grimiest low-ceilinged taproom, a truly savage and barbaric 'tap' wherein is dispensed the thinnest and flattest beer I have ever yet come across. They are nasty, suspicious dens, to say the least of it, and I fear that the over-refreshed bargee is by no means a lamb when he gets home to his unfortunate family.

Alcohol was the reason that John and Jane Probert ended up at Chester Assizes in July 1877, both charged with murdering young Charles Moston, who was found dead on the towpath at Waverton. Probert was master of the Shropshire Union Company's boat *Usk* and had been among a group of men drinking from a cask of liquor in the cargo. Some of them claimed it was only the dregs from an empty cask they had washed out, containing liquor 'not much better than sherry'. Later that evening, the Proberts said their boat hand, Charles, had fallen into the canal drunk but managed to get out onto the bank and refused to come on board. Three men went to look for him but gave up as it was nearly dark.

The *Usk* went on to Chester, where Mrs Probert was heard to say that 'she could not rest in her bed until that chap came home', adding, 'somebody would be sure to find him dead in the morning'.

When Charles' body was found with dislocated vertebrae which could only have been caused by extreme violence, the Proberts were arrested for wilful murder. The judge at their trial ruled there was no evidence to convict them – a decision that was greeted with applause in court by a large group of the couple's friends. A report in the *Illustrated Police News*, headlined 'SHOCKING REVELATIONS OF CANAL LIFE', noted that of sixteen boatmen called as witnesses, only two or three could sign their name on depositions and one had never heard of the Bible.

Cases like this seemed to corroborate many of George Smith's claims. The *Burton Chronicle* was appalled by the accounts contained in his book:

> How few amongst us know even of the existence of such a population as a separate class! How very few have the slightest idea of the seething mass of ignorance and vice which floats up and down our canals in boats! Their state is simply terrible to contemplate.

Some boatmen returned to their houses on land between trips, while others lived aboard family boats passed down through successive generations. The number of vessels on the waterways had never been even approximately counted, but the *Examiner* thought there were 20,000 barges, the majority 'the permanent homes of a large population, wandering about like water gypsies, over the 4,000 miles of canal in England'. It was difficult to be certain of the true figure. Smith estimated the canal-boat population was between 80,000 and 100,000 men, women and children. Others believed it was much smaller, perhaps only 40,000, and suspected he deliberately exaggerated some of his findings for greater impact. The tactic was certainly effective and so was all the publicity.

By 1877 Parliament was preparing a bill to improve canal-boat conditions, and the *London Evening Standard* ran a series of investigative reports on the waterways, which were syndicated in many other newspapers. The special correspondent travelled by narrowboat on different canals, talking to bargemen about the new proposals. He noted that 'the men as a rule eat well, drink well, and smoke well' and at Braunston he was impressed by the tempting supper on one captain's table – a joint of ham, corned beef, a freshly baked crusty loaf, a dish of pickled onions with cucumber and a large can of ale. Clearly, life was not too bad for everyone on the water. The writer concluded that conditions varied greatly on different canals, with the worst to be found in Staffordshire and at Wigan in Lancashire. Other trading centres that required most improvements included Paddington, Birmingham, Etruria on the Trent & Mersey, Wolverhampton, Manchester, Leeds, Liverpool, Coventry and Oxford.

In January 1878, the Canal Boats Act became law, introducing registration of all boats and new sanitary standards. However, it was not tough enough to ensure enforcement and very little changed. Undeterred, George Smith addressed more public meetings, wrote constantly to the papers and published another book, *Canal Adventures by Moonlight*, with lively descriptions of his journey from London to Leicester and the characters he met on the cut.

One of them was 85-year-old Ben the legger, who claimed to have walked more than 50,000 miles, the equivalent of twice round the world, during half a century spent legging boats through Braunston Tunnel. He was forthright in his opinion of families on boats, telling Smith bluntly:

> I say the same now as I've said all along, that a boat cabin is no place for women and childer. It is neither right nor decent. When I went a-boating at first, the men were not allowed to take the women and childer wi' them. Now they can take as many as they loiks. For the life of me I canna tell how they packs 'em. There inna room for them to stand up, much more to lie down.

A short story published the same year as the new Canal Boats Act and dedicated to George Smith gave a poignant account of childhood suffering. *Rob Rat: A Story of Barge Life* by Methodist preacher and popular author Mark Guy Pearse was a sentimental tearjerker about two hungry, ragged children living with their abusive father in a wretched hole of a barge named *Water Rat*. It described the muddy wharf littered with heaps of brick, manure, slabs of slate and rotting refuse, where the only cheerful refuge was the Bargeman's Rest Inn, with its ruddy light streaming out onto the bleak darkness, 'But such a bad name [it] has for ribald talk, brutal fights, horrible drunkenness of men and women too, that it adds only to the weird terrors of the place.' By the end of the tale, the youngsters had been rescued by kindly Old Noah and had a chance of a better life. Fiction though it was, it must have struck a chord with many readers who felt genuine sympathy for children stuck in hopeless deprivation.

One letter writer to the *Examiner* in January 1879 explained he lived in that part of London running alongside the canal called Venetia (known today as Little Venice), which:

> ... has been one of the most unsavoury in a moral as well as a physical sense, in the whole metropolis. It will take some time before the sanitary and educational authorities can thoroughly overhaul Venetia ... The difficulty of catching and teaching these small nomads must be very great.

Boat families undeniably put up with real hardship, and when boatwoman Martha Smith was seen jumping in the canal with a young child in her arms, everyone thought she had given way to despair. On 29 September 1882, she was seen walking along the bank of the Rochdale Canal near London Road, Manchester, at night in a drunken and highly excitable state. The police were called, but when a constable approached Mrs Smith, she swore at him and plunged into the water holding her daughter. They were soon rescued and Mrs Smith, aged 45, was charged with attempting to commit suicide and the attempted murder of 4-year-old Elizabeth Ellen. In court, she insisted it was simply an accident, she had slipped in, and the jury believed her – the verdict was not guilty. More than seventy newspapers reported the case.

It was a boatman's word against his accuser in another odd case that summer, when Joseph Thay was arrested for kidnapping 9-year-old James Howe. The boy had been playing truant from school with his friends and was on the canal bank when Thay passed in his boat and offered them a ride. After a short distance, the other boys jumped off and James started crying for his mother, but Thay said he would not let him go as he needed a boy to mind the horse.

James claimed he spent the first night under a hedge, soaked through from the rain. Then for the rest of that week he had to look after the horse by day, sleep outdoors and was given only dry bread and boiled turnips to eat. When the boat reached Wolverhampton, James made his escape and walked back to Derby, which took two days. At Derby Quarter Sessions, Thay alleged the boy had refused to go home. The court decided to give him the benefit of the doubt, and he was acquitted.

Despite sympathetic murmurings in some quarters, people were still shocked at the casual violence of canal life that was exposed in court hearings. The *Wigan Observer* ran a story headlined 'LIFE ON THE CANAL', recounting how boatwoman Margaret Collins arrived at the local magistrates' office in an agitated state, clutching her two children. The boy's forehead was bleeding and Margaret had ugly marks on both arms. She said her husband had beaten her about the legs with a crowbar and had taken all their clothes to throw into the canal.

A warrant was issued for John Collins' arrest, but at the hearing the next day, Margaret was reluctant to give all the facts. She told the magistrate they ran a pair of boats, and she managed one of them but wanted to leave her husband and earn her own living. He had already sold one horse to buy drink and was about to sell another. She did not want to do him any harm, if the bench would only give her some protection.

Collins was found guilty of assault and of another separate attack on a stranger. The magistrate, Mr Hopwood, sentenced him to one month's imprisonment on each count in the indictment, saying it would have been six months if his wife had given evidence more fully. Collins would be free in two months, but it was never going to be easy for Margaret to escape from her own life sentence of hard labour and drunken abuse.

Finally, in 1884 an amended Canal Boats Act was passed, with strict measures in place to enforce registration and annual inspections of all boats, together with compulsory school attendance. George Smith was not given the job of inspector, as some had expected, but the following year he was awarded a grant from the royal bounty fund in recognition of his tireless efforts to promote child welfare. He used the money to buy a house in the peaceful canal-side village of Crick, near Rugby, where he spent the rest of his life.

Some of his claims had wrongly given the impression that all boat families lived in terrible slum conditions, yet he had exaggerated the facts to achieve his goal and admitted, 'There are many kind-hearted, clean and respectable people amongst them.' In the wake of publicity about George Smith's campaign came realisation that poor boatmen could be seen not as villains, but as victims themselves – prisoners of the canals and a brutal lifestyle they were born into. After his first tour of the waterways, the new Chief Inspector of Canal Boats, John Brydone, reported that, although he did not want to reiterate what was said so often about the prevalence of vice and immorality, 'It exists! I have found it to be the case.' He remarked:

The one great cause underlying the whole of the matter is the old, old story, drink. The lingering about for hours at a time, day after day, in the public house, spending money, time and energy, soon induces poverty, strife, blasphemy, vice, squalor and misery, besides cruelty of many sad descriptions.

14

GANGS OF RUFFIANS

The George and Dragon wasn't a bad place to be on duty, especially on a chilly winter's day. Set right beside the canal wharf in the Warwickshire village of Fenny Compton, it was a popular watering hole, better known to locals as the Wharf Inn, for obvious reasons. Police Constable William Hine arrived mid-morning on Monday, 15 February 1886, with orders from his superiors to keep a discreet look-out for any trouble at the cattle sale being held there. But the day proved to be uneventful.

After waiting to see the last customer off the premises, he said good-bye to landlord Joseph Hardman, and about 10 p.m. set off to walk the mile back to his cottage and waiting family. By midnight, he had not returned home.

Next morning, when there was still no news of him, a team of police officers began to search the fields and surroundings of the pub with its wharf buildings, boathouse and stabling, while men positioned on both banks of the canal with long ropes began systematically dragging the water in 2ft sections. Eventually, on Saturday night, a large pocket-knife was found lying in a ditch hidden under a thick bramble hedge. The weapon had two blades – one was open and smeared with con-gealed blood. Six feet away, near a footpath, they found spots of blood and signs of a violent struggle. Seven yards further on, a police helmet with a long dent across it was lying on the ground. Superintendent George Hinde went to break the bad news to Mrs Emily Hine, who identified the bloodstained knife as her husband's and then fainted from the shock.

Reinforcements from other Warwickshire Police divisions soon joined a full-scale hunt for the missing constable, together with villagers and labourers who combed coppices, canal banks, reservoirs and bye-lanes. Plain-clothes officers searched several cottages in Fenny Compton, examining the householders' clothes and bedding. A pair of well-trained bloodhounds, loaned by Mr Gibbins of Ettington, were taken out to investigate a clue discovered at Priors Hardwick, but by this time the scent had gone cold. There was no trace of the murdered man or the murderers, and with no fresh leads to investigate, police confessed they were baffled.

Gossip was now running wild in the neighbourhood. A coachman recalled hearing a horse and trap driven through a nearby village at a mad pace at 11 p.m. on the previous Monday night. Locals knew of a hovel sheltering fowls in the field where traces of blood were discovered, and rumour had it that a gang of fowl-stealers were the most likely suspects and must have killed Police Constable Hine when he disturbed them.

Press interest in the murder mystery spread rapidly, with reports appearing in the *London Evening Standard* and *Pall Mall Gazette*, among many others. The *Birmingham Daily Post* despatched someone for an exclusive interview with William Hine's parents at their home in Shottery, near Stratford-upon-Avon, to get the full story. The couple were more than willing to co-operate. Mr Hine was a shepherd at Shottery Farm and explained that their 30-year-old son worked as a labourer in the village before joining Warwickshire Constabulary six years earlier, initially serving at Henley-in-Arden. Later, he was stationed at Shipston-on-Stour, where he narrowly escaped with his life when two notorious poachers savagely attacked him with a shovel. Since then, William had feared they would come after him for revenge. About ten months ago, he was posted to Fenny Compton, and recently told a friend, 'You may depend upon it they mean to do for me some time; that will be my end.'

Finally, nine days after Police Constable Hine disappeared, the drag lines being deployed by the search party on the Oxford Canal snagged on something submerged beneath the water at a bend a quarter of a mile from the pub. The hooks of the drags had caught on his greatcoat and brought the body to the surface, fully clothed in a police uniform plastered with mud, the left trouser leg torn. Both hands were tightly clenched, and his face was covered with blood.

In the stables of the Wharf Inn, Dr Elkington carried out a post-mortem examination and found abrasions on the fingers of the left hand, a large bruise on the left ankle, marks of a blow to the forehead, and a deep cut to the jugular vein. Speaking later at the inquest, he said:

> My opinion is that the wound in the neck was alone the cause of death, and there is no reason to suppose that wound was self-inflicted. The concussion of the brain was sufficient to cause unconsciousness. The wound could not have been inflicted while the man was in a standing position, and it also appeared as though the head had been held whilst the blood drained away.

Top brass from Warwickshire Police, including Chief Constable Robert Kinchant (who, a few years later, fled to India to escape bankruptcy and was dismissed from the force), attended the inquest at the Wharf Inn, which was crowded with spectators for the occasion. Among the witnesses was Superintendent George Hinde, who described how he had searched the body after it was brought out of the water and retrieved Police Constable Hine's staff, handcuffs and whistle, together with a pocket-book from the breast pocket that was quite dry but did not contain any notes that might have been helpful in the case. He also found a few small coins, a Co-operative cheque for threepence and a watch in the left waistcoat pocket which had stopped at six minutes past eleven.

Superintendent Hinde said he last saw the deceased officer on Friday, 12 February, when he made no complaint and did not say he was dissatisfied with his position in the force. 'He never said anything which would lead me to suppose he was likely to commit suicide – quite the reverse. He was particularly happy with his wife, and in very comfortable circumstances.' He was a very provident, careful man with a £30 deposit in the bank, and was a trusted officer with an excellent conduct record. 'I specially recommended him to Fenny Compton, where special care was necessary.'

One potential suspect seemed to be unemployed farmer William Albert Kingerise, who was called to give evidence at the request of Superintendent Hinde and was examined at length. He admitted that he left the Wharf Inn at ten o'clock on the Monday night, but could not state positively what time he arrived home in the village. Nothing could be proved, and at the end of the inquest the jury returned a verdict of wilful murder against some person or persons unknown.

The *Police Illustrated News* ran a full report with a photograph of the dead officer and said there was no doubt he had been brutally murdered, though robbery was obviously not the motive. The body had been discovered halfway between the public house and Police Constable Hine's cottage. From the nature of the injuries, it appeared he was attacked unawares, as his whistle and staff remained inside his pockets. It was most likely that an unexpected severe kick brought him to the ground, where he was struck on the head with a blunt instrument, stabbed in the neck and thrown into the canal at exactly 11.06 p.m. – a time which could be fixed from the officer's stopped watch. In the absence of any conclusive evidence, it was just guesswork, of course. And despite a thorough investigation, the case was never solved.

A large deputation of officers from Warwickshire Constabulary was present at Police Constable Hine's funeral on 1 March, which went ahead in heavy snow. More than £800 was collected on behalf of his widow and three young children, which was paid out to them at £1 a week.

He was the first man in the county's force to be killed on duty, but police work everywhere was dangerous, and violent attacks by drunken rowdies or suspects resisting arrest were all too common. By the 1890s, almost a quarter of prosecutions for assault were offences against the police.

In addition to the natural hazards of the job, it entailed long hours on the beat for low pay, harsh discipline was enforced by superiors, with dismissal or fines, and until 1887, policemen were not even allowed to vote – a rule intended to prevent political bias. Although the job had its downsides, plenty of young men were attracted to steady employment with a free uniform and boot allowance, which offered excitement, promotion prospects and a more satisfying alternative to the mundane drudgery of factories or farm labour.

Patrolling isolated rural areas had its risks, as Police Constable Hine was well aware. Poachers posed a particular threat and their violent skirmishes with gamekeepers, farmers or police officers were regular occurrences. The game laws provoked widespread hostility in the countryside, especially after the Poaching Prevention Act authorised police to stop and search likely suspects or anyone carrying a gun, snares or nets. Villagers complained that police used these powers without reasonable grounds for suspicion.

However, trying to catch poachers often led to fruitless games of hide and seek, which were never going to deter persistent offenders who wanted fresh meat for the pot, like 85-year-old Cheshire boatman Thomas Gayter. He had already served an eight-year prison sentence for wounding and was well known for poaching in the Manchester area, when the *Police Gazette* published his description as a wanted man on a charge of fowl stealing, noting that he could be identified by a burn mark on the calf of his left leg and a blue spot between each thumb and forefinger. How long he managed to evade capture and remain a free man is not known.

†††

Since the earliest days of the waterways, boatmen had never been afraid to stick up for themselves when necessary. And by the late nineteenth century, they were determined to fight for better pay and conditions. There was a great deal at stake for men defending their livelihood, and years of simmering resentment against employers grew into a righteous anger which could spill over into violence.

When canal carriers Messrs Gerrish & Company announced they were cutting the wages of second mates on all their boats, some of the workforce came out on strike. But others, including Thomas Davis, employed on the barge *Enterprise*, decided to keep working. On a trip to Bristol one morning, he was confronted by six striking boatmen at Weston Lock near Bath, who demanded he come out and join them. When he refused, they jumped on board, shouting abuse, and began to beat about the cabin with sticks. One of them picked up a heavy stone and said he would throw it down the hatchway. Thomas Davis seized a hatchet to defend himself and threatened to chop the legs off the first man who came near him, as William Bowler lashed out with a stick and William Gregory hurled a large tack pin made of iron. No one was injured, but the strikers were later prosecuted by Gerrish & Co., with Gregory and another man sent to prison for one month, while Bowler was fined £1 with costs.

Up north, on the Lancaster Canal, forty boatmen began a strike in May 1887 when several employers reduced their allowance by a penny a mile and warned they had the choice of returning to work or removing their possessions from the boats and losing their jobs. Every penny counted for the men, who said their wages averaged only 30 shillings a week and, besides keeping their horses, they had to board their younger children with town families in order to send them to school and abide by the Education Act.

By 1889, feelings had hardened among working men in many parts of Britain, and newspapers were reporting 'MORE LABOUR DISPUTES: AN EPIDEMIC OF STRIKES', including East End tailors, shipyard labourers on the Wear and colliers in the coalfields of Lancashire and Wales. London's tramway and omnibus drivers met to protest at their long hours, and a walkout by factory hands at Messrs Thornycrofts' torpedo works was settled when employers agreed to a partial settlement of their demands.

Canal boatmen were among the thousands of workers who decided to take action that year. In mid-November, a packed meeting in the billiard room of the Catherine Wheel public house in Brentford High Street listened to a representative from the Amalgamated Society of Watermen, who urged the canal men present to join a union and remedy their miserable rates of pay, which during the last five years had been cut to almost starvation wages. There were hopes that every boatman passing through Brentford would enrol in an association which could have 2,000 members.

On Tuesday, 26 November, the new Amalgamated Society of Canal Boatmen met at the same pub, and in a speech punctuated with indignant cries of 'Shame' and bursts of applause from the audience, General Secretary Mr Pearson said he regretted the state to which things had degenerated, and it was time the masters paid boatmen better so they could clothe, feed and educate their children. 'Their masters might well afford to live in great houses and ride in carriages, whilst [they] had gone from bad to worse, and must insist on their condition being improved.'

Mr Pearson pointed out that boatmen often had to travel more than 100 miles, passing through 179 locks, yet when they reached Brentford, frequently had to wait days until the barges were ready for loading, for which they received no compensation. Another society official, Mr Raynor, summed up the mood of the meeting, saying, 'I hope the day is not far distant when the wages of boatmen will be high enough to enable them to keep their wives and families in decent homes, and not in boats.' By December, at least some canal companies operating in Birmingham and the Black Country districts had conceded an advance of 10 per cent on long voyages, improved rates for day work and also agreed to provide stoves and cabins in all boats.

It was not only pay and excessive hours that created grievances, but the unacceptable working conditions that, in some places, exposed men to terrible dangers. One of these was the last great Victorian inland waterway scheme, the Manchester Ship Canal, designed to boost the city's fortunes by providing a direct link to the Irish Sea. Altogether, more than 16,000 navvies were employed on the 35-mile canal to excavate millions of tons of earth and stone. They were big, tough men, who knew the risks of work which, at four and a half pence an hour, paid better wages than the average labourer could expect.

However, the sheer scale of the project resulted in far higher numbers of deaths and injuries than anyone had foreseen. Three field hospitals and a series of first-aid posts were erected along the route at the start of construction, and by the time work finished six years later, medical staff had dealt with more than 1,400 accident victims, many severely injured. According to official figures, 154 men were killed during the project, although John Ward, President of the new Navvies' Union, claimed there were over 1,000 fatalities, most of them unrecorded. He blamed the high number of casualties on the use of cheap, unskilled labour.

Steam engines, locomotives and 6,000 wagons were used for the heaviest work, but gangs of men still carried out punishing manual labour with the same basic picks, shovels and wheelbarrows that navvies had used a century earlier. And like their predecessors, they too needed a drink when they returned to their makeshift camps at the end of a ten-hour day. With such vast numbers of migrant labourers in the area, it was difficult for the police to keep tabs on any troublemakers. But they did try.

In April 1889, the Cheshire force planned a raid on the illicit drinking shops known as shebeens, which usually sprang up on navvy encampments. A superintendent and twelve constables hid in a furniture van taken to the site and leaped out when they reached the line of huts. Inside four of them, they seized large quantities of whisky and casks of beer. Four navvies were summoned to appear at Daresbury Petty Sessions and fined for selling drink without a licence. The penalty was unlikely to be much of a deterrent – after all, there was strength in numbers.

A mob of between 700 and 800 navvies surrounded police at Ellesmere Port, one Saturday night in the summer of 1890, to try to stop Thomas Partridge being arrested for assaulting local boy William Gray, who had thrown stones at him. In retaliation, Partridge had hit him and pushed him to the ground, kicking the boy until he was unconscious. When Sergeant Wilkinson went to make an arrest, he was attacked by Partridge and two others before the crowd of navvies closed in on him.

At Chester's City Police Court, Chief Superintendent Hindley told magistrates that, with 4,000 navvies on the Eastham section of the canal, 'it was a matter of impossibility for the police in their present strength to do their duty'. The chairman of the bench said they were determined to put a stop to assaults on the police and sent Partridge to gaol for five months.

Construction leaders on the Manchester Ship Canal had to contend not only with all the problems of managing a volatile workforce, but also with serious flooding and harsh winter weather that repeatedly delayed progress. Finance was also a problem and money ran out half-way through the project. Cost-cutting and delays put extra pressure on contractors, who were sometimes tempted to cut corners on even the most rudimentary safety procedures.

In August 1891, 16-year-old George Pratt, who was working as a pointsboy on the Ince section of the Ship Canal, appeared at Chester Castle Petty Sessions, charged with causing the death of ten navvies. An engine was struggling to pull twenty-three wagons up an incline, and as it was making a third attempt, Pratt moved the points at the wrong moment and the train shot into a dead-end siding and crashed down into the cutting below, killing ten men working there. A ganger who had engaged the lad for the job said he gave him no special instructions on how to operate the points as he looked a very intelligent lad.

Magistrates decided that there was no case to answer and discharged the prisoner, saying the instructions given to Pratt were insufficient for such an important post. And they stressed that the employment of young boys, especially at night, as pointsmen was to be deprecated.

The socialist weekly newspaper *Justice* ran an angry piece headlined 'THE SYSTEMATIC SLAUGHTER OF NAVVIES ON THE MANCHESTER SHIP CANAL', commenting on yet another accident:

> It is not at all surprising that thirteen 'navvies' – not men – have been killed and five or six injured upon the Manchester ship canal. But it is peculiar that the press and public should go into hysterics over thirteen deaths and forget the thirteen hundred corpses whose mangled bodies testify to the reckless criminality of the superintendents of these works.

Manchester Ship Canal eventually opened to boats on 1 January 1894, and in May, Queen Victoria performed the official opening ceremony. It was the largest inland navigation in the world, with towering bridges, enormous locks and vast docks, which had cost a stupendous £15 million to complete.

†††

Far away from triumphant celebrations of extraordinary industrial achievement, ordinary people toiled for long hours in exhausting jobs which were at least preferable to unemployment. Life in the overcrowded urban districts remained grim, and where there was poverty and deprivation, inevitably, there was crime.

Respectable citizens in various parts of Britain had for some time noticed groups of rough lads running wild. Perivale rector Charles Hughes wrote a letter to the *Middlesex County Times* describing an incident he had witnessed, when innocent passengers on a canal excursion from Paddington were set upon by three or four ruffians by the bridge near Horsington Hill. They knocked down some women sitting quietly in the boat, attacked a young boy and assaulted a constable who intervened. Reverend Hughes commented:

It is some satisfaction to know that the ringleader got nine months hard labour, and the others six months, and 14 days, but that satisfaction would be much greater if they had had a good flogging as well. These scenes I hear are common on the canal ... the great days for these occurrences being Sunday and Monday. Surely some very energetic measure should be taken to put down these scenes, strangely out of harmony with the peaceful surroundings.

In Birmingham, out-of-work domestic servant Elizabeth Littlewood was hustled by a gang of youths as she walked along the canal towpath near Fazeley Street, one evening in May 1889. She was the worse for drink and an easy target for the jeering lads, who knocked her to the ground, tore off nearly all her clothes and threw them into the water, while about 100 others watched her humiliation.

The commotion was heard by boatman Samuel Smith at Fazeley Street Wharf, who battled his way through the crowd to help, receiving several blows on the head from stones and belt buckles. He managed to reach the nearest lock, and one lock-keeper went to Elizabeth's rescue while another fetched the police. When he returned with an officer from Duke Street, the roughs had fled.

Samuel Smith, aged 47, was treated in hospital for cuts and bruises to the face and a suspected broken jaw. Four men charged with criminal assault were later discharged by the Birmingham stipendiary magistrate, because no one could corroborate they had actually taken part in the attack. Apparently, five defence witnesses could prove that the accused men were at the theatre when it happened.

In Camberwell, police carried out a raid on a gambling gang which had been meeting regularly at a secluded spot on the banks of the Surrey Canal in the summer of 1890. Officers seized cards, a dice tin and other gaming paraphernalia they were using and arrested eleven men, although the ringleaders escaped by swimming across the canal.

Even in cases where the police managed to make an arrest, for three-quarters of the crimes committed, no one was ultimately sent for trial. Official figures for twelve months to the end of September 1892 reported 39,021 offences in England and Wales with 319 cases of murder, attempted murder or manslaughter, 819 violent assaults and 12,635 assaults on peace officers.

Drunkenness continued to be blamed for social disorder. The number of licensed premises had been growing steadily, and by the 1890s there were more than 100,000 (twice the number today), or one for every 316 people. And that was on top of countless illicit drinking dens supplying cut-price booze. In a fresh attempt to address concerns about alcohol consumption, a Royal Commission on Licensing was set up in 1897, and after a two-year inquiry concluded that the government must introduce legislation to force large numbers of pubs to close, with compensation paid to their licensees.

Meanwhile, landlords who did a roaring trade could sometimes find themselves in a difficult situation – they wanted to sell as much beer as possible, but reluctantly had to deal with the consequences when customers drank too much and became disruptive. In the Newbridge Arms, beside the canal at Coedpenmaen in south Wales, six men and an escaped prisoner named Enoch Thomas were behaving so badly one Monday night that at 10 p.m. the landlord sent for the police.

Two officers arrested Thomas, but 10 yards from the pub he refused to go any further, kicking and trying to break free, then throwing stones. Fifty men gathered round with shouts of 'Don't you go Enoch, they shall not take you!' and 'Let's give it the bastards now!' Several blows and kicks were delivered by the crowd. One constable was hit behind the right ear with a piece of brick and fell, senseless, to the ground. When he came to, he was being kicked to the canal side and just managed to make it inside the pub, bruised and bleeding. The culprits were later gaoled for a month at Pontypridd Police Court.

In another 'DESPERATE AFFRAY ON THE CANAL-SIDE', reported by the *Cheshire Observer* in January 1896, a boisterous group of seven or eight boatmen surrounded a police constable near Queen Street, Chester, where a dozen boats were moored. The officer had arrived to sort out a disturbance shortly before midnight and was obstructed as he tried to arrest boatmen John Owen and William Lloyd, who were drunk and making a row. Owen struggled violently and struck out with a tiller, but missed his target and dropped the makeshift weapon in the water. Lloyd grabbed a second constable's staff, then smashed a hammer down onto his knuckle and foot. When back-up arrived, police overpowered the two assailants, who were each given a twenty-one-day prison sentence.

Out on the streets or on canal banks, drinking and fighting bolstered male self-esteem and won the respect of other men. Tough, outlaw figures who were not afraid to defy authority had almost legendary status, like John Sadler who was known as the King of Canal Boatmen because of his fearsome reputation.

An army reservist and captain of the *Wren*, he was among a group of boatmen who arrived at a public house in Barbridge, Cheshire, one day in July 1896. The men were already well oiled and publican Thomas Colley refused to serve them, asking Police Sergeant Ratcliffe to remove Sadler from the premises.

A few minutes later, Sadler was being escorted along the road back to his boat when he suddenly dealt Sergeant Ratcliffe a terrific blow on the jaw, flooring him, then, with one knee holding him down, tried to throttle the officer. Thomas Colley and his brother pulled Sadler off and eventually he was handcuffed, but even then, he fought like a madman, head-butting the sergeant in the stomach.

Three-quarters of an hour later, Sadler was manhandled into a trap, where he had to be held down by an officer and two civilians as a farmer drove them to Nantwich. The assault brought Sadler a month in prison with hard labour, plus a fine of 32s 6d, but no doubt the King of Canal Boatmen went on to fight another day.

Canals had long ago earned their own dubious reputation, and in December 1897 the *Pall Mall Gazette* reported that many miles were becoming derelict as virtually no money had been spent on repairs in the past forty years. It described the sad state of neglected waterways in some parts of the country, with weedy backwaters, overhanging trees, moss-covered ancient bridges and dilapidated towpaths beside long stretches of stagnant water. The success of the railways meant that shortly after the inland navigation had been completed, its doom was sealed. The *Gazette* remarked, 'Nowadays the very word canal, as representing the engineering enterprise of a day that is past, would seem to be replete with a certain, sluggish suggestiveness peculiarly its own.'

The ghostly remains of glorious canals, once the pride of Britain, were now creeping through deprived urban slum districts on the very edge of society, inhabited by the disenchanted and the dispossessed. Restless youths, living in cheap lodgings nearby, liked to congregate on canal banks in these God-forsaken places.

Sometimes they were simply larking about and having a bit of harmless fun. One Sunday in July 1898, churchgoers who had been attending morning service in the Winson Green area of Birmingham were shocked to see lots of young men running down the street, stark naked. Some policemen on duty nearby had spotted them bathing illegally in the canal and decided that the safest way to secure their arrest would be to take all their clothes. Undeterred, the lads made off home, leaving the garments in the hands of the law.

But all too often, large groups of young men loitering outside with nothing much to do spelt trouble. Incidents of antisocial behaviour involving unruly youths were becoming more frequent in the 1890s, mostly in major cities where organised street gangs ran riot, fighting rivals for control of the neighbourhood and terrorising local inhabitants. Pitched battles took place at night between working-class lads in their teens armed with sticks, stones and heavy, studded, brass-buckled belts, sometimes even with knives and pistols. Onlookers were afraid to come forward to give evidence, intimidated into silence by threats about the likely consequences.

One letter writer to the *Birmingham Mail* described what was happening:

> In spite of all the energy of the Birmingham Police, the present time is a veritable reign of terror, owing to the conduct of the Professional Rough-cum-Peaky Blinder. One in a neighbourhood is enough to set the whole district in a flame, as he is sure to have a following, and the younger Peakies emulate his disorderly conduct. … they look after market people and others who have been selling their wares, and who are a little market merry; and then beat them, rob them, and leave them on the ground to the tender mercies of the police, who finish by locking them up for being drunk and disorderly, while the culprits are drinking the health of society in a neighbouring public house.

The *Globe* labelled such brutal ruffians 'criminal young animals', commenting:

> They stop at nothing; for the sake of a few shillings they will, to use their own vernacular, 'out a man'. Indeed, several deaths have already to be laid at their door, but up till now luck has been on their

side, and no member of these brotherhoods has as yet found his way to the gallows.

Public feeling on the matter was summed up by a correspondent to another publication, who said:

The rapid development of Hooliganism has attracted the attention of all classes of men and women. According to one set of comfortable critics the Hooligan is born in the Board Schools and developed in the music halls. The majority, however, are content to shake their heads, and remark that the times are very evil, and think it is best to let well alone. The one fruitful cause of Hooliganism is – neglect.

In London, the Hooligan gang was the most notorious, alongside lesser-known groups such as the Chapellers and the Lion gang in Islington, the New Cut gang from Lambeth and the Pooley gang from Leather Lane. Liverpool had its Cornermen, Manchester and Salford had Scuttlers, while in Birmingham, the young ruffians were nicknamed Peaky Blinders for the distinctive fringe and peaked flat cap worn across one eye.

A spate of rowdy incidents with dozens of assaults, robberies and drunken violence over the August Bank Holiday in 1898 drew well over 400 outraged newspaper reports on Hooligans. There was heated debate on the origins of the name (said to be derived from an infamous Irish family) and ideas on the best punishment for riotous young bullies, ranging from stiffer sentencing to reintroducing military service.

Letters from readers in the *Morning Post* criticised magistrates for being too lenient and suggested wider use of the lash. Flogging with the cat-o'-nine-tails was a favourite remedy, and in a comment piece, the *Globe* noted:

It is not quite so pleasant to be a Hooligan as it was. Sentences of three years, eighteen and twelve months are being distributed with most encouraging freedom at Clerkenwell Sessions, and we regret the cat cannot be included in sentences. At any rate, this is a good beginning in the excellent work of suppressing London ruffianism. Even your experienced Hooligan does not do three years' penal servitude 'on his head'.

Fifty policemen were transferred that August, from Westminster to those parts of south London where gang warfare was at its worst.

An intrepid correspondent for the *Pall Mall Gazette* made a midnight tour of the district, walking from York Road along Great Charlotte Street and the New Cut, swarming with disreputable loiterers, across Waterloo Road and into Oakley Street, where the cockney Hooligan gang was rampant. A Lambeth tobacconist told him they mostly fought among themselves, only attacking and robbing strangers who were under the influence of drink. And a policeman on the beat confirmed this opinion, adding that it was very difficult to hunt them down to their lairs.

The popular press seemed to be awash with sensational accounts of youth knife and gun crime, and the violence spilled over onto stretches of canals running close to the dingy backstreets. There were reports of vicious stabbing matches between opposing gangs of English and Italian youths on the streets of Clerkenwell, renowned as the home of Hooligans and one of the dirtiest parishes in the city.

Clerkenwell lads Fred England, a 16-year-old costermonger, and 13-year-old Michael Kenna were wandering along the Regent's Canal one Wednesday afternoon, each carrying a gun. Kenna was playing truant from school and revelling in the freedom. Near Muriel Street in Islington, they confronted two youths on the towpath. England said, 'I'm going to shoot you', and pulled the trigger, but his revolver did not go off. Full of bravado, Kenna said, 'I'll show you how to shoot him' and, taking a pistol from his pocket, shot George Stringle in the right leg. He fell to the ground bleeding.

England ran off and Stringle's companion grabbed Kenna, who offered 2 shillings if he would keep quiet. But the game was over. Kenna was arrested, and a few days later, when England was brought to court charged with stealing boots, he was recognised and remanded for wounding. The *Islington Gazette* commented:

No provocation seems to have been given for the act, it was one of those deliberate cases of Hooliganism for which the School Board is directly responsible. It is a terrible thing that life should be sacrificed by an urchin of this type rather than his delicate sensibilities should be wounded by corporal punishment. This is the cant of present-day philosophers, and terrible wickedness it is in practice.

At Hackney, in London's East End, there was always trouble. In one alarming incident, sixty to eighty youths rampaged through the streets, some armed with guns, knocking down pedestrians and trampling on them. The gang was on the look-out for members of the rival Broadway mob. Watchmaker's assistant Joseph Norton was at the corner of Granville Road about 6 p.m. on Sunday when the gang ran past, shouting, 'There is one, fire at him!' Six shots rang out from revolvers carried by 19-year-old Thomas Curtis and Joseph Fitzpatrick, aged 17, one bullet hitting a lad named Charles Luton in the leg. Curtis ran over to the edge of the Regent's Canal and flung the weapon into the muddy depths.

Another Hackney lad, Fred Millard, was also a target and lost his job at a sugar refinery because of the case. He later described what happened:

Between three and four on Sunday I saw Curtis and twenty or thirty others – they said, 'Here is two of the Broadway' and ran after me and fired five shots. I ran for a policeman and when I came back they had gone. The same evening I saw Curtis again, with others, spread out across the footpath. They fired several shots towards where I was standing. I went to Dove Road and made a complaint to two constables.

Six gang members went on trial at the Old Bailey charged with riot and unlawful assembly and malicious wounding. Police told the court there had been a great deal of trouble over the past two years from youths fighting with sticks, but not with revolvers before this incident. Gangs carrying firearms had been patrolling the streets of Hackney for two or three weeks, and Inspector Charles Pearn said, 'These revolvers can be bought for from seven shillings and sixpence to ten shillings at any pawnbroker's, and as cheap as one shilling in the cattle market.' Curtis and Fitzpatrick were sentenced to six months' hard labour, two others, aged 16 and 17, were given two months and the last two lads on trial were acquitted.

Many people attributed the outbreaks of gang violence to a lack of proper education. At a packed meeting in Leigh, Lancashire, Mr Pickles from the National Union of Teachers' Executive said children should be in school and not left running about the streets. Only five out of every six children in England attended school, while a million others could be found instead 'on canal boats, in the alleys of our big cities and elsewhere ... these are the people that make our "Hooligans"'.

The thoughtful comments of the government School Inspector for Birmingham, Mr Airy, seemed to resonate with the public, and were widely reported in newspapers across the country from the *Birmingham Daily Argus* to the *Leeds Times*, *South Wales Echo* and *Daily Mail*. He blamed organised ruffianism on the law allowing boys to leave school after five years' education, saying:

> The 'peaky-blinder' is an off-shoot of a bad educational system. They drift to the canal bank or to the gates of railway stations; they will carry a bag or hold a horse, but regular work soon becomes intolerable to them. It is from this five-year attendance class that the great 'peaky-blinder' brigade and the bands of night ruffians in the streets are recruited; and they constitute the greatest danger of a city.

In every courtroom Justice and Mercy confronted each other head on, fighting as bitter rivals locked in a perennial battle for supremacy. But crime was never going to be defeated and, after all, the law had its limits. At the end of the century, canals were darker and more dangerous than ever.

NOTES ON SOURCES

Chapter 1

Northampton Mercury, 4 April 1795; *Gentleman's Magazine*, August and September 1795; *Derby Mercury*, 13 August 1795; *Chester Courant*, 13 January 1795.

Wild Nathan: *Stamford Mercury*, 7 April 1815.

John Hassell, *Tour of the Grand Junction* (1819).

For more on canal construction, useful sources are Antony Burton, *The Canal Builders* (1972) and *Navvies* (2012), also Alan Faulkner, *The Grand Junction Canal* (Newton Abbot, 1971).

Sampford Peverell sources include Reverend C. Colton, *Sampford Ghost: A Plain and Authentic Narrative* (1810); *Taunton Courier*, 30 August 1810 and 25 April 1811; *London Evening Mail*, 3 September 1810; *Oxford University & City Herald*, 22 September 1810; *St James' Chronicle*, 7 May 1811.

Blisworth report: *Sun*, 29 March 1805; George Smith, *Canal Adventures by Moonlight* (1881).

Chapter 2

A full history of canal boatmen can be found in Harry Hanson, *The Canal Boatmen 1760–1914* (Gloucester, 1984). Other useful sources include Charles Hadfield, *British Canals* (London, 1966); Anthony Burton, *The Great Days of the Canals* (London, 1989); and Stuart Fisher, *Canals of Britain: A Comprehensive Guide* (London, 2012).

Gibbert case: Old Bailey Proceedings Online, 12 January 1803.

China theft: *The Star*, 9 July 1811.

Reverend Stebbing Shaw, *A Tour of the West of England in 1788* (London, 1789).

'Vile rogues' letter: Lea to Langton, 22 October 1818, cited in Gerald Turnbull, *Pickfords 1750–1920: A Study in the Development of Transportation* (PhD thesis, 1972), p. 199.

'Decided wickedness' quotation: *Canal Boatmen's Magazine*, 20 May 1829, cited in Hanson, *Boatmen*, p. 64.

Will the Waterman ballad (London, 1780–1802).

Geese theft: *Oxford Journal*, 29 January 1803.

Hay theft: Old Bailey, 14 July 1813.

Whipping: Clive Emsley, *Crime and Society in England 1750–1900* (Abingdon, 2018), p. 259.

Larceny: Drew Gray, *Crime, Policing and Punishment in England 1660–1914* (London, 2016), pp. 111–12.

Geese trial: Old Bailey, 14 September 1808.

Birmingham Canal Navigation notice: March 1770, cited in Hanson, *Boatmen*, p. 40.

Lock cottages: detailed in Nigel Crowe, *Canals* (London, 1994), pp. 82–8.

Lock-keepers: Hanson, *Boatmen*, pp. 35–40.

Lock offence: Birmingham Canal Navigation, Houghton to lock-keepers, June 1797, cited in Hanson, *Boatmen*, p. 36.

Alcohol and pubs: Patrick Colquhoun, *A Treatise on the Functions and Duties of a Constable* (London, 1803) and *A Treatise on Indigence* (London, 1806).

Seventeenth-century drinking and pamphlet: Richard Rawlidge, *A Monster Late Found Out and Discovered* (Amsterdam, 1628), cited in James Nicholls, *The Politics of Alcohol* (Manchester, 2011), p. 5.

Chapter 3

Foster case: *The Times*, 15 January 1803; *Morning Chronicle*, 28 December 1802; *Morning Post*, 15 January 1803; *Sun*, 4 and 19 January 1803; Andrew Knapp and William Baldwin, *The New Newgate Calendar: Being Interesting Memoirs of Notorious Characters*, Volume IV (London, 1810).

For more on execution, see Vic Gatrell, *The Hanging Tree: Execution and the English People 1770–1868* (Oxford, 1996), specifically pp. 7, 32, 255–6; *The Times* letter, 13 February 1804; Patrick Colquhoun, *A Treatise on Indigence* (London, 1806).

Thomas Done case: *Chester Chronicle*, 4 May 1810.

Drowning: *Lancaster Gazette*, 17 January 1807; *The Times*, 27 April 1802.

Park bench: *Caledonian Mercury*, 26 October 1801.

Navvy murder: *Staffordshire Advertiser*, 20 April 1805.

Lost boy: *The Times*, 1 September 1800; *Oxford Journal* and *Staffordshire Advertiser*, 24 January 1801.

Chapter 4

Letters in *Gloucester Journal*, 23 June 1794 and *Gentleman's Magazine*,
   November 1795.

Thomas Pennant, *The Journey from Chester to London* (London, 1782).

Reverend Stebbing Shaw, *Tour of the West of England* (London, 1788).

Warehouse fire: *The Times*, 4 July 1793.

Cotton trade: Boyd Hilton, *A Mad, Bad, and Dangerous People? England 1783–1846*
   (Oxford, 2006), p. 23.

Ledbury opening: *Gloucester Journal*, 2 April 1798.

Paddington Basin opening: *Oxford Journal*, 18 July 1801.

Hutchinson: Old Bailey, 11 April 1804.

Goodenough: Old Bailey, 14 Jan 1801.

Reward notice: *Derby Mercury*, 11 November 1802, 23 August 1804.

Thefts: Turnbull, *Pickfords*, pp. 200–1.

Caseltine: Old Bailey, 22 April 1789.

Miles trial: Old Bailey, 2 April 1800.

Howarth: Old Bailey, 9 December 1789.

Pyman: Old Bailey, 12 September 1804.

Harpur: *Oxford Journal*, 24 August 1799.

Fenton: Old Bailey, 9 July 1800.

Peterson: *Aberdeen Journal*, 30 December 1801.

Larceny figures: Colquhoun, *A Treatise on Indigence*.

Glover: *Derby Mercury*, 15 January 1807.

Horse: *Manchester Mercury*, 12 December 1809.

Boatman robbed: *Oxford Journal*, 25 May 1805.

Heath: Old Bailey, 4 December 1811.

Conliffe: Old Bailey, 26 October 1814.

Arson: *Derby Mercury*, 7 October 1802.

Gunpowder: *Morning Advertiser*, 3 April 1809.

Chapter 5

Augustus Cove, *The Tocsin Sounded* (London, 1813).

Tobias Smollett, *The Critical Review: Or, Annals of Literature*, Vol. 3
   (London, 1813).   .

Cove case: *Statesman*, 29 June 1812; *Leicester Journal*, 3 July 1812.

John Hassell, *Tour of the Grand Junction*, pp. 5–6.

Porter attack: *The Times*, 2 September 1815.

Pleasure boats: *Morning Chronicle*, 4 July 1804; Faulkner, *The Grand Junction Canal*.

Messenger trial report by Chairman, Aylesbury Quarter Sessions, 20 October 1810.

Painter trial: Old Bailey, 11 January 1809.

Booth petitions: Middlesex Sessions, January, February and April 1811.

Objection to canal: Parliamentary debate, 7 May 1812, cited in Michael
  Essex-Lopresti, *Exploring the Regent's Canal* (Studley, 1998), p. 5.

Fight on Agar's land: *The Times*, 22 March 1815.

Homer fraud: Regent's Canal Company Minutes, April and June 1815;
  Caledonian Mercury, 6 May 1815; *Oxford Journal*, 27 May 1815.

Useful sources on the Regent's Canal include Herbert Spencer, *London's Canal*
  (London, 1976); Alan Faulkner, *The Regent's Canal: London's Hidden Waterway*
  (Burton-on-Trent, 2005); and Robert Philpotts, *When London Became an Island:
  The Story of the Building of the Regent's Canal 1811–1820* (London, 2008).

White-collar crime: Emsley, *Crime and Society*, pp. 55–6.

Pickpockets Keith and Eves: Old Bailey, 14 September 1814.

Dundas trial: *The Times* and *Public Ledger*, 22 April 1817.

John Sutcliffe, *A Treatise on Canals and Reservoirs* (Rochdale, 1816).

Report of the Alarming Increase Committee (London, 1816), pp. 12–13, 25.

Morris and Showell: Old Bailey, 6 December 1820.

Indecent bathing: *Public Advertiser*, 16 August 1820.

London crime: Gray, *Crime*, pp. 185–86; Emsley, *Crime and Society*, p. 62.

Witham riot: *Stamford Mercury*, 11 August 1815; *Bury & Norwich Post*,
  24 May 1815; Burton, *Navvies*, p. 36.

Lord Morton cartoons: British Museum Catalogue of Prints, Volume 9, 13382,
  13383.

Regent's Canal opening and robberies: *Morning Chronicle*, 2 August and
  21, 22 September 1820; *National Register*, 6 August 1820; *Daily Advertiser*,
  3 August 1820; *Globe*, 3 August and 22 September 1820; *Sun*, 3 August 1820;
  Statesman, 4 August; *Public Advertiser*, 5 and 8 August 1820.

Ellinger trial: Old Bailey, 18 September 1820.

Boatmen riot: *The News*, 28 July 1822; *Morning Advertiser*, 26 July 1822; *Morning
  Chronicle*, 23 September 1822; *The Examiner*, 29 September 1822.

Chapter 6

Osborne and Cooke: *Birmingham Journal*, 9 December 1826; *The Times*,
  22 March 1827; *Pierce Egan's Life in London*, 25 March 1827; Martin Wiener,
  Men of Blood (Cambridge, 2006), pp. 83–6; Gray, *Crime*, pp. 145–8.

James Pattern: *St James' Chronicle*, 13 August 1825; *The Times* and *Globe*,
  13 August 1825; *Morning Post*, 16 August and 6 September; *Warwick Advertiser*,
  10 September; *Birmingham Chronicle*, 8 September.

Strawmen: Gray, *Crime*, p. 262.

Bloody Code: Gray, *Crime*, pp. 275–95.

James Hughes: *Lancaster Gazette*, 26 July and 30 August 1828; *The Times*, 22 July;
  Yorkshire Gazette, 6 September.

Crime figures: Gatrell, *The Hanging Tree*, p. 574. Gatrell suggests the pragmatic reason for reducing the number of capital offences.

For more on punishment and the end of the Bloody Code: Gray, *Crime*, pp. 275–95; Wiener, *Men of Blood*, pp. 19–23.

Bell and Connor: *Aberdeen Press and Journal*, 29 October 1828; *Morning Chronicle*, 22 September 1828. Full details of the case and its context can be found in Rachel E. Bennett, *Capital Punishment and the Criminal Corpse in Scotland, 1740–1834* (London, 2018), pp. 110–11.

Colquhoun, *A Treatise on Indigence*, p. 43.

Further details on policing: Gray, *Crime*, pp. 223–34 and Emsley, *Crime and Society*, pp. 231–3.

Morning Herald comment on police reprinted in *Cheltenham Journal*, 27 July 1829.

Naked bathing: *Morning Advertiser*, 30 July 1829.

Boatmen attack police: *London Evening Standard*, 30 November 1829.

Male victimisation: *Morning Chronicle*, 31 July 1829 (cited in Wiener, *Men of Blood*, p. 86).

Judge's comment: *Morning Advertiser*, 15 August 1829.

Matilda Parker: *Morning Chronicle*, 12 March 1829.

Warning to boatmen: *Worcester Journal*, 9 April 1829.

Holdmoes: *Morning Chronicle*, 18 June 1829.

Chapter 7

Pub details: Smith, *Adventures by Moonlight*, pp. 7, 19; Crowe, *Canals*, pp. 94–5.

Beer shops: Hilton, *Mad Bad*, pp. 576–77; Nicholls, *Alcohol*, pp. 46–8, 80–95.

Gin consumption: Nicholls, *Alcohol*, pp. 35–37.

Quote 'this fascinating poison': John Lettsom, *Hints Respecting the Effects of Hard Drinking* (London, 1798), cited in Nicholls, *Alcohol*, p. 68.

Dickens: cited in Nicholls, *Alcohol*, p. 46; *The Examiner*, 3 January 1830.

Beer bill debate: *St James' Chronicle*, 3 July 1830.

Hodgkiss and Cooke: *Worcester Herald*, 28 July 1832.

Elizabeth Sutton: *Globe*, 29 August 1833; *Morning Post* and *The Times*, 30 August 1833.

Robert Paviour: *Morning Chronicle* and *The Times*, 14 March 1833; *Oxford Journal*, 23 March; *London Evening Gazette*, 12 April; trial Old Bailey, 11 April 1833; *Essex Standard*, 20 April.

Barratt: *Sporting Chronicle*, 4 August 1833.

1834 Select Committee quote: cited in Emsley, *Crime and Society*, pp. 64–65.

House of Commons debates: Hansard, April and June 1834; *London Evening Standard*, 24 April; *Morning Post*, 4 June 1834.

Youth's warning: *Bucks Gazette*, 16 August 1834.

Alehouse windows: Hilton, *Mad Bad*, p. 577; *Essex Standard*, 15 August 1834; *Leamington Spa Courier*, 18 October 1834.

Drunkenness Committee: *The News*, 29 September 1834.

Metropolitan drunkenness: *Worcester Journal*, 2 April 1835.

Dykes: *Morning Advertiser*, 19 October 1836; *St James' Chronicle*, 20 October; *Evening Chronicle*, 21 and 28 October; *Morning Post*, 27 October.

Nairey bridge fight: Old Bailey, 16 September 1824.

Beer shop numbers: Nicholls, *Alcohol*, p. 92.

Fights: Gray, *Crime*, pp. 82–83.

Parker and Blower: *London Evening Standard*, 19 April 1837.

Bishop: *Worcester Journal*, 23 March 1837.

Reverend William Baker, *The Curse of Britain: An Essay on the Evils, Causes and Cure of Intemperance* (London, 1838).

Pub closing: *The Times*, 10 September 1839.

Townsend: *Morning Post*, 28 September 1838.

Giles and Payton: *Worcestershire Chronicle*, 19 July 1838; *Wolverhampton Chronicle & Staffordshire Advertiser*, 11 July.

Greenacre: *The Times*, 10 January 1837; Old Bailey trial, 3 April 1837; *John Bull*, 30 April. For an account of the Greenacre case as public entertainment, see Judith Flanders, *The Invention of Murder* (London, 2011), pp. 91–8.

Chapters 8–10

Christina Collins letter: *Staffordshire Gazette*, 6 July 1839.

Brown family: *Nottingham Review*, 20 March 1840 and 23 May 1828.

Ingleby references: *Nottingham Review*, 8 February 1828; *Sheffield Independent*, 15 December 1821; *New Times (London)*, January 1822; *Morning Herald*, 4 May 1824; *Belfast Chronicle*, 20 August 1832; *Morning Post*, 23 March 1837.

There is some doubt whether Christina was legally married to Ingleby, the master of deception. After his death, a Rachael Ingleby claimed to be his widow and that he had deserted her thirty years earlier (*Berwick Advertiser*, 14 April 1838). A court case revealed Ingleby's unconventional love life, when a Leicestershire baker named Pratt was acquitted of bigamy, after alleging Ingleby ran off with Mrs Pratt and lived with her in Nottingham for several years before she left town with her paramour and disappeared (*Leicestershire Mercury*, 25 March 1837 and *Morning Post*, 23 March 1837).

For more on Ingleby and the Collins murder, sources include eminent historian of magic, Professor Edwin A. Dawes, *A Rich Cabinet of Magical Curiosities* (2005); and John Godwin, *The Murder of Christina Collins* (1990). For locations and reference to Colin Dexter's fictional reworking of the case, see his Inspector Morse novel, *The Wench is Dead* (London, 1989). See also John Godwin and Antony J. Richards, *The Murder of Christina Collins* (Cambridge, 2011).

Inquest, trial reports and comments on the case: *Staffordshire Advertiser*, 22 and
29 June 1839, 27 and 31 July 1839, 21 and 28 March 1840, 11 and 18 April 1840;
Staffordshire Gazette and County Standard, 6 July and 24 August 1839, 21 March
and 18 April 1840.

The case was covered in many other newspapers, including *Morning Chronicle*,
25 July 1839; *Derby Mercury*, 31 July 1839; *Wolverhampton Chronicle*,
7 August 1839; *Morning Herald*, 18 March 1840; *Leicester Herald*, 21 March
1840; *Morning Advertiser*, 6 April 1840; *Liverpool Mail*, 16 April 1840; *Worcester
Journal*, 14 March 1840.

Sunday working: *Worcester Journal*, 2 April 1835; *Leeds Intelligencer*, 19 March 1836;
Derby Mercury, 28 June 1837; *Staffordshire Advertiser*, 3 August 1839; *Staffordshire
Gazette*, 24 August 1839.

Camden Pelham, *The Chronicles of Crime; or, The New Newgate Calendar*
(London, 1841).

Chapter 11

Northern Star and *Leeds General Advertiser*, 28 March 1840; *Manchester Courier*
and *Lancashire General Advertiser*, 4 April 1840; *London Evening Standard*,
27 August 1840; *Southern Reporter*, 3 September 1840.

Canal Police Act: *Preston Chronicle*, 19 September 1840.

Candiliffe: *Leicester Herald*, 3 April 1841.

Brentford flood: *Chelmsford Chronicle*, 22 January 1841.

Aliases: Hanson, *Boatmen*, p. 169; letter to *Staffordshire Advertiser*, 17 August 1839.

Sunday traffic: House of Lords debate, 26 April 1841 (Vol. 57, cc 1069–72).

Evidence of the Select Committee on Sunday Trading on Canals and Navigable
Rivers and Railways, *House of Lords Journal*, Vol. 73, 1841; *Wolverhampton
Chronicle & Staffordshire Advertiser*, 15 September 1841 and 4 May 1842;
Hanson, *Boatmen*, pp. 49–50, 71–82.

Crime and unemployment: Emsley, *Crime and Society*, pp. 34–37.

Williams: Old Bailey trial, 12 June 1843.

Sams: Old Bailey, 16 December 1844.

Norman: Old Bailey, 4 March 1844; *Staffordshire Advertiser*, 3 August 1839.

*First Report of the Commissioners Appointed to Inquire as to the Best Means of Establishing an
Efficient Constabulary Force in the Counties of England and Wales*, 1839 (169) XIX.

Salmon and Palin: *Wolverhampton Chronicle*, 16 August; *Sun* (London), 15 August 1843.

Patmore and Jerram: *Weekly Chronicle* (London), 7 January 1844; *The Atlas*,
24 February 1844; *Hereford Journal*, 3 April 1844; *Morning Post*, 5 November 1842;
The Patriot, 13 November 1843.

Floating chapels: *Wolverhampton Chronicle*, 30 September 1840; *Morning
Post*, 10 June 1844; *Oxford Chronicle*, 4 May 1850; *Aris's Birmingham
Gazette*, 8 May 1848; *Liverpool Mail*, 6, 13, 20 and 27 December 1845 and
3 January 1846; Hanson, *Boatmen*, pp. 80–81.

Malt theft: *Derbyshire Advertiser and Journal*, 9 October 1846.
Harefield Lock fight: *London Evening Standard*, 29 September 1846; *Leeds Intelligencer*, 3 October 1846.
Thomas: Old Bailey trial, 14 June 1847; *Morning Post*, 17 June.
Judge's words: *Hampshire Advertiser*, 8 May 1845.
Drinking: Nicholls, *Alcohol*, p. 112.
Bolton meeting: *Lancashire Advertiser* and *Bolton Chronicle*, 25 August 1849, *Yorkshire Gazette*, 8 February 1845.
Liverpool Assizes comment: *Liverpool Mercury*, cited in Wiener, *Men of Blood*, p. 257.
Parliamentary debate on Sale of Beer Act: HC, 20 March 1839, Vol. 46; HL, 3 June 1839, Vol. 47.
Temperance: Nicholls, *Alcohol*, pp. 99–107; Paul Jennings, *The Local: A History of the English Pub* (Cheltenham, 2021), pp. 165–81.
Thorpe murder: *Morning Post*, 27 August 1847; *Wolverhampton Chronicle*, 24 November 1847; *Sun*, 18 March 1848; *Leicestershire Mercury*, 19 January 1850.

Chapter 12

Francis: *Cheshire Observer*, 19 April, 3 May and 9 August 1856.
Mackett: *Examiner*, 12 February 1853; *The Times*, 8 April; *Daily News*, 14 May 1853.
Moore: *The Times*, 9 September 1853; *Preston Chronicle*, 17 December 1853.
Letters in Henry Mayhew's survey of the poor were published in the *Morning Chronicle* from October 1849 to December 1850, later published in four volumes as *London Labour and the London Poor* (London, 1861–62).
Alcohol and crime: Emsley, *Crime and Society*, pp. 69–72; Alexander Mackay and Shirley Brooks, *The Morning Chronicle's Labour and the Poor: The Rural Districts* (London, 1983).
Charles Dickens, *Hard Times* (London, 1854), Chapter 5.
Useful sources on the development of the canal carrying trade include Hanson, *Boatmen*, pp. 85–100; and Anthony Burton, *The Great Days of the Canals* (London, 1989); *Manchester Courier*, 10 January 1852; *Morning Advertiser*, 6 November 1856.
Boatmen behaving badly: *Morning Advertiser*, 17 February 1853; *London Evening Standard*, 9 December 1854; *Fife Herald*, 30 April 1868; *Cardiff and Merthyr Guardian*, 21 August 1852.
John Hollingshead, *Odd Journeys In and Out of London* (London, 1860).
Murders: *Derby Mercury*, 19 March 1851; *London Evening Standard*, 4 March 1858, 14 and 22 May 1858, 24 August 1858, 25 November 1858 and 1 April 1862; *Morning Chronicle*, 15 and 17 May 1858; *North Devon Journal*, 27 May 1858; *Rugby Advertiser*, 28 August 1858; *Bristol Daily Post*, 4 April 1862.
Drink: Nicholls, *Alcohol*, pp. 121–6. For details of the licensed trade, see Jennings, *The Local*, pp. 73–86.
Mr Justice Mellor: *Leeds Mercury*, 27 March 1866.

Shooting: *Illustrated Police News*, 10 October 1868; *Alcester Chronicle*, 27 July 1867.

For more on crime reporting in the media, see Gray, *Crime*, pp. 21–49.

Further discussion of the Victorian interest in violence can be found in Rosalind Crone, *Violent Victorians: Popular Entertainment in Nineteenth-Century London* (Manchester, 2012).

Cheshire rumour: *Globe*, 28 August 1865; *Herts Guardian*, 29 August; *Leicester Journal*, 1 September; *Leeds Mercury*, 2 September; *Cheshire Observer*, 2 September.

Blood-stained knife: *Morning Post*, 7 November 1867.

Kidsgrove Boggart origins: *Staffordshire Sentinel*, 6 December 1879.

Victorian folklore: Karl Bell, *The Legend of Spring-heeled Jack: Victorian Urban Folklore and Popular Cultures* (Woodbridge, 2012).

Lapworth drowning: *Leamington Spa Courier*, 24 May 1862.

London murders: *Pall Mall Gazette*, 27 June and 24 August 1872, 19 February and 13 June 1873, 9 September and 10 October 1873; *Islington Times*, 30 July 1872; *Daily Telegraph*, 2 August 1872; *London Evening Standard*, 20 August 1872; *Eastern Daily Press*, 11 September 1873; *Leicester Chronicle*, 13 September 1873; *Huddersfield Chronicle*, 13 September 1873; *Manchester Evening News*, 21 November 1873.

Chapter 13

Tilbury explosion: *Daily News*, 2 and 6 October 1874; *Morning Post*, 3 October 1874 and 15 May 1875; *Globe*, 3 October 1874; *London Evening Standard*, 20 October 1874 and 13 May 1875; Herbert Spencer, *London's Canal*, pp. 65–8; Faulkner, *The Grand Junction Canal*, pp. 175–6.

Shoebottom: *Illustrated Police News*, 14 December 1867.

Arnold Bennett, *Clayhanger* (London, 1910).

Walmsley: *Preston Herald*, 8 September 1875.

Margaret Evans: *Illustrated Police News*, 7 May 1881.

Mincher: *Shields Daily News*, 29 January 1870.

Prisons: Gray, *Crime*, pp. 297–314.

Spencer: *Manchester Evening News*, 8 March 1875; *Bicester Herald*, 12 March 1875.

Worthington: *Manchester Evening News*, 10 and 14 September 1874 and 4 January 1875; *York Herald*, 11 September and 18 December 1874; *Huddersfield Chronicle*, 11 September 1874; *Wigan Observer*, 12 and 18 September 1874, 11 and 18 December 1874; *Birmingham Daily Post*, 16 September 1874; *Pall Mall Gazette*, 16 September 1874.

Executions: Emsley, *Crime and Society*, pp. 290–1; and Gatrell, *The Hanging Tree*, pp. 589–611.

George Smith, *Our Canal Population: A Cry from the Boat Cabins* (London, 1875) and *Canal Adventures by Moonlight* (London, 1881).

Boat families: Hanson, *Boatmen*, pp. 120–38; *Coventry Herald*, 14 April 1876; *Globe*, 3 June 1876; *Star*, 27 January 1876.

John and Jane Probert: *Illustrated Police News*, 5 and 12 May 1877; *Liverpool Mercury*, 24 July; *Gloucester Citizen*, 25 July 1877.

Canal-boat conditions: *Burton Chronicle*, 4 May 1876; *Examiner*, 5 May 1877; *London Evening Standard*, 21 April 1877; *Cheshire Observer*, 8 September 1877; *Wigan Observer*, 15 September 1877.

Mark Guy Pearse, *Rob Rat: A Story of Barge Life* (London, 1878).

Venetia letter: *Examiner*, 25 January 1879.

Martha Smith: *Illustrated Police News*, 14 October 1882; *Manchester Courier*, 7 November 1882.

Thay: *Leeds Times*, 1 July 1882.

Collins: *Wigan Observer*, 22 October 1881.

John Brydone: 14th Report of the Local Government Board for 1884, p. 74 (cited in Hanson, *Boatmen*, p. 128).

Chapter 14

William Hine murder: *Birmingham Daily Post*, 22 February 1886; *London Evening Standard*, 24 and 25 February 1886; *Warwick and Warwickshire Advertiser*, 27 February 1886; *Banbury Advertiser*, 4 March 1886; *Illustrated Police News*, 6 March 1886.

Kinchant bankruptcy: *London Evening Standard*, 9 January 1892.

Police work: Emsley, *Crime and Society*, pp. 45, 247–51.

Poaching: Pamela Horn, *Labouring Life in the Victorian Countryside* (Stroud, 1995), pp. 230–3, 238; Emsley, *Crime and Society*, p. 80.

Gayter: *Police Gazette*, 26 August 1898.

Gerrish boatmen strike: *Bristol Mercury*, 22 December 1884.

Lancaster Canal strike: *Lancaster Gazette*, 21 May 1887.

Labour disputes: *Wiltshire Times*, 12 October 1889.

Brentford boatmen: *Middlesex Independent*, 16 and 27 November 1889.

Birmingham boatmen: *Gloucestershire Chronicle*, 14 December 1889.

Manchester Ship Canal: *Clarion*, 5 November 1892; *Bradford Weekly Telegraph*, 20 April 1889; *Derby Daily Telegraph*, 2 May 1889; *Liverpool Weekly Courier*, 2 August 1890; *Lancaster Gazette*, 1 August 1891; *Justice*, 25 July 1891.

Liz McIvor, *Canals: The Making of a Nation* (London, 2015), pp. 145–98.

Ruffians: *Middlesex County Times*, 28 August 1886; *Birmingham Daily Post*, 23 May 1889; *Birmingham Mail*, 4 June 1889; *Eastern Evening News*, 14 July 1890.

Crime figures: Hansard, House of Commons debate, 10 March 1893.

Drink: Jennings, *The Local*, p. 167 and Nicholls, *Alcohol*, p. 144.

Thomas: *Pontypridd District Herald*, 7 January 1893.

Owen and Lloyd: *Cheshire Observer*, 18 January 1896.

King of Canal Boatmen: *Cheshire Observer*, 1 August 1896.

Derelict canals: *Pall Mall Gazette*, 30 December 1897.

Naked youths: *Birmingham Mail*, 30 July 1898.

Useful sources on street gangs are Heather Shore, *London's Criminal Underworlds, c. 1720–c. 1930: A Social and Cultural History* (Basingstoke, 2015), and Carl Chinn, *Peaky Blinders: The Real Story* (London, 2019).

Ruffians: *Birmingham Mail*, 8 January 1896; *Globe*, 9 August 1898; *Pall Mall Gazette*, 15 August 1898; *South Wales Echo*, 15 August 1898; *Justice*, 20 August 1898; *Leeds Times*, 27 August 1898; *Globe*, 7 September 1898; *Dundee Evening Telegraph*, 3 October 1898; *Daily Telegraph*, 18 August 1899; *Morning Post*, 28 November 1900.

Education: *Leigh Chronicle and Weekly District Advertiser*, 7 October 1898.

England and Kenna: *London Evening Standard*, 28 October and 7 November 1898; *Islington Gazette*, 31 October 1898.

Hackney gang: Old Bailey Online, 5 April 1897.

SELECT BIBLIOGRAPHY

Baker, Reverend William, *The Curse of Britain: An Essay on the Evils, Causes and Cure of Intemperance* (London, 1838).

Bell, Karl, *The Legend of Spring-heeled Jack: Victorian Urban Folklore and Popular Cultures* (Woodbridge: The Boydell Press, 2012).

Bennett, Rachel E., *Capital Punishment and the Criminal Corpse in Scotland, 1740–1834* (London: Palgrave, 2018).

Burton, Anthony, *History's Most Dangerous Jobs: Navvies* (Stroud: The History Press, 2012).

Burton, Anthony, *The Canal Builders: The Men Who Constructed Britain's Canals* (Barnsley: Pen & Sword, 2015).

Burton, Anthony, *The Great Days of the Canals* (London: David & Charles, 1989).

Chinn, Carl, *Peaky Blinders: The Real Story* (London: John Blake, 2019).

Clark, P., *The English Alehouse: A Social History 1200–1830* (London: Longman, 1983).

Colquhoun, Patrick, *A Treatise on Indigence* (London, 1806).

Colquhoun, Patrick, *A Treatise on the Functions and Duties of a Constable* (London, 1803).

Colton, Reverend C., *Sampford Ghost: A Plain and Authentic Narrative* (1810).

Cove, Augustus, *The Tocsin Sounded* (London, 1813).

Crone, Rosalind, *Violent Victorians: Popular Entertainment in Nineteenth-Century London* (Manchester: Manchester University Press, 2012).

Crowe, Nigel, *Canals* (London: Batsford, 1994).

Emsley, Clive, *Crime and Society in England 1750–1900* (Abingdon: Routledge, 2018).

Essex-Lopresti, Michael, *Exploring the Regent's Canal* (Studley: Brewin, 1998).

Faulkner, Alan, *The Grand Junction Canal* (Newton Abbot: David & Charles, 1971).

Faulkner, Alan, *The Regent's Canal: London's Hidden Waterway* (Burton-on-Trent: Waterways World, 2005).

Fisher, Stuart, *Canals of Britain: A Comprehensive Guide* (London: Adlard Coles, 2012).

Gatrell, Vic, *The Hanging Tree: Execution and the English People 1770–1868* (Oxford: Oxford University Press, 1996).

Godwin, John, *The Murder of Christina Collins on the Trent and Mersey Canal* (J.F. Godwin, 1990).

Gray, Drew, *Crime, Policing and Punishment in England 1660–1914* (London: Bloomsbury, 2016).

Hadfield, Charles, *British Canals: An Illustrated History* (Newton Abbot: David & Charles, 1966).

Hanson, Harry, *The Canal Boatmen 1760–1914* (Gloucester: Sutton, 1984).

Harrison, Brian, *Drink and the Victorians: The Temperance Question in England 1815–1872* (Keele: Keele University Press, 1994).

Hassell, John, *Tour of the Grand Junction* (London, 1819).

Hilton, Boyd, *A Mad, Bad, and Dangerous People? England 1783–1846* (Oxford: Oxford University Press, 2006).

Hollingshead, John, *Odd Journeys In and Out of London* (London, 1860).

Horn, Pamela, *Labouring Life in the Victorian Countryside* (Stroud: Sutton, 1995).

Jennings, Paul, *The Local: A History of the English Pub* (Cheltenham: The History Press, 2021).

Knapp, Andrew, and William Baldwin, *The New Newgate Calendar: Being Interesting Memoirs of Notorious Characters, Volume IV* (London, 1810).

Lettsom, John, *Hints Respecting the Effects of Hard Drinking* (London, 1798).

McIvor, Liz, *Canals: The Making of a Nation* (London: BBC Books, 2015).

Mackay, Alexander, and Shirley Brooks, *The Morning Chronicle's Labour and the Poor: The Rural Districts* (London, 1983).

Nicholls, James, *The Politics of Alcohol: A History of the Drink Question in England* (Manchester: Manchester University Press, 2011).

Pearse, Mark Guy, *Rob Rat: A Story of Barge Life* (London, 1878).

Pelham, Camden, *The Chronicles of Crime; or, The New Newgate Calendar* (London, 1841).

Pennant, Thomas, *The Journey from Chester to London* (London, 1782).

Philpotts, Robert, *When London Became an Island: The Story of the Building of the Regent's Canal 1811–1820* (London: Blackwater, 2008).

Shaw, Reverend Stebbing, *A Tour of the West of England in 1788* (London, 1789).

Shore, Heather, *London's Criminal Underworlds, c. 1720–c. 1930: A Social and Cultural History* (Basingstoke: Palgrave, 2015).

Smith, George, *Canal Adventures by Moonlight* (London, 1881).

Smith, George, *Our Canal Population: A Cry from the Boat Cabins* (London, 1875).

Spencer, Herbert, *London's Canal* (London: Lund Humphries, 1976).

Sutcliffe, John, *A Treatise on Canals and Reservoirs* (Rochdale, 1816).

Turnbull, Gerald, *Pickfords 1750–1920: A Study in the Development of Transportation* (unpublished PhD thesis, 1972).

Wiener, Martin, *Men of Blood: Violence, Manliness and Criminal Justice in Victorian England* (Cambridge: Cambridge University Press, 2006).

Newspapers

Aberdeen Journal
Belfast Chronicle
Berwick Advertiser
Birmingham Chronicle
Birmingham Daily Post
Birmingham Journal
Bolton Chronicle
Bradford Weekly Telegraph
Bristol Daily Post
Bristol Mercury
Bucks Gazette
Burton Chronicle
Bury & Norwich Post
Caledonian Mercury
Cardiff and Merthyr Guardian
Chelmsford Chronicle
Cheltenham Journal
Cheshire Observer
Chester Chronicle
Coventry Herald
Daily Advertiser
Daily Telegraph
Derby Mercury
Derbyshire Advertiser and Journal
Dundee Evening Telegraph
Eastern Daily Press
Eastern Evening News
Essex Standard
Evening Mail
Examiner
Fife Herald
Globe
Gloucester Citizen
Gloucestershire Chronicle
Hampshire Advertiser

Hereford Journal
Herts Guardian
Huddersfield Chronicle
Illustrated Police News
Islington Gazette
Islington Times
Justice
Lancashire Advertiser
Lancaster Gazette
Leamington Spa Courier
Leeds Intelligencer
Leeds Mercury
Leeds Times
Leicester Journal
Leicestershire Mercury
Leigh Chronicle and Weekly District Advertiser
Liverpool Mail
Liverpool Weekly Courier
London Evening Gazette
London Evening Standard
Manchester Courier
Manchester Evening News
Manchester Mercury
Middlesex County Times
Middlesex Independent
Morning Advertiser
Morning Chronicle
Morning Post
National Register
Northampton Mercury
North Devon Journal
Northern Star and Leeds General Advertiser
Nottingham Review
Oxford Journal

Pall Mall Gazette
Police Gazette
Pontypridd District Herald
Preston Chronicle
Preston Herald
Public Advertiser
Shields Daily News
South Wales Echo
Sporting Chronicle
Staffordshire Advertiser
Staffordshire Gazette
Staffordshire Sentinel
Stamford Mercury
Statesman

St James' Chronicle
Taunton Courier
The Atlas
The Patriot
The Times
Warwick and Warwickshire Advertiser
Wigan Observer
Wiltshire Times
Wolverhampton Chronicle
Worcester Herald
Worcester Journal
Worcestershire Chronicle
Yorkshire Gazette

INDEX